Spirituality and the Curriculum

Theology in Dialogue Series
Series Editor: Ian Markham

The Theology in Dialogue series is an internationally supported response to a pressing need to explore the relationship between theology and the different, ostensibly secular, academic disciplines which appear within the degree programmes of colleges and universities. It has been developed by The Council of Church and Associated Colleges (CCAC), a network of UK-based colleges and universities which have Church foundations.

Each volume begins with a chapter and a reply, providing a thoughtful justification for the interaction of theology and each subject. This is followed by a theoretical analysis of this interaction, and a range of case studies illustrating the difference this makes in the classroom. All volumes contain contributions from the most highly respected scholars in their field.

Other books in the series:

English Literature, Theology and the Curriculum edited by Liam Gearon
The grand narrative of theology and the many narratives of literature have interacted with complex and culturally enriching results over the centuries. This volume provides an enlivened, interdisciplinary debate between the fields of English literature and theology. The analysis of this textual dynamic ranges from varied, historical case studies in theology and literature, to practical concerns centring upon effective models of curriculum innovation, especially, but not exclusively, in higher education.

Sociology, Theory and the Curriculum edited by Leslie J. Francis
The innovative essays in this dialogue demonstrate how sociology can be enriched by the scrutiny and insights of theology, and how the proper subject matter of theology can be illuminated by the theories and empirical methodologies of sociology. A focus is placed on the particular case of the church college, as an institution which teaches sociology, but which is also of sociological interest itself.

Theology in Dialogue Series
Series Editor: Ian Markham

Spirituality
and the Curriculum

Edited by Adrian Thatcher

CASSELL
London and New York

Cassell

Wellington House, 125 Strand, London WC2R 0BB
370 Lexington Avenue, New York, NY 10017-6550

© Adrian Thatcher and the contributors 1999

An earlier version of Chapter 10 was published in John Beck, *Morality and Citizenship in Education* (Cassell, 1998).

The extracts from children's writing in Chapters 7 and 13 are used with the permission of the authors' parents.

First published 1999

British Library Cataloguing-in-Publication Data
A catalogue record for this book is available from the British Library.

ISBN 0-304-70484-9

Typeset by BookEns Ltd, Royston, Herts.
Printed and bound in Great Britain by Biddles Ltd,
Guildford and King's Lynn

Contents

Contents

Series Editor's Foreword

One of the central questions facing theological discourse must be its relationship with other discourses in the academy. For the academy this issue is acute. The twin pressures of secularization and plurality have inhibited theological reflection; theology has been confined to a 'department'; the result being that students on different degree programmes do not explore the overall framework and assumptions of their study. Certain fundamental value questions are entirely neglected.

This series is a challenge to the confinement of theological reflection to a single department. We believe that a full and rounded education ought to provide the space for wide-ranging reflection. Education is not value-free: all students ought to be encouraged to confront questions of value.

Each volume examines both questions of approach and questions of content. Some contributors argue that an overtly Christian or religious framework for higher education actually affects the way we approach our study; a religious framework supports faith, while the secular framework is opposed to faith. Other contributors insist that a religious framework simply makes the curriculum wider. The approach will be the same as our secular counterparts; however, where the content of a course has a religious implication this will be included. Each volume brings out the diversity of positions held within the academy.

We have attracted the best writers to reflect on these questions. Each volume concludes by reflecting on the curriculum implications – the precise implications for educators in our schools and higher education colleges.

Ian Markham

The Contributors

John Beck is Head of Education Studies Department at Homerton College, Cambridge.

Andrew Bolton is Co-ordinator for Peace and Justice Ministries at the International Headquarters of the Reorganized Church of Jesus Christ of Latter Day Saints, Independence, Missouri.

Catherine Bowness is Senior Lecturer in Religious Education at the College of St Mark and St John, Plymouth.

Marian Carter is Tutor for Adult Theological Education at the College of St Mark and St John, Plymouth.

Clive Erricker is Reader in the Study of Religions, Chichester Institute of Higher Education; co-Director of the Children and Worldviews Project; and co-Editor of the *International Journal of Children's Spirituality*.

Jane Erricker is Director of Research in the School of Education, King Alfred's College, Winchester; co-Director of the Children and Worldviews Project; and co-Editor of the *International Journal of Children's Spirituality*.

Mary Grey is Professor of Theology at Sarum College, Salisbury.

Paul Grosch is Senior Lecturer in Philosophy at the College of St Mark and St John, Plymouth.

Ian Markham is Liverpool Professor of Theology and Public Life at Liverpool Hope University College.

David Nixon is St Luke's Chaplain at the School of Education, University of Exeter.

The Contributors

Vanessa Parffrey is a lecturer at St Luke's School of Education, University of Exeter.

A. Elizabeth Ramsey is a Senior Lecturer in Religious Education at Liverpool Hope University College.

Philip Sheldrake is Vice-Principal of Sarum College, Salisbury.

Adrian Thatcher is Professor of Applied Theology at the College of St Mark and St John, Plymouth.

Theology, Spirituality and the Curriculum – An Overview

Adrian Thatcher

There has been an upsurge of interest in spirituality in many, perhaps all, late capitalist societies. This is a strange phenomenon indeed. Is there an inverse relation between increased secularization and increased attention to spirituality? Now that spirituality has floated free from religion, are individuals enabled to explore a spiritual dimension to their lives without the dubious benefit of religious or ecclesiastical mediation? Or does preoccupation with spirituality merely mirror the importance which is attached to the individual, to the self and its rights, needs, pleasures and projects?

Whatever the answers to these questions may be, the spiritual and moral development of children has received unparalleled attention among teachers, lecturers, curriculum-makers and theorists in the 1990s throughout the English-speaking world. Some advocates of the new spirituality promise consensus between the different world faiths; between believers and unbelievers; between religious faith and secular humanism; between different Christian traditions; even between religious traditionalists and New Age enthusiasts. In societies which sit light towards the social and religious traditions that have made them what they are, might not the attention given to 'spiritual development' actually make the problem worse? Is it not a convenient pretext for turning away from the past, from the demands of social justice, from moral and environmental imperatives which call us to change our priorities and our lives, and turning instead towards a preoccupation with 'the self', the private individual in his or her interiority?

Why has the spiritual and moral development of children assumed so much importance at all stages of the curriculum? Is there a perceived religious and moral hiatus in late modem societies which these preoccupations are supposed to address? In the schools of Britain collective worship, religious education and the spiritual and moral development of children are compulsory. Do these activities provide soothing reassurances that continuity remains between the post-Christian society Britain may have become, and earlier generations when living faith was a reality for many more people than now? Does the language of spiritual and moral development maintain the convenient fiction that the religious and moral education of children (and in Britain the experience of worship) continues as it always did, except that now it is controlled by humanists instead of Christians?

This volume addresses a further puzzling feature of the preoccupation with spiritual and moral development, viz., the absence of any contribution from Christian theology to the shaping either of policy or of practice. Since the Christian faith has long traditions of spirituality, and the term is historically associated with religious traditions, is it not odd that theology has contributed little and Christians have generally contented themselves with a place in the secular consensus? There appear to be several reasons for this. First, changes in education are influenced by the social contexts in which they take place, and theology generally does not handle social change well. Fundamental social changes are brought into sociological discourse by means of core concepts like *secularization, pluralism, relativism, modernity, postmodernity, de-traditionalization* and *globalization*. While there is a theological literature which engages and deploys these concepts, it is not well known. Much theology merely evades the need to engage with social change by its stolid preoccupation with bygone ages.

Second, theology has been partly supplanted by religious studies, and the methodology of religious studies copes better with religious pluralism, distances itself from the phenomena studied, and is more obviously at home within the secular environment which largely gave rise to it. Third, historically theology has grouped itself with philosophy and the humanities in preference to the social sciences. But while the social sciences immerse themselves in examining and seeking to understand the·social world, theology (with the notable exception of liberation theology) does not. Fourth, and as a consequence, there is little work done in 'applied theology' (despite a proliferation of degree programmes in this subject). The 'theology of education', which itself has a small literature, is generally ignored by theologians and educators alike.

Fifth, it seems indisputable that the social changes just alluded to make learning about, and from, religious traditions more problematic. People have a much reduced knowledge of the Bible and the Christian tradition and are likely to find religious language and talk of God odd, or authoritarian, or oppressive. Theology has itself been slow to speak in new contexts with the required humility and to find a language for speaking about God which is received as good news, even for those people for whom all talk of God is problematic. Sixth, theology has made a negligible contribution to educational theory in general, and to religious education in particular. Lack of confidence in theology and a lack of perceived relevance of its contribution has led to the development of religious education, at least since the Second World War and probably before, outside of theological influence. Seventh, and on the educational side, the presuppositions which practising theologians make when they enter the realm of education are not shared by educators, even if the educators are themselves Christians.

Despite these difficulties it is far from obvious that the removal of theology from the discussion of the meaning of spiritual and moral development has been beneficial to either. Spirituality is an immediate victim of the conceptual chaos surrounding it. Once wrenched from its religious meaning, it has to be *assigned* a meaning by its advocates, and there is lack of agreement among them about what it signifies. Those who follow Rudolph Otto's *Idea of the Holy* and speak of 'awe and wonder' at the existence of a world or puzzling features of it, ignore that in the Judaeo-Christian tradition the holy is often associated with the *common*, not the *uncommon*. The use of bread and wine in Christian worship makes that clear. Those who identify spirituality with numinous or extraordinary experiences would seem to invest them with a significance denied to ordinary experiences such as receiving kindness, the sharing of love, or solidarity in suffering. Those who identify spirituality with individual inwardness appear to endorse the cultural value placed on individualism which religious or morally sensitive people do well to oppose. Those who identify spiritual development with human or individual or personal development seem to have capitulated to former dogmas of a psychological or psychotherapeutic kind which see people as individual units of human being. Those who identify spirituality with a non-material dimension to life seem to have become prey to a philosophical and religious dualism which ignores the material conditions which are needed for a spiritual life to be a possibility. Indeed, the belief in a God who becomes flesh provides the ultimate refusal of a theology or theory of human nature which does not begin with embodiment. It is far from obvious that spirituality without theology is even coherent.

This volume is an attempt to speak theologically about spirituality, and also about morality, in a way that engages directly with the international emphasis on both of them in an educational context. The theological approach was safeguarded by the commissioning of an essay by an eminent theologian linking theology and spirituality with the curriculum. It was stipulated that the essay should be around 5,000 words in length, accessible to theologians, non-theologians, teachers and educators, and that it should be sufficiently open-ended to evoke a range of responses. Mary Grey accepted the invitation to write the paper. Her chapter provides a unity of theme and a common purpose for the whole book.

Grey notes that the mission statements of Church colleges and schools embody a vision of learning and nurturing communities. To the extent that these institutions display a commitment to theological truth they are able to play a 'formative part' in 'human enrichment'. Grey deploys what have been called 'transformation theologies' and chooses from them liberation theology, ecological theology and feminist liberation theology. The method of these theologies, listening to marginalized groups, hearing lost voices, recovering memories, and so on, prompts a greater willingness to listen to children and their stories, and achieves a deep sense of the human subject, whether adult or child, as connected to others in community.

The content of transformation theologies is also able to influence the curriculum. They provide a new contribution to pastoral care through the importance of story and the ethics of care. Ecological theology resists the 'myth of cosmic homelessness' which sees people as belonging essentially to some other world than this one, and as being essentially unconnected to the earth which is their home. Ecological theology challenges the anthropocentrism of much Western thought, religious and secular, and builds bridges between religious faith and the imaginativeness of the scientists who work with the new cosmologies. Feminist theology brings a 'hermeneutics of suspicion' to tradition, not just to religious tradition, whilst at the same time setting free the liberating potentialities to be found there. Educators influenced by the transformation theologies may become 'mystics', who 'recover their own potential for contemplation, wonder, stillness, relationship with the natural world, and a thirst for learning which transcends narrow curriculum limits'. They in turn may help students and children to become mystics and dreamers.

Adrian Thatcher contrasts Grey's chapter with the attempt of the recent British School Curriculum and Assessment Authority to produce and implement an agreed statement on 'values'. Criticisms are made of its ahistorical method, the fragility of its claim to have achieved a moral consensus, and its calm banishment of God in the name of a humanistic morality. The ideology of the consensus is shown to rely on five dubious polarities of thought. The relationship between the value statements and the principles of action allegedly generated by them is discussed, and each of the four contexts for the values is analysed. It is shown that the humanist consensus is deeply flawed. Church-related schools and colleges are advised to have confidence in the resources which faith provides for the spiritual and moral development of children, not least the Great Commandments of Jesus to love God with all our hearts and our neighbours as ourselves. Grey and Thatcher appropriate Christian tradition critically, willing both to acknowledge the complicity of that tradition in its contribution to exploitation, oppression and fanaticism, and to affirm the transforming power of Jesus Christ in social and personal life, and therefore in the learning and teaching which education provides.

Reference has already been made to the diversity of meanings which are allocated to the term 'spirituality'. Philip Sheldrake considers the prospects for spirituality as an academic discipline. His 'working definition' is drawn from the Christian tradition. It is 'the study of how individuals and groups appropriate traditional Christian beliefs about God, the human person, creation, and their interrelationship, and then express these in worship, fundamental values and life-style. Thus, spirituality is the whole of life viewed in terms of a conscious relationship with God, in Jesus Christ, through the indwelling of the Spirit and within the community of believers.' Sheldrake has no time for the 'great divorce' between affectivity and conceptual knowledge which reduces spirituality to academically superfluous devotion. Theology has to be 'performative' not merely 'informative', and criticism is 'the servant of good theology'. Some striking agreements may be found between Grey's and Sheldrake's essays. Three of these concern *transformation*, *mysticism* and *experience*. The search for spiritual knowledge is itself said to be transformative. Should anyone think that mysticism is miles from the milieu of postmodernism, Sheldrake reminds us that the mystic and the postmodern person 'live in a movement of perpetual departure', each being 'wanderers and pilgrims lost in "the totality of the immense"'. And by grounding itself in experience (inevitably expressed and mediated in part by cultural context), spirituality keeps theology close to human concerns and vetoes its failure to connect.

David Nixon and Vanessa Parffrey muse upon Mary Grey's vision, in the last sentence of her essay, of educators as mystics. Drawing on the Ignatian vocabulary of *consolation*, *desolation* and *discernment*, they remind us that there is more to spirituality than the generalized instillation of awe and wonder. The contemplative world is contrasted with the language and practice of education which is inevitably utilitarian and performance-oriented. Even the continued professional development of the teacher, with its cycle of practice, reflection (alone and with others) and engagement with relevant literature is paralleled by the movement of the soul toward God in contemplative practice. The Christian educator is someone who is well aware that contemplative and calculative rationalities present two different worlds of experience, and who will seek to 'enhance points of convergence' between them.

Andrew Bolton adds a further theology of transformation to the three described by Mary Grey. Drawing on the history and theology of non-conformist Christianity, Bolton finds the heritage of Dissenters an empowering stance against what he calls the new 'Constantinian shift'. Bolton makes a series of hard-hitting parallels between state control of the Church in former times and state control of education in the present. 'The school is the new parish church. The new prayer book, designed to bring national uniformity to education, is the holy national curriculum, but without Cranmer's beauty of language. The Chief Executive of the Qualifications and Curriculum Authority is our new Archbishop – as subservient to government as any Erastian Anglican'. Non-conformity in past centuries is said to have emphasized, variously, freedom of conscience, equality between men and women, economic solidarity, non-violence, democracy, and so on. Non-conformists are needed now in the new 'Church of Education'. Like their predecessors they will begin with the biblical witness, including the witness of Jesus to children. Bolton's vision for the Church college as a learning and nurturing community coincides with Grey's, described earlier.

The necessity for a child-centred approach to spirituality is taken up by Elizabeth Ramsey and by Clive and Jane Erricker. Ramsey notes the conceptual hiatus into which spirituality has fallen and warns against purely verbal constructions which ignore 'the reality of the child's world'. Attention to case-studies provided by real children leads her to seek to 'resolve the conflict between vague spirituality and political tragedy'. At one level this conflict is located between curriculum theory and children's actual experience: at another level the conflict is illuminated by the disturbing contrast with the relationship between Christians and Jews seeking to come to terms with the tragedy of the Holocaust. The tragedy of the Holocaust, like the tragedies of deprived children, requires an accommodation beyond soothing words, but rather a deep sensitivity to suffering and a willingness to be engulfed by questions about 'the very foundation of our humanity'. When the Jewish–

Christian dialogue is informed by 'a renewed humility and willingness to rediscover', both traditions are changed for the better, and the light generated by them then becomes appropriate content for religious education. Themes are drawn from the learning which comes from this dialogue and which for that very reason also makes sense of 'the reality of the child's world'.

Clive and Jane Erricker situate themselves 'beyond' religious traditions. Pushing further Grey's admission of the ambiguous impact of the churches on contemporary consciousness, they want to take the 'conversation' she seeks into new areas. Tradition-specific understandings of spiritual development must be set aside in favour of 'learning experiences that develop an individual's sense of self-understanding and his or her awareness of the nature of human existence in a way that can affirm or deny the sense of the Transcendent'. Increasing pluralism and secularization have left uncertainties about what spiritual and moral development might mean. An 'inclusivist' definition of each is sought based on the 'love of humanity', howsoever derived. The experience of faith is said to be 'spiritual progress' in the task of realizing this love. Their research in their Children and Worldviews Project leads them to conclude that 'loving relationships and time spent listening and responding to children' lie 'at the heart of spiritual and moral education' and that this task is to be taken on by schools.

Some of the theological grounds for the Errickers' post-traditional position are clearly controversial. Is the humanism to which they aspire genuinely inclusive? Is not the quest for an inclusive humanism a good example of the type of discourse from which postmodernity announces a break? Does it not exemplify the ideology already castigated by Thatcher? Educationally, would not the increasing transfer of attention within the curriculum from religious content to personal relationship actually increase religious ignorance? Ian Markham takes up some of these issues in his reply. He thinks they rely too heavily on a straight reading of the secularization thesis and that their account of pluralism is vitiated by their unwillingness to see how their proposals for spirituality 'would appal other faith communities'. Markham proposes his own model of 'engaged diversity' in relation to spirituality. While the Errickers appear to wish to eliminate religious difference,

Markham want to 'enjoy' it. He proposes four partially incompatible accounts of spirituality, from Islam, Judaism, Hinduism and Buddhism. Placed before children, the facts of difference are able to promote children's religious learning.

John Beck's approach to spirituality differs from any so far considered. Writing from a perspective outside religious traditions, he delivers an incisive and trenchant critique of the use of the concept in British curriculum theory and Government documents, concluding it would be 'worse than misguided' to build a 'curriculum domain' based on the loose and contradictory meanings indicated by it. A telling comparison between the lobbying groups which were responsible for the insertion of spiritual development in the 1944 and 1988 Education Acts concludes that each believed in the conflation of doctrinal Christianity, an ambiguous concept of 'spiritual', and the use of education to promote 'national moral virtue'. Matthew Arnold's *Culture and Anarchy*, in particular its insistence upon religion as the source and guarantor of morality, stands behind the aspirations of both groups. But discourse which links spiritual and moral development 'like Siamese twins' is itself shown to be 'vague', 'platitudinous' and equivocal. Attempts to locate spirituality in 'our deepest humanity' as official humanism does are equally doomed, since all manner of evil issues from our deepest humanity also. The 'symbolic presence' of the spiritual in the curriculum merely provides opportunity 'to have recourse to deliberately ill-defined and inclusive uses of the term' which are intellectually indefensible and ought to be abandoned.

Beck's essay invites comparison with the earlier stances adopted towards spirituality in the book. The arguments of Grey are based in Christian liberation theology and so would appear to escape identification with the 'neo-conservatives' and advocates of 'national cultural restoration' whom Beck criticizes. Since Markham thinks the consensus view of spirituality is 'doomed to failure' he too escapes the charge of attempting, impossibly, to arrive at any consensus or inclusive view of spirituality. Rather, the religious humanism of the Errickers might appear to be more vulnerable to his critical insights, and a *rapprochement* between overt Christian theology and critical philosophy remains an interesting open question.

Adrian Thatcher

The confusion and equivocation in the language of
spirituality described by Beck is partially explained by Paul
Grosch. Prior to the period of Scholastic theology and
philosophy, in which those disciplines separated from each
other, the practice of spiritual exercises by theologians and
philosophers was one of the means by which theology and
philosophy were held together. Thereafter spirituality was
believed to be within the province of theology only, and as
theology weakened, a spiritual void arose which was filled by a
preoccupation with the autonomous self and a fascination with
Eastern religions and philosophies. Wittgenstein's *Tractatus*
represents a culmination of philosophical development which
acknowledges the crucial importance of 'the mystical' while
claiming that nothing about it can sensibly be said. In an
analysis which confirms some of Sheldrake's insights, Grosch
believes that the conditions of postmodernity provide an
auspicious time for a rediscovery of the spiritual exercises
which both disciplines have abandoned. These exercises are
'learning to live', 'learning to dialogue', 'learning to die' and
'learning how to read'. As Grey has spoken of transformative
theologies, Grosch speaks of transformative philosophy, since
the practice of the exercises is 'an acknowledgement of the
spiritual dimension of our inconsequential physical existence'.
Since the exercises are all about learning, it is tragic that
educators have forgotten about them. Renewed concentration
upon them may re-integrate theology and philosophy: more
urgently, it may transform the vision of what is ultimately
worth learning (and contribute to Grey's vision of educators as
mystics).

David Nixon, writing from the perspective of a university
chaplain, draws overtly from the traditions of faith and in so
doing resolves the problem of the 'mutually contradictory
concepts' which 'spirituality' brings together. His essay is a
theological reflection on what chaplains do. The incarnation of
God in Christ is divine 'permission to share the lives of
particular human beings around us in their myriad dimensions'.
As in Grey's essay, moral development is rooted in the
university community rather than the individual person. Since
public-sector educational institutions are increasingly short of
money and increasingly accountable to internal and external
audit, their corporate culture is likely to be competitive and

10

bureaucratic. Chaplains press on with their vision of the university as a community. They share the sufferings of others who are bruised and damaged by their employment. 'The alternative ... in a world of fragmented individuals is to create a solidarity, a community of compassion in which we all may grow.' Time 'wasted' with students is necessary for effective ministry (and e-mail is a useful replacement for the confessional). Chaplains are 'people who provide a still centre'. In the culture of competition 'our worship may begin as an encouragement to share gifts and resources', to be welcoming (and to adapt buildings so that they are warm, bright and usable for the 'multiplicity of community needs'). Universities and churches have much in common. While student populations have increased and the size of congregations has generally diminished, both types of institutions are short of money. The experience of education offered by the University and the experience of worship offered by the churches have not kept pace with the social changes which have profoundly affected each. Nixon's profound question to both sets of institutions is 'Without losing the heart of what it is to be a university or a church, how can we set up new models or paradigms which are sustainable economically yet will also nourish us spiritually and morally for the next and subsequent generations?'

Finally, Cathy Bowness and Marian Carter address three very broad questions: Where in the curriculum of schools and colleges are opportunities for emphasizing spirituality to be found? How are they to be explored and emphasized? Do the official guidelines characteristic of the British context help or hinder? Bowness and Carter describe the environment within which education happens, and show how its psychological, social and physical character may be made conducive to the spiritual development of learners. They give examples illustrating how this might be done, basing them in the different areas of the curriculum. They show how spiritual development is able to contribute to children's sense of identity at the different curriculum stages and within collective worship.

2

Christian Theology, Spirituality and the Curriculum

Mary Grey

I t is an illusion to think that theology and spirituality emerge from a timeless, context-free vacuum, or that there is a consensus as to how their insights should be used for education. Before delving into their significance for the curriculum in Church school and college, this paper draws together some of the most striking challenges which the current social and cultural scene present, before sketching appropriate theological responses. Postmodernism – even if it presents disputed territory – has at least made us aware that values, choices and cultural priorities are influenced by such social factors as economic situation, position in society, gender, race, historical and community memories, as well as the personal factors of heredity, and psychological and developmental influences. But the down side of this is that religious faith and its credal expressions have felt particularly threatened by postmodernist claims that truth is context-dependent and partial, and that universalist claims of all-embracing truth are without substance.

Secondly, Christian theology – in Western Europe at any rate – has felt doubly challenged and forced on to the defensive by its increasingly marginal status in a continent, on the one hand secular, and on the other, multi-faith and multicultural. (The fact that these two statements are inconsistent should give a clue that another 'reading' of the situation is possible.) Nor has the mushrooming of such sensational religious phenomena as

'The Toronto Blessing' and the rising of new fundamentalisms[1] contributed to the taking seriously of the contribution that theology makes to the educational scene.

Thirdly, the educational scene itself throughout Western Europe is rapidly being affected for the worse by increased competition for scarce resources, the undervaluing of scholarly research which is not income-generating,[2] and the vast pruning exercise which many faculties of humanities are undergoing.[3]

Fourthly, the disaffection with regard to all the main denominations of the institutional Church continues. The combination of financial and sexual scandals (including child abuse by clergy), the continuing rejection of the gay communities (even if the Lesbian and Gay Christian Movement is steadily winning more support), and the alienation of young people and of women of all ages, means that the climate of opinion in which theology and spirituality are approached is for many highly negative. Finally, we live in a world context where some of the most serious conflicts and tragedies – the Balkans, Northern Ireland and Palestine, for example – are fuelled by religious tensions. Religion is seen as the problem, not the solution.

Despite this bleak *mise-en-scène* there are still some positive considerations of specific interest for the churches' involvement in education. The mission statements of Church colleges and schools express a sincere commitment to caring for the student and child in a way directly inspired by religious faith. They (we) are committed to creating the kind of educational communities where the whole person-in-relation is respected.[4] The quality of these relationships is – in theory, at least – inclusive of family and neighbourhood, and within school or college of all non-academic staff, from cooks to gardeners and cleaners. The motivating factor behind this is the notion of the school and college as both learning and nurturing communities.[5] It is no accident that many students, when asked why they chose such a college, frequently reply that the 'community atmosphere' and the quality of interaction between staff and students were what drew them. But perhaps the most important feature of the Church college is its commitment to truth, and the conviction that theology and spirituality have a vital commitment to make to this search.[6] There is no way that we aim to turn the clocks back, attempting to reinstate theology once more as the 'queen of the sciences'. It is rather that theological truth, rightly interpreted, learns from, and contributes to other fields of learning, *in such a way as to enable them to play a formative part of human enrichment*. In the words of Cardinal Newman:

> Religious truth is not only a portion but a condition of general knowledge. To blot it out is nothing short of ... unravelling the web of University teaching. It is ... to take the Spring out of the year.[7]

The search for truth then, is no abstract enquiry, but embodied in the structures and lived experience of the learning community – at least, that is the hope. It is a truth which is dynamic in making the links between theory and practice, between so-called academic objectivity and the implications of scholarship for the lives of ordinary people. The disciplines of theology and the praxis of a spirituality which embraces the whole person, personally and socially, in a justice-building context, contribute to the transformation of society. I wrote elsewhere:

> The point at which the agendas of faith communities, the needs of society and the role of theology – seen from the experience of the praxis of transformation – coincide, is at the nodal point of creating just communities and structures which facilitate this.[8]

So, although post-Enlightenment individualism has in fact fuelled currents within spiritualities we have inherited – ranging from the extremes of over-indulgence to a narrow, body-denying asceticism – yet there are richer moral sources to be mined from the traditions, as well as new dimensions being discovered. These are both in continuity with the roots of Christianity as well as challenging the dominant strand.[9]

To respond to the contemporary context, this essay uses what Mark Kline Taylor in his book *Remembering Esperanza* calls the postmodern threefold trilemma:[10] this he names as the need to resist oppression, engage responsibly with tradition, and react creatively to a pluralist society.[11] He argues that a response to culture, such as Alasdair MacIntyre's, is a *postmodernism of reaction*, which fails to engage with society in a fully responsible manner. MacIntyre, it will be recalled, argued for

> local forms of community within which civility and the intellectual and moral life can be sustained through the Dark Ages which are already upon us.[12]

The danger here is that a one-sided recourse to tradition – MacIntyre calling for a new St Benedict much as black South Africa called for a new Moses – both ignores the damaging aspects of mainstream tradition and neglects the urgency of making a response to the multi-layered oppressive contexts of contemporary life.[13] Taylor brings up front what theologians frequently ignore – often relegating liberation theology to a minority group in the so-called Third World: that we actually live and work in a culture of violence. The students and children we educate do experience many levels of oppression and exploitation. The categories of domination and submission are not just theories for textual analysis, but actual discursive practices in institutional situations as well as in the home. Taylor chooses to focus on the interlinked oppressions of classism, sexism, racism and heterosexism, arguing that all four are expressions of a supremacist logic endemic in North American society. In a strategy which is at the heart of the argument I am putting forward, he argues for resisting domination together with, at the same time, engaging responsibly with tradition; and recognizing that the same struggle for justice is being engaged with in many faith communities: conversely, to celebrate difference without resisting oppression or engaging with tradition can produce a blindness as to how colonialist policies have rigidified unjust structures. And above all, to make connections between plurality and resistance to domination without engaging tradition is to stress tolerance and freedom without the resources of myth, ritual and memory, which engaging tradition can bring:

> Without these resources of tradition, the rhetorics of tolerance may often retain their appeal and inspiration, even their power to affect social-political

practice, but their appeal and power to nurture the common good is likely to be short, like the life and beauty of a cut flower.[14]

The response to this three-fold dilemma also bears in mind that the young people with whom we are concerned are growing into adulthood after society has undergone roughly fifty years of the secularization process, a process which has in fact taken many diverse forms in the last few hundred years. The most threatening form, which concerns us here, is the way that secularism breeds a society increasingly impervious to Gospel values, ultimately opposed to the Transcendent and to God.[15] *We can write the human narrative with no reference to the Transcendent* is the implication. But rather than accept this counsel of despair, I argue that a new configuration of the sacred and the secular is called for and indeed already experienced within theology lived as the praxis of transformation.

Moreover, the fundamentalistic expressions of religion which are on the increase – manifested in Christianity, Judaism, Islam, Sikhism, Hinduism – are themselves fuelled by the prevalent consumerist individualism of the current 'world order'. (Or they are in reaction to it.) So to propose insights from theology and spirituality based on the threefold trilemma is to recall Christian theology to its evangelical roots as counter-culture, as prophetic alternative to the domination of money and the profit motive, to the loss of integrity in public life, and the acquiescence given to violence in private.

To resist the 'unfinished symphony' of oppressions has become associated with a group of theologies designated as 'transformation theologies'. Thus, Professor David Ford, in his inaugural lecture as Regius Professor of Divinity at the University of Cambridge, wrote:

> ... a growing number of theologies of liberation (largely within Christianity but also in Judaism and Islam) insist that genuine theology must be rooted in resistance to oppression ... These highly controversial theologies have changed the consciousness and agenda of the theological world even where they have been largely rejected.[16]

Whereas it should be true that *all authentic theologies have transforming potential*, here I select and illustrate three examples from the 'transformation theologies', the best of which unite personal growth/nurture with the struggle for justice on the political scene, in order to offer insights for engaging the curriculum on a wider basis.[17] The selected three are (a) liberation theology (which also acts as an umbrella term for all), (b) ecological theology and (c) feminist liberation theology.

Liberation theology[18]

The diverse liberation theologies – black,[19] Latin American, Asian,[20] Afro-Caribbean, feminist, womanist,[21] gay, mujerista,[22] minjung[23] ... all have in common the struggle at a systemic level against the injustices which kill both body and spirit on an immense scale and on a global level. They are fearless in making the links between poverty, marginality, and the four areas which Mark Kline Taylor took as priorities in his call to resist domination. They take with utmost seriousness the words of the Vatican Instruction:

> It is not possible for a second to forget the situations
> of dramatic poverty from which the challenge set to
> theologians springs – the challenge to work out a
> genuine theology of liberation.[24]

Far from reducing theology to politics, the liberation theologians offer a widened vision of the Transcendent, because the revelation of God and the following of Christ are embodied in all the struggles to achieve justice for the poorest and most despised categories within all societies. For example, many would argue that AIDS sufferers are today's outcasts, and mentally handicapped and disturbed people tend also to be a forgotten category. Here, rather than attempt to define what is specific to each liberation theology, certain common features are discussed, as making connections with curriculum areas of the mission of the Church in education.

The first point is methodological: it is the crucial value of *listening* as a tool for liberation theology.[25] The very success of the supremacist logic of domination/subjugation depends on not hearing anything other than the prevailing patterns of reasoning and content of arguments. At its worst, it means being deaf to anyone else; whoever is 'other' to those who speak the discourse of power becomes stereotyped as misguided, unfortunate, undeserving of charity, lacking in intelligence, less than human, criminally responsible for their own misfortune, congenitally incapable of enjoying 'quality of life' and so on. And yet it is frequently from this corner that a genuine alternative is being voiced. The very diversity of marginalized groups and the complexity of making links between gender, class, race, power, health, culture, sexual preference and religious background underscore both the difficulty and the urgency of 'hearing' the lost voices, buried narratives and memories. Robert Bellah has called this 'an ascesis of listening'.[26] The poet Adrienne Rich asks for 'a severe listening'.[27] Newman's phrase was *cor ad cor loquitur* (heart speaks to heart), which evokes the quality of listening essential for genuine mutuality in relation. Because logic has lost its listening quality, which, arguably, was its original meaning,[28] because philosophy has lost the ability to be midwife to an idea which was Plato's challenge in the dialogue *Theaetetus*,[29] the post-Enlightenment model of rationality has become a confrontational mono-logic, creating cultures of silence, exclusion and marginality. Hence also the importance in feminist liberation theology of the metaphor of 'hearing into speech' of silenced voices.[30] The philosopher Hans-Georg Gadamer speaks of the need for openness in listening:

> ... this openness exists ultimately not only for the person to whom one listens, but rather that anyone who listens is fundamentally open. Without this kind of openness to one another there is no genuine human relationship. Belonging together always also means being able to listen to one another.[31]

What also needs stressing is the need to listen to children themselves, engaging with the world-view(s) of children as they emerge from our multi-faith context. *But voices are silent because they have been silenced.* Discourses are lost or buried not through carelessness, but through a systemic amnesia. Hence the second point about a liberation method is the activity of remembering.

Remembering as 'dangerous memory' has long been at the heart of liberation theology, from the early work of Walter Benjamin and Johann-Baptist Metz to the way in which all the theologies of liberation, each in its own unique way, base their theological reflection on story, narrative, recovery of narratives obscured or destroyed by oppressive regimes and so on.[32] Hence, resisting domination is at the same time engaging responsibly with tradition. That God's saving work in Christ has been incarnate in diverse ways among suffering and rejected peoples is the theological point: but its significance across the curriculum is not fully understood. The Republic of Ireland in 1995 began to remember the Great Famine of 1845–48. When participating in a conference where I was asked to speak on 'the silence of God in the face of the famine' I stumbled upon what could only be called amnesia on the part of theology. But, to my surprise, this was also the message of the economist, the historian and the literary scholar. A systemic amnesia covered the lost narratives of the famine. Hence the importance of remembering as a communitarian activity of recovering and discovering suppressed narratives, myths, rituals, which not only satisfy the need to be rooted in culture and history, but are also resources for the current struggle against the many-layered oppressions. Elisabeth Schüssler Fiorenza has made the 'dangerously remembering' of both memories of oppression but also those of freedom and of women's leadership in the New Testament the touchstone of her theological method.[33]

In fact, it is difficult to over-emphasize the importance of remembering as a communal activity and as a counter-cultural contrast to society's excessive individualism. Sharon Welch writes:

> This memory leads Christianity to a critique of what is commonly accepted as plausible; dangerous memory leads to political action. Dangerous memories fund a community's sense of dignity; they inspire and empower those who challenge oppression. Dangerous memories are a people's history of resistance and struggle, of dignity and transcendence in the face of struggle.[34]

The way that primary memory of spiritual vision can be recalled to develop a more mature spirituality in adulthood has long been recognized.[35] There is now, also, far more recognition of so-called cultural minorities, although the linguistic needs of these children are far from being met. But the attempt to integrate the theological theme of remembering as communal task confronts the inadequacy of the present narrow view of 'the subject' through insisting that any textual study must be rooted in communitarian praxis. This lonely 'I' of post-Cartesian dualism, this wandering hero (the Ulysses model), pirate and conquistador, is in reality embodied, gendered, located within a specific societal position, and inheriting community memories which may have been suppressed.[36]

Relying on tools of liberation theology brings a new concept of pastoral care,[37] an area of importance across the curriculum. The importance of story – both personal and communal narratives – has been stressed. But this can be developed in three ways. What might be called 'spiritual autobiography', or scripting the soul, can be integrated with theories of personal and social development, and explored through 'the spiritual quest in literature', in a way appropriate to students' needs and identities. It can be mind-blowing for students to *follow the novel as pilgrim*, tracing the geography of the novel through the cities of the world, from Russia in the nineteenth century to Latin America in the twentieth. It is again another way of countering individualism, of earthing the spiritual search in a social and political context. Secondly, 'scripting the soul' can be seen as a communal activity: the psychologist James Hillman in his prolific writings laments the fact that psychology as a discipline has shrunk to a narrow individualism. (He is especially thinking of analysis and psychotherapy[38]). Soul-language has all but disappeared in a culture which (rightly) has re-envisioned spirituality in an embodied way. 'Souls', wrote the Jewish Etty Hillesum, a few years before she died in Auschwitz, 'are simply wasted on us westerners.' We simply do not know what to do with them! She herself worked quietly on a 'landscape for the soul', a balance between interior and exterior dimensions.[39] Hillman's appeal for the recovery of the soul for psychology (seen as the *logos* of psyche-soul) is important for the theme of this book in that it is through collectively-held values like integrity in public and personal lives, accountability, search for truth, sensitivity to suffering and solidarity with the sufferers, willingness to develop sustainable life-styles, in other words, *deeply theological values*, that transformative possibilities are offered to society. In the communal adopting of these, lies the recovery of soul.

The third area of importance for pastoral care is the new ethical basis offered. The debate between the late Lawrence Kohlberg and Carol Gilligan in terms of the relative merits of ethics based on justice or care is well known.[40] But the way this has developed in the last ten years is both to show how the two approaches complement each other (and for a liberation theology approach the justice-making dimensions of both are vital), but also to show that two different notions of the subject are involved. Each notion brings enormous consequences for education.[41] The post-Enlightenment individualist tradition has encouraged a separatist notion of self. This is the lonely hero-self referred to above: ethical obligation implies that 'he' is detached from emotional ties, traditionally seen as 'the world of the female', in order to fulfil his task as culture builder. The contrasting notion of the relational self, or in my terms the 'connected self', sees its ethical obligations on the basis of a rich web of relations, respecting the often conflicting demands of each, particularly the demands of groups perceived as 'other' to the dominant group, and remaining faithful to a sense of interiority.[42] This is, in fact, creating more holistic forms of 'landscapes of the soul'. It is at the same time celebrating difference by paying attention specifically to the needs of minority groups for respect and inclusion into structures of justice.

Ecological theology

The pastoral care ideas developed above are also connected with the insights of ecological theology. Whereas the particular oppression being struggled against here is, of course, the exploitation of the environment, this is interlinked in a complex manner with all human experience. First, the presupposition which grounds all ecological theologies is that this planet is our home, here is where our theologies of creation, our notions of human origins and destiny are constructed. The locus of divine revelation is here. Here is where God is experienced as both immanent and transcendent. Hence what has to be resisted throughout education is the myth of *cosmic homelessness*. This is the all-pervading acceptance – for which Christianity must take some blame – that 'man's' true home lies beyond the earth, in the heavenly city, where the dimension of the material, the physical, sexual and bodily, will cease to have significance. They will yield to a disembodied 'spiritual' existence. Although Christianity has officially always preached the resurrection of the body, in the popular imagination this has never taken on the meaning that this world matters, that any notion of Heaven must somehow be grounded here.[43] Consequently, attempts to create sustainable, less consumptive life-styles have not been grounded in Christian theology as they could have been; at the same time, deeply ecological themes such as sacrament, Eucharist, theology of creation, have not been ecologically interpreted.[44]

Five points are significant for our theme: the first links with and develops the richer notion of subjectivity suggested in the previous section. 'The ecological self' is important for pastoral care, because, in addition to the personal, psychological, social and economic factors which are important for growth and nurture, relationship with nature and the quality of the environment with which the child interacts are also vital. Joanna Macy urges that the individual and the environment, the species and the environment, are essentially symbiotic.[45] A sound environmental context is crucial for health, for the ability to learn at all, and for developing the sense of appreciation and reverence for the world which is at the heart of all religious education. Nor is this a uniform task: in many parts of the world nature is terrifying, destructive, to be feared, its limits learnt. This diversity of possible responses must be taken seriously.

The second area is epistemological and philosophical. It is the challenge to rid education of anthropocentric presuppositions, the belief that 'man' is king of the environment, with the power – certainly 'he' has this – and the right, even the duty, to subdue 'nature' on the grounds of a presumed superiority. An organic approach will see humanity as part of the great web of life, yes, with particular responsibilities, but also needing to learn a certain humility as to its part in the greater whole, and to allow other species also to play their part. It is epistemological because it affects the entire process of perceiving and knowing the world. It is philosophical in opposing the dominant oppositional dualisms of the Western tradition, for example, humanity/ nature, man/animal, body/mind.[46]

The third area is the ethical area, which is probably the best known. It concerns the challenge to integrate into education a concern for the environment in all its aspects – not merely the disaster areas – as well as being able to give students an ethical framework for responding to such issues as animal rights, experiments on animals[47] or saving the rain forest. Theology has a particular role here, as providing a less functional approach to ethical issues, grounding ethical decisions in a creation theology, and stimulating an ecological spirituality of respect for and wonder at creation.

This links with the fourth area, which is the particular alliance that has sprung up between theologians and scientists working with new cosmologies.[48] Instead of the now sterile approach of the 'God of the gaps' – letting God fill the gaps which science cannot yet explain – theologians are increasingly entering into dialogue with cosmologists who envision the world in a profoundly reverential manner, with a deep sense of wonder. At the same time these same theologians, such as Thomas Berry, are making us sharply aware that at a certain point Christian theology lost a cosmology. Hence the human being became, in this warped consciousness, the kingpin of creation, with all the consequences we have been discussing. To recover a cosmology for theology entails another Copernican shift. It involves such attempts as Grace Jantzen's and Sallie McFague's to see the world as the Body of God, to link the so-called 'death of God' to the extinction of the species, to give theological content to loss, ambiguity and tragedy in nature, and to dialogue with the cosmologies within other faith traditions.[49] The effects for spirituality have been to recover creation spiritualities from Christian and other faith traditions which inspired a closer relation to nature – like the Celtic or the Benedictine, and Buddhist traditions of non-violence – and can provide a resource for sustainable life-styles today. This is, at the same time, recovering strands from tradition as well as engaging in a pluralistic dialogue.

Finally, an ecological theology poses a challenge affecting all three horns of the trilemma: this is the work of constructing an aesthetic theology, a theology of beauty based concretely on eco-

Mary Grey

justice. But it will be a theology reaching beyond the bounds of the religions, in dialogue with poets, artists and musicians from many cultures and traditions. As the Jesuit theologian Robert Murray has remarked: when theologians have neglected the earth and creation, poets and artists remained faithful:

> In *The Cosmic Covenant* I remarked that all too often and especially since the rise of industrialism, 'it has been poets rather than theologians who have been the prophets of reverence for creation' ... A whole theology of creation and the human place in it, of its right use and abuse and its destiny, could be constructed from the works of poets and artists of many cultures and faiths.[50]

Such an aesthetic theology would have a theology of the Holy Spirit in a central place: the Spirit of creativity, life-breath and beauty. Not only is this mining the tradition for buried resources, as well as being open to the Spirit beyond the boundaries of the religions, but it would also be manifesting the Spirit at work in communities of the oppressed: it would be a grassroots theology of culture which focused on the celebration, joy and creativity of poor communities which have actually been providing resources for their healing and transformation.

Feminist liberation theology[51]

The reason for selecting feminist liberation theology as a separate area for discussion is that as a discipline it brings together many of the points mentioned earlier and develops them further. It also contains an implicit inclusive capacity for the interlinking of as yet unnamed oppressions, for example, making connections between militarism and violence against women in the recent tragic events in Bosnia.[52]

The particular value for the understanding of the spirituality of education is the challenge which feminist theological theory – in dialogue with other disciplines – makes to the parameters in which the educational agenda is constructed. Elsewhere, I have described the four linchpins of feminist theology as new awareness, academic discipline(s), new culture and ethic, and new spirituality.[53] But because feminist theology consistently crosses the boundary between theory and practice, resists simplistic categorization, is consistently trying to maintain relationship while respecting and celebrating difference, and maintains a hermeneutic of suspicion in the face of all dominant strands of the intellectual Western tradition, it offers a paradigm for all liberation theologies, exposing the blindness or one-sided approach of many of these.

In fact, the situation is becoming increasingly complex. Since the emergence of the theology of Third World women of EATWOT (Ecumenical Association of Third World Theologians) – what Mercy Amba Oduyoye referred to as the 'irruption within the irruption'[54] – women from all continents have begun the analysis of the systemic oppressions present in their diverse contexts. It was the result of their achievements that an invitation came to a group of women theologians from Europe and North America to a global dialogue on the theme of 'Women struggling against global violence – a spirituality for life' in Costa Rica in December 1994. What is significant here is that the thematic approach included economic, cultural, ecological, military, domestic and political forms of violence. A focus on just one of these would have missed important connections. So the dialogue embraced analyses across many disciplines of learning. Yet it was incorporated in a method which explored alternative forms of life-styles, cultural analyses, and rituals which celebrated solidarity across diversity. It was a powerful indication of the extent of the educational task needed.

Feminist liberation theology also enables a nuanced attitude to tradition. Rather than totally dismissing Christian tradition as patriarchal ('kyriarchal' is the category suggested by Schüssler Fiorenza[55]), many scholars have insisted that tradition has been a source of liberation as well as of oppression. The Bible is used as a source of empowerment for women by setting free its liberating potential.[56] But tradition is also re-envisioned, not as a burden which must be dragged from one age to the next, given a new cultural face-lift, and used as a judgemental tool or criterion of orthodoxy. Tradition, from the perspective of the underside of history, is seen rather as nurturing and sustaining memory, another reason why the theme of 'dangerously remembering' is so vital. Tradition offers us strands where 'the other', 'the stranger' can be met as friend, where the truth of the other can be heard, acknowledged and even celebrated: and this is a now a process being engaged with across the world faiths. Not for nothing did Hans Küng say that there can be no world peace without peace between the world faiths.[57]

Conclusion: the once and future child[58]

All these themes come together in considering the significance of the young person in the educational process. Discovering the 'once and future child' is discovering the child as mystic, the child as dreamer. It means recovering the inspiration of Christ, who said that the child was the very stuff of the Kingdom of Heaven. But this means entering the world of the child and being willing to learn the language that the child speaks. If we believe that faith traditions have something to offer, we have to develop ways of moving easily in and out of the many discourses which are part of the child's world – the language of advertising, vernacular, dialect, slang, science fiction, TV thrillers and so on. Being bearers of tradition does not mean loading archaic concepts onto a child. Rather, 'offering the word of life' is empathizing imaginatively with what is possibly already a spirituality capable of wonder, of fierce capacity for justice-making, a spirituality where story-telling and listening to dreams are still trusted pathways, and where curiosity has not yet been stifled. The emphasis in this chapter has been strongly on a liberation spirituality, interpreted in the broadest possible way: this is because, as educators, we may not be in the forefront of political decision-making. But as theologians and as teachers we have unique responsibilities to explore the symbols, myths and language we use, to allow their liberating potential to unfold. Even more strongly, there is a moral imperative to eliminate forms of language which perpetuate harmful dualisms and degrading tensions.

The stories we tell are never innocent or free-floating, but are always rooted in a specific historical context (long forgotten), and are involved in a particular power dynamic: they convey a particular world view. The stories which Jesus told, the Rabbis told, the Sufi mystics told, subverted the dominant power dynamics, and (in the case of the Kingdom of

God) raised up the child and the little ones of culture. In order to play the prophetic role which education for liberation desperately needs, educators first need to become mystics, to recover their own potential for contemplation, wonder, stillness, relationship with the natural world, and a thirst for learning which transcends narrow curriculum limits. And that could be the service which theology offers the curriculum.

Notes

1. See Martyn Percy, *Words, Wonders and Power: Understanding Contemporary Christian Fundamentalism and Revivalism* (London: SPCK, 1996).
2. I do not wish in any way to plead for the return of the 'ivory tower' academic: research must relate in some way to the needs of the human – and non-human – community. But something of great value is lost if all is reduced to the profit motive.
3. The faculty of theology of the Catholic University of Louvain, to give but one example, is undergoing a budget reduction of 33 per cent. In Britain, the Research Assessment exercise has had drastic effects on small departments, noted for excellent teaching, but unable to compete, research-wise, with the 'giants'.
4. This is not to make any comparison with the mission statements of state-run institutions, many of which reflect a high degree of commitment to care. The point here is that in Church colleges, the commitment is a concrete way of living out Christian discipleship.
5. This will be developed further. See David Clark, *Schools as Learning Communities: Transforming Education* (London: Cassell, 1996); M. Grey, 'Disturbing the comfortable? Or the wisdom of the disturbed? Liberating truth and theological education' in Stephen Barton (ed.), *Where Shall Wisdom Be Found?* (Edinburgh: T. and T. Clark, 1999), 335–47.
6. It would almost seem to be a living proof of this statement that in the transformation (August 1997) of the Church college La Sainte Union into a secular college of the University of Southampton (New College) the first sections of college life to be axed were the chaplaincy and then the chapel.
7. John Henry Newman, *The Idea of a University* (London: Longmans, Green and Co., 1910), p. 70.
8. See M. Grey 'From cultures of silence to cosmic justice-making – a way forward for theology?' Inaugural Lecture, University of Southampton (1993), p. 14.

Mary Grey

9. Cf. Charles Taylor, *Sources of the Self* (Cambridge: Cambridge University Press, 1986).
10. Mark Kline Taylor, *Remembering Esperanza: A Cultural-Political Theology of North American Praxis* (Maryknoll, NY: Orbis, 1990).
11. Ibid., pp. 40–5.
12. Alasdair MacIntyre, *After Virtue: A Study in Moral Theory* (Notre Dame, IN: University of Notre Dame Press, 1981), p. 245.
13. Mark Kline Taylor also takes a critical stance with regard to the postmodernism of George Lindbeck, *The Nature of Doctrine: Religion and Theology in a Post-Liberal Age* (Philadelphia: John Knox, 1984). Lindbeck calls for theology to own up to its cultural-linguistic specificity, to give up its liberal and modern tendencies to generalize about humanity and religion and to develop the particularity of its ecclesial-communal rule, particularly its narrative texts. Taylor accuses him of a 'utopian textualism' which fails to engage with the more complex interpretive strategies which actually engage with the complex worlds of the reader: Taylor, *Remembering Esperanza*, p. 34.
14. Ibid., p. 42.
15. I have argued this in M. Grey, *The Shaking of the Foundations – again! Is there a Future for Christian Theology?*, the Von Hügel Lecture, St Edmund's House, Cambridge (Von Hügel Institute, 1994). The different expressions of secularism have been described by Charles Davis, *Religion and the Making of Society* (Cambridge: Cambridge University Press, 1994).
16. David Ford, *A Long Rumour of Wisdom: Re-describing Theology* (Cambridge: Cambridge University Press, 1992), p. 19.
17. It is not possible to engage here with the detailed socio-economic analysis on which these theologies are based and through which their unique qualities are obtained. In many cases they show how arbitrary are the classification and periodicization on which traditional scholarship is based. For example, to claim that we are now in a postmodern era, whereas in many parts of the world *modernity itself has not yet dawned*, reveals the limited value of such labelling, as well as calling attention to the power dynamics behind the process of naming.
18. For basic introductions to liberation theology, see Philip Berryman, *Liberation Theology* (London: I. B. Tauris and Co., 1987); José Miguel Bonino, *Doing Theology in a Revolutionary Situation* (Philadelphia: Fortress, 1975); Leonardo Boff and Clodovis Boff, *Introducing Liberation Theology*, tr. Paul Burns (Tunbridge Wells: Burns and Oates, 1987). For a recent

assessment, see Ian Linden, *Liberation Theology: Coming of Age?* (London: CIIR, 1997).

19. For black theology see Gayraud S. Wilmore and James Cone (eds), *Black Theology: A Documentary History*, 1966–1979 (Maryknoll, NY: Orbis, 1984).

20. For Asian liberation theology see Virginia Fabella and Sergio Torres (eds), *Irruption of the Third World: Challenge to Theology* (Maryknoll, NY: Orbis, 1983).

21. For womanist theology see Dolores Williams, 'Womanist theology: Black women's voices' in Ursula King (ed.), *Feminist Theology from the Third World: A Reader* (London: SPCK, 1994), pp. 77–86.

22. For mujerista theology see Ada Maria Isasi Diaz, 'The task of Hispanic women's liberation theology – mujeristas: who we are and what we are about' in *Feminist Theology from the Third World*, pp. 88–102. In the category 'Hispanic women' are included women whose cultural and historical roots are in Cuba, Puerto Rico or Mexico, but who at present are living in the USA.

23. For minjung theology see Fabella and Torres, *Irruption of the Third World*, p. 70.

24. Vatican Instruction, *Some Aspects of Liberation Theology* (6 August 1984).

25. See Gemma Corrado Fiumara, *The Other Side of Language: A Philosophy of Listening* (London: Routledge, 1990). Also M. Grey, 'Towards a listening logic' in *The Wisdom of Fools?* (London: SPCK, 1993), pp. 89ff.

26. Robert Bellah, *Habits of the Heart: Individualism and Commitment in American Life* (Berkeley: University of California, 1985).

27. See Adrienne Rich, 'A Transcendental Etude' in *The Dream of a Common Language* (New York: W. & W. Norton, 1978), p. 73.

28. This is argued by Gemma Corrado Fiumara in *The Other Side of Language*.

29. See *Theaetetus* in *The Dialogues of Plato* (Oxford: Clarendon, 1953).

30. The phrase is that of the late Nelle Morton. See *The Journey Is Home* (Boston: Beacon, 1986).

31. Cited by Fiumara, *The Other Side of Language*, p. 8.

32. For 'dangerous memory' see Johann-Baptist Metz, *Faith in History and Society: Towards a Practical Fundamental Theology* (New York: Crossroads, 1980), pp. 66–7. For its development by feminist theology, see Sharon Welch, *A Feminist Ethic of Risk* (Minneapolis: Fortress, 1990), pp. 154–5. For recent articles on its importance in work for justice generally, see M. Grey,

'Liberation theology and the bearers of dangerous memory', *New Blackfriars*, 75/887 (November 1994) pp. 512–24; Marsha Hewitt, 'The redemptive power of memory: Walter Benjamin and Elisabeth Schüssler Fiorenza', *Journal of Feminist Studies in Religion*, 10/1 (Spring 1994), pp. 73–89.

33. See especially Elisabeth Schüssler Fiorenza, *Bread Not Stone: The Challenge of Feminist Biblical Interpretation* (Boston: Beacon, 1984).
34. Sharon Welch, *A Feminist Ethic of Risk*, pp. 154–5.
35. See Edward Robinson, *The Original Vision* (Oxford: The Religious Experience Research Centre, 1977).
36. In some parts of Europe, for instance the Netherlands, it is rapidly becoming the case that memories of Christianity itself are being lost. Ignorance as to ancient devotions, saints' names or the liturgical year, lack of consciousness of Church history, use of words like 'salvation' only in a loose metaphorical sense, are becoming the norm.
37. The importance of incorporating an environmental dimension will be discussed in the next section.
38. See especially James Hillman, *Re-envisioning Psychology* (New York and San Francisco: Harper and Row, 1975).
39. Etty Hillesum, *An Interrupted Life: The Journals of Etty Hillesum* (New York: Washington Square Press, 1980).
40. See Carol Gilligan, *In a Different Voice?* (Cambridge, MA: Harvard University Press, 1980).
41. See Carol Gilligan, 'Mapping the moral domain: new images of self-in-relationship' in Carol Gilligan, Jane Victoria Ward and Jill McClean Taylor (eds), *Mapping the Moral Domain* (Cambridge, MA: Harvard University Press, 1988), pp. 3–19; Judith Jordan, Alexandra Kaplan *et al.* (eds), *Women's Growth in Connection: Writings from the Stone Centre* (New York and London: The Guilford Press, 1991); Catherine Keller, *From a Broken Web: Separatism, Sexism and Self* (Boston: Beacon, 1986); M. Grey, 'The separate self and the denial of relation' in *The Wisdom of Fools*, ch. 5.
42. Two recent books which open up a richer notion of pastoral care are Larry Kent Graham, *Care of Persons, Care of Worlds* (Nashville: Abingdon, 1992); and Valerie de Marinis, *Critical Caring: A Feminist Model for Pastoral Psychology* (Louisville, KY: Westminster John Knox Press, 1993).
43. It was for this reason that Mark Kline Taylor based the climax of his book *Remembering Esperanza* – a new Christology – on *Christus Mater*, linking with mothers, matter, material reality, and the notion that *matter matters*.

44. Priests have confessed to me that they have celebrated Mass all their priestly lives without making any ecological connection!
45. Joanna Macy, 'Awakening to the ecological self' in Judith L. Plant, *Healing the Wounds: The Promise of Eco-feminism* (Philadelphia: New Society, 1989), p. 205.
46. For a developed account of the damaging effects of these dualisms, see Val Plumwood, *Feminism and the Mastery of Nature* (London: Routledge, 1992).
47. See Andrew Linzey, *Animal Theology* (London: SCM, 1994); *Theology in Green*, 5/2, is devoted to articles on animal rights.
48. For example, Matthew Fox, *Original Blessing* (Santa Fe: Bear and Co., 1982); Thomas Berry, *The Dream of the Earth* (San Francisco: Sierra Books, 1990); Brian Swimme, *The Universe Is a Green Dragon* (Santa Fe: Bear and Co., 1985); Brian Swimme and Thomas Berry, *The Universe Story* (San Francisco: HarperSanFrancisco, 1992); Rupert Sheldrake, *The Rebirth of Nature: The Greening of Science and God* (London: Century, 1990).
49. See Grace Jantzen, *God's World, God's Body* (London: Darton, Longman and Todd, 1984); Sallie McFague, *The World as the Body of God* (London: SCM, 1992).
50. Robert Murray SJ, "A poetry for the peaceable kingdom", *Theology in Green*, 5/2, pp. 38–43.
51. Early key texts are, for example, Letty Russell, *Human Liberation in a Feminist Perspective: A Theology* (Philadelphia: Westminster Press, 1974); J. O'Connor, "Liberation theologies and the women's movements: points of comparison and contrast", *Horizons*, 2 (1975), pp. 103–13; Letty Russell, Kwok Pui Lan *et al.*, *Inheriting Our Mothers' Gardens* (Louisville, KY: Westminster, 1988).
52. The Report of the European delegation to the Costa Rica dialogue, December 1994 (which I co-ordinated), highlighted the interlinking between sexism, poverty, imperialism and militarism in the tragedy of the rape of the mainly Muslim Bosnian women. This tragedy also drew attention to the fact of a dominant Christian and neo-imperialist culture unwilling or unable to understand the situation of Muslim communities as 'other' to the powerful Christian majority.
53. See M. Grey, "Feminist theology – a critical theology of liberation" in *The Cambridge Companion to Liberation Theology* (Cambridge: Cambridge University Press, 1999).
54. Mercy Amba Oduyoye referred to the fact that this new Association had ignored the voice of women. At this point (New Delhi, 1981), the Women's Commission was founded. See

Virginia Fabella, *Beyond Bonding: A Third World Woman's Theological Journey* (Manila: EATWOT and The Institute of Women's Studies, 1993), p. 27.

55. Elisabeth Schüssler Fiorenza, *But She Said: Feminist Practices of Biblical Interpretation* (Boston: Beacon, 1992). 'Kyriarchal' is literally 'the rule of the Lord' and, in a more complex way than 'patriarchal', focuses on the logic and the practices of domination which are prevalent in most societies.

56. See, for example, John Pobee and Barbel Wartenburg-Potter (eds), *New Eyes for Reading* (Geneva: WCC, 1996); Elsa Tamez, *The Bible of the Oppressed* (Maryknoll, NY: Orbis, 1992).

57. See Hans Küng, *Global Responsibility: In Search of a Global Ethic*, tr. John Bowden (London: SCM, 1990).

58. This image is taken from T. H. White's famous story *The Once and Future King* (London: Collins, 1958), where the climax of the story is that King Arthur is free to die because a child will carry forward his vision of Camelot and the Round Table.

3

Values – Secular or Christian?: A Response to Mary Grey

Adrian Thatcher

The theological approach

I t will be obvious that Mary Grey's essay is a deeply Christian writing. Indeed it can be read purely as a fine example of 'applied' or contextual theology. It is able to advocate listening and remembering as a theological method because it first listens and remembers. It understands the 'marginal status' of Christianity in postmodern Europe and so is able to speak 'from the margins'; it recognizes that many Christians today live in societies which are paradoxically secular and multi-faith. It admits both the widespread 'disaffection' with the institutional churches, and the identification of religion as a human problem instead of a divine solution.

Critical first of the Christian tradition and its connivance with oppression, it is for this reason able to criticize oppression wherever it is found. Anchored within the Christian tradition, it can both speak for it and contribute to the task of its continual renewal. Drawing on the resources of that tradition, it discerns the work of God's Spirit beyond the Christian religion, indeed beyond all religion. Rooted explicitly in faith, it is able to perceive, as rival accounts cannot, that dominant world-views are routinely constructed in order to exclude all reference to 'the Transcendent'. Recalling Christian theology to its 'evangelical roots as counter-culture', it is able to articulate an alternative way of being which exposes violence, selfishness, individualism and injustice. Affirming Christ's risen body, it earns the authority to reaffirm the sacredness of human bodies and the body of the earth, ravaged by exploitation, greed and waste. Rooted in human connectivity, it is able both to confront narrow individualism and genuinely to celebrate difference. Celebrating human unity with the whole organic world, it is able to deal with the advanced prejudice of anthropocentrism which regards nature as ours to exploit. Just because it affirms the gospel of God's love for everyone and everything, it can offer real hope and actual 'transformative possibilities'. And so on.

It will be equally obvious to the reader that the task of spiritual development is itself exposed to transformative possibility by the arguments offered in the paper. The settled consensus in the relevant literature, that individual children are the beneficiaries of attempts to develop them spiritually, is shaken by the counter-assertion that communities are the locations within which spiritual development occurs, or fails to occur. The 'search for truth' is 'embodied in the structures and lived experience of the learning community'. Belonging to a community which owns and practises spirituality is the *sine qua non* of the spiritual development of its members. Yet schools and colleges, whether formally Christian or not, often embody 'discursive practices' which oppress the human spirit. Remembering, like 'scripting the soul', is a communal activity. The values of spiritually developed people will be communal values. Even Christianity will find itself enriched by dialogue with partners in the community of world-faiths.

The secular approach

The process of values production

Many educationalists throughout the world are interested in how a consensus on values may be reached in schools. Events in the UK in the 1990s may provide an interesting case study of one such attempt. In 1993 a Government agency, the National Curriculum Council, circulated to schools so-called 'guidance notes' on spiritual and moral development.[1] Another agency of Government, the Office for Standards in Education (Ofsted) required spiritual and moral development to be assessed, and issued further notes to the new army of inspectors on how this would be done.[2] The Government also issued a circular to schools warning them explicitly that they were paying 'insufficient attention' to 'the spiritual, moral and cultural aspects of pupils' development'.[3] It became increasingly obvious that the concepts of spiritual and moral development could not begin to bear either the political or the curricular weight that was being loaded on to them. The spiritual and moral development of children was supposed to occur through collective worship (a uniquely British phenomenon), religious education, and as a cross-curricular theme, embedded in the whole curriculum. These prescriptions were unpopular. Teachers had not been prepared to deal with them. There was no consensus, either in the teaching profession or outside in the broader society, about what these terms might mean, who should interpret them, and how the curriculum might accommodate them. In the absence of such a consensus, civil servants had a breathtaking idea: they would invent one, and invite people outside the schools to help them.

So the Government, acting through another newly-formed agency, the School Curriculum and Assessment Authority (SCAA) convened a conference 'Education for Adult Life'. This conference endorsed the view 'that although society has the ultimate responsibility for the spiritual and moral development of young people, schools have a vital role to play and that they would be better able to play this role if they could rely on a *commonly agreed framework of values*'.[4] The Authority then created a forum, grandiosely entitled 'The National Forum for Values in Education and the Community', and mandated it to make recommendations to the Authority on 'ways in which schools might be supported making their contribution to pupils' spiritual and moral development', and on 'whether there is any agreement on the values, attitudes and behaviours that schools should promote on society's behalf'.

The Forum consisted of about 150 people, a deliberately 'representative section of society' which included 'representatives from the teaching professions, school governors, parents, teacher trainers, principal religions, academics, the legal professions, youth workers, employers and the media'. International interest in spiritual and moral development provided an important context for the Forum's work:

The Forum noted that interest in spiritual and moral development is currently a matter of concern world-wide. Members drew attention to similar projects in Australia, Canada, Germany, the Netherlands, Norway, Scotland, Spain and the USA. There was a general view within the Forum that England has devoted less official attention to these areas of education than have other countries, and that we have a great deal to learn from international thinking.

The Authority entertained high hopes for any common statement of values which the Forum might have been able to produce. Among the 'perceived benefits' of any such statement was the demonstration 'that despite the many differences between members of a pluralistic society, there are certain values upon which we can all agree'. A common values statement would also be a 'corrective to the claim' so disliked by espousers of liberal moral theories, 'that we "respect" or "tolerate" every view', irrespective of its content, just because it happens to be held by someone. The Forum divided into groups, met three times, and, strongly encouraged by the Authority, produced the desired goods. Undoubtedly a remarkable consensus was produced. The 'value-statements' from it are reproduced later in this chapter.

A change of government in the United Kingdom made no difference either to the strategy of the consensus-makers or to its momentum. Schools were sent more 'guidance notes' and sent two matrices, one full, one empty! The first of these, 'A Statement of the Overall Goals of Promoting Pupils' Spiritual, Moral, Social and Cultural Development', was a 30-page, highly detailed, completed matrix, disarmingly offered to schools as 'an illustration of how a school might complete the process described in the guidance' and 'not offered as an ideal'. The second matrix, 'The Empty Matrix – a Management Tool' was intended 'to be used by schools, in consultation with their immediate and extended communities, to guide thinking about the promotion of pupils' spiritual, moral, social and cultural development'. Once completed, the matrix would become a complete statement of school policy in this area. After further consultation between the Authority[5] and the schools, 'final guidance will be issued'.

The method of values production

Perhaps the most striking feature of this consensus-seeking venture of a powerful Government agency is its entirely *ahistorical method*. There is to be no discussion of the troublesome historical, social, ethnic, economic and religious differences and inequalities which constitute the actual society on whose behalf spiritual and moral development is being fostered. Attention to these may have thrown light on the perceived social crisis which the focused promotion of spiritual and moral development is supposed to address. The consensus is likely, then, to be pretty superficial. This wilful bracketing-out of our separate histories is scarcely appropriate for an Authority bidden to promote 'cultural development', for an appreciation of the importance of history is usually deemed central to it. When Alasdair MacIntyre in *After Virtue* famously compared the collapse of science in the imaginary world of the Know-Nothing party with the collapse of moral discourse in the real world, he noted that 'a prerequisite for understanding the present disordered state of the imaginary world was to understand its history',[6] and that the tools of enquiry for an investigation of the present (his examples were phenomenology, existentialism and philosophical analysis) would not 'be able to discern anything wrong'.[7] No such difficulties impeded the National Forum. All they needed to do was meet three times and write a few papers for each other. A task was set: a consensus was required, so one was produced.

Attention to history might yield reasons why there is moral disagreement and perhaps a moral hiatus within society. 'It is only through knowledge of its history that a society can have knowledge of itself.'[8] Grey warns about 'systemic amnesia' with regard to the Irish famine. The encouragement of collective amnesia is morally dangerous. Yet amnesia is being organized, processed, solemnly agreed, and passing into the curriculum, with all the apparatus for policing and enforcement that state bureaucracies possess. And what is easier to enforce than a policy which can be depicted as agreed by everyone it affects?

Equally alarming is the mode of moral discourse which the Report endorses. The *normalization* of the term 'values' as a core concept of postmodern moral language seems fraught with unheeded danger signals. Have we not already had four centuries of dogmatic separation of facts from values, immortalized by Dickens' Thomas Gradgrind in *Hard Times*,[9] with values confined to the realm of fiction, fantasy, opinion and what science had no time for? Does 'values' slip so easily into the curricular vernacular because of its usefulness in economics? Is the word which means 'an amount, a fair price or return, monetary or material worth in usefulness or importance to the possessor, utility or merit, etc.', really an appropriate synonym for personal beliefs, whether religious or moral? Is not the attraction of the word its sheer emptiness? An indicator of moral earnestness without content? And does not the plural form trip off the tongue because it merely confirms the nebulousness of its supposed referent?

Is not the strategy of seeking *consensus* also suspect? Well, it is 'good' and 'pleasant' to 'live together in unity' (to paraphrase Psalm 133:1) but the prospects for this consensus seem slight. This is no committed attempt to edge towards some synthesis after due process of painful listening and stock-taking, perhaps with space for repentance and 'amendment of life'. That would be a consensus worth having. There is no proposal here for facing disagreements and differences, resolved to live without violence in recognition of the other's 'otherness'. No hint that there may be a Transcendent source for living in peace, where difference does not threaten community, and which Christians recognize as the Triune life of God?[10] Indeed what point is there in recognizing and owning our differences since, as it turns out, we are really in agreement about morals anyway?

Social theorists often do useful work for theologians, and the work of Zygmunt Bauman is useful here. Developing his own particular account of what separates postmodern from modern ethics, he uses the term *aporia* ('in a nutshell, a contradiction that cannot be overcome, one that results in a conflict that cannot be resolved')[11] and argues that 'it was a characteristic, perhaps the defining, feature of modernity that the aporia was played down as a conflict not-yet-resolved-but-in-principle-resolvable'. 'Modernity', he continues, 'is about conflict-*resolution*, and about admitting of no contradictions except conflicts amenable to, and awaiting resolution.' The very treatment of difference in the methodology of the Forum, after the civil servants have completed their work, is exposed by Bauman's analysis. There is a determination to find a lowest common denominator of beliefs and to promote these, whatever distortions, erasures, or equivocations may be necessary on the way. An admitted lack of consensus about 'sources of authority for values' and 'the application of values to life' was no difficulty for the consensus-seekers. They were able to turn this lack of agreement into a new and important agreement ('There was agreement that there was not consensus ...').[12] And the problem of disagreement about 'the application of values to life'? The consensus-seekers don't find that a problem at all. 'Shared values' are what count, irrespective of the diversity of sources and applications. 'Between the sources of authority and the application there is room for agreement.'

No one is supposed to ask what happens to 'values' when they are extrapolated from their sources and before they are applied to life, nor whether much is gained by this manufacture of artificial space between value-sources and value-applications, space which is about to be occupied by the new curriculum for personal and social education, and spiritual and moral development. Unfortunately, other important preliminaries about the method of this report deserve to be brought into the light. Let us consider the appeal to something called 'society in general'. Schools will be aided if 'they could rely upon a framework of values supported and agreed by society in general'.[13] Support 'from society in general'[14] will provide a 'secure basis' for the spiritual, moral, social and cultural education of children. Let us hope that beyond relativism there may be 'a universalism of love' which we may discern by common human agreement, as opposed to party, selfish, sectarian, or national interests. The doctrine of natural law says something like that. If there is such a universalism, it is unlikely to be found in the 'totalizing' appeals to 'society in general'. Such generalizations permit the covering up of real social differences, differences with a real capacity for social disruption, in the name of a purely verbal unity.

The consensus remains undisturbed about the lack of fit between what people agree about and what is most important to them. The strategy here is to note the problem and carry on. The lack of consensus over the 'sources of authority for values' is code for saying that religious traditions are disallowed from contributing overtly to the secular consensus. God is banished, as we shall see, from the value-statements, and a further reason for banishing God is the disagreement in 'society in general' about the importance of God. Since only consensus is to be admitted into the value-statements, God is an early casualty. This is a further outstanding example of what I have elsewhere called (borrowing Milbank's phrase) 'policing the sublime'.[15]

The banishment of God from the statement of values is, on any analysis, an amazing achievement. Jews, Christians and Muslims presuppose the reality of God, whose presence pervades the natural and human worlds. Here is a breathtaking assumption. In the interests of securing moral agreement in a multi-faith society, all believers in God are expected to concur in the Great Divine Removal. That which is of ultimate importance to them offends against the Great Secular Consensus, so, while yet being expected to participate in this consensus, they must also agree to the marginalization of the Deity. Ironically, they are expected to consent, in the name of morality, to the inability of the secular society to live before God; to the optionalization of the Ultimate; to the reduction of God to the status of a consensus-threatening non-problem. When Nietzsche proclaimed the death of God, he at least was consumed by the horror of what had occurred – 'Who will wipe this blood off us? ... Is not the greatness of this deed too great for us? Must not we ourselves become gods simply to seem worthy of it?'[16] No such horror afflicts the secular curriculum-makers. The living God is now proclaimed to be an obstacle to the new, agreed, secular humanism.

How has this great deed, apparently with the loyal support of believers in God themselves, been done? How have believers in God succumbed to the charm offensive of the new humanism? How have the teachings of the Holy Office been supplanted by those of the Holy Office for Standards? The answer to these questions lies in the Preamble to the values and, as we shortly see, in unquestioning adherence to the Five Polarities. The values, we are told,

> are not exhaustive. They do not, for example, include religious beliefs, principles or teachings, though these are often the source from which commonly-held values derive. The statement neither

implies nor entails that these are the *only* values that should be taught in schools. There is no suggestion, in particular, that schools should confine themselves to these values.

Agreement on the values outlined below is compatible with disagreement on their sources. Many believe that God is the ultimate source of value, and that we are accountable to God for our actions; others that values have their source only in human nature, and that we are accountable only to our consciences ...

There is a lot going on in the warm-up here that precedes the unveiling of the Values. We have already noted the separation of facts from values; that is the first polarity. The second polarity is the separation of the past from the present. Those theorists who believe that 'de-traditionalization' is a feature of postmodernity will find the Preamble a verifying primary source. The third polarity is that between common and 'uncommon' values. Underlying the disclaimer to an exhaustive list, and the denials that SCAA's values are the only values or that schools should confine themselves to these, is a fairly obvious identification of beliefs held in common and the others, the 'uncommon' ones, which, just because they may be religiously generated, are thereby not common. The fourth polarity is an extreme disjunction between religious and secular values. There is no possibility even of an overlap between religious and non-religious values. 'The values ... do not ... include religious beliefs, principles or teachings ...' The relationship of secular beliefs to religious beliefs is not just that between common and uncommon, but also between derived and the 'underived' source or origin.

'Source' suggests a point at which something springs into being, or a point of origin, such as a spring, of a stream or river. In physics it means the point or part of a system where energy or mass is added to the system. This is the fifth polarity, between the source of values and the present, particular, apprehension of them. A damaging admission now begins to appear: secular values may be sourced, after all, in religious values. Well, the neglect of the source of, say, a river, can lead to its pollution or destruction, just as the neglect of a source of energy can lead to the collapse of an energized system. The entire enterprise of values-production, coupled with neglect of the very sources which make the enterprise possible, cannot be a serious rational undertaking. Belief in God as the source of values now appears as a phenomenological remark about human oddness. 'Many believe that God is the ultimate source of value' becomes a report about one of the myriad of optional beliefs that informed individuals are entitled to hold, akin to 'Many people believe their horoscopes' or 'Many people believe they can win the national lottery'.

The content of values production

What about the value-statements themselves? The first thing to say is that some revolutionary concepts, in particular, love, justice, community, the environment, and the common good of society, having been expunged from the strident humanism of the 1993 guidance notes,[17] have been re-admitted into the secular canon of moral consensus. This is most welcome and partially restores faith in the process that has just been criticized. The moral landscape of 1997 is different from that of 1993, and supporters of the consensus can point to the contributions they have made to the changes.

There are 'four specific contexts' where 'values are seen to operate',[18] viz., 'values related to society, values related to relationships, values related to self, values related to the environment'. During and after the consultation, the order of the contexts was changed, along with some of the detail in each. This is the most recent statement which, because it will be discussed extensively, is quoted in full:[19]

The self

> We value ourselves as unique human beings capable of spiritual, moral, intellectual and physical growth and development.
> On the basis of these values, we should:
>
> - develop an understanding of our own characters, strengths and weaknesses;
> - develop self-respect and self-discipline;

- clarify the meaning and purpose in our lives and decide, on the basis of this, how we believe that our lives should be lived;
- make responsible use of our talents, rights and opportunities;
- strive, throughout life, for knowledge, wisdom, and understanding;
- take responsibility, within our capabilities, for our own lives.

Relationships

We value others for themselves, not only for what they have or what they can do for us. We value relationships as fundamental to the development and fulfilment of ourselves and others, and to the good of the community.

On the basis of these values, we should:

- respect others, including children;
- care for others and exercise goodwill in our dealings with them;
- show others they are valued;
- earn loyalty, trust and confidence;
- work co-operatively with others;
- respect the privacy and property of others;
- resolve disputes peacefully.

Society

We value truth, freedom, justice, human rights, the rule of law and collective effort for the common good. In particular, we value families as sources of love and support for all their members, and as the basis of a society in which people care for others.

On the basis of these values, we should:

- understand and carry out our responsibilities as citizens;
- refuse to support values or actions that may be harmful to individuals or communities;
- support families in raising children and caring for dependants;

- support the institution of marriage;
- recognise that the love and commitment required for a secure and happy childhood can also be found in families of different kinds;
- help people to know about the law and legal processes;
- respect the rule of the law and encourage others to do so;
- respect religious and cultural diversity;
- promote opportunities for all;
- support those who cannot, by themselves, sustain a dignified life-style;
- promote participation in the democratic process by all sectors of the community;
- contribute to, as well as benefit fairly from, economic and cultural resources;
- make truth, integrity, honesty and goodwill priorities in public and private life.

The environment

We value the environment, both natural and shaped by humanity, as the basis of life and a source of wonder and inspiration.

On the basis of these values, we should:

- accept our responsibility to maintain a sustainable environment for future generations;
- understand the place of human beings within nature;
- understand our responsibilities for other species;
- ensure that development can be justified;
- preserve balance and diversity in nature wherever possible;
- preserve areas of beauty and interest for future generations;
- repair, wherever possible, habitats damaged by human development and other means.

It is necessary to comment on the general form of the value statement before moving to each of the four areas. Since there is intentionally something here for everyone, it would be churlish not to acknowledge it. However, this is a further difficulty that secular consensuses generate: they marginalize their critics, especially religious ones, because, after all, the people who have agreed these statements are all reasonable, and schools and teachers have been told 'they can have confidence that there is general agreement in society upon these values'.[20] Given the reluctance of schools and teachers to handle explicit religious and moral teachings on the grounds of their controversiality and lack of consensus, who but a dissenting nutcase would want to disturb this new and entirely unanticipated creation, a values-statement that everyone supports?

We might note the confidence with which the values generate particular and precise 'principles for action', wondering how the consensus has so easily solved the problem of the relationship between beliefs and practices, and how it is able to predict procedural public outcomes from privately held 'values' with such accuracy. Values apparently generate their own procedural moral imperatives: 'on the basis of these values we should ...' Might not the link between a good moral character and the dispositions to act well which it generates have occurred to the consensus-makers? Whatever the answer, there is an obvious and fatal flaw in the Authority's own reasoning. It is already admitted that there is no consensus about 'the application of values to life', but the application of values to life now flows unanimously and profusely. Another case of amnesia?

Next we might ask about the values featured in the statement, Whose are they? On whose behalf are they articulated? The statement 'We value ...' occurs four times. But who are 'we'? Everyone? The National Forum? The Qualifications and Curriculum Authority? The 94 percent of adults confronted by the Authority's opinion researchers? Christians familiar with saying the creed ('We believe ...') may want to ask whether these value-statements function as secular versions of the Christian creeds, enabling the 'strong desire among schools to take a firm stand on values and behaviour',[21] rather as orthodox Christians used the Nicene creed to take a firm stand against the values of the Arians. Since it has been admitted that religious beliefs are the unacknowledged sources of many of the values in the statement, the similarity may not be accidental. But now we might want to press a *dis*similarity between the two types of belief-statements, those of the Christian Church and those of the secular Authority. The creeds were at least embedded in religious communities whose identity the creeds expressed. A problem with the consensus is that *everyone*'s identity, *per impossibile*, is supposed to be expressed by it.

There are other difficulties with 'We value ...'. It becomes a transitive verb, expressing an action that is carried from the subject to the object. 'We' (a group of subjects) 'value' ourselves, relationships, truth, etc., and the environment: the subjects value some object for some further derivative reason, 'as'. Such statements were called by Gilbert Ryle 'avowals',[22] and as such they presumably express some feature of the mental states of the people doing the avowing. The epistemological question whether these beliefs and values are subjective states, or whether a claim to more serious moral knowledge, appropriately objective, and rooted, say, in moral traditions or sources of wisdom, now becomes open. And since sources of value are relegated to the periphery of discussion, the suspicion that the value statement does not provide genuine moral knowledge must be justified.

Each of the value-contexts appears to bristle with difficulties. During revisions, the statement about 'the self' has moved into first position. This new ordering, admits the Authority, 'reflects the belief of many that values in the context of the self must precede the development of other values'.[23] One needs to ask why 'the self' does come first. Is it in response to the criticism, often made by feminists, that women in patriarchal societies find themselves lacking in self-worth, and so need to seize control over their lives as a precondition of moral agency of any kind? Such a thought does not appear to be present in this section of the statement. Indeed, the development of 'a sense of self-worth', present in earlier versions, did not survive (just because of its resonance with feminist insights?). Let us imagine (no more than that) a narcissistic, selfish, deeply uncaring society which always put the interests of individuals above those of relationships, society and the environment. Such a society might cease to be aware of, or actually remove, correctives which could expose collective self-interest as the evil state of affairs it is. Individuals advocating self-interest might then think it self-evidently true. Is not the statement that 'values in the context of the self must precede the development of the other values' too disconcertingly congruent with such a society to escape comment? Opponents of the minuscule British overseas aid budget still mask their meanness with the slogan 'Charity begins at home'. And that is where it generally ends.

The values are clearly self-centred, despite the disclaimer that 'the ordering of the values does not imply any priority or necessary preference'.[24] Has there ever been a moral statement which begins by affirming the value it places on the utterers' own self-importance? Once the Five Polarities are invoked, reasons why human beings are 'unique' recede, because they cannot be agreed. 'All human beings are unique' is compatible with 'No human being is unique'. Does the statement mean that each human being is unique? Probably. But that would not by itself entail moral imperatives about how human beings should be treated, for it might be claimed equally that in relation to species, each member, whether dog, dolphin or human being, is unique. Is the potentiality for growth the reason for valuing ourselves, as the statement suggests? That would be an odd reason.

Agreement with the principles of action in this section is consistent with disbelief that the principles are derived from the values, or that the majority of them can be located within 'the context of the self'. This is because the boundaries of 'the self' may be unable to be drawn in the way the statement presumes. None of the self-actualization envisaged in 'the context of self' is even possible without communities of people surrounding, holding and nurturing the self in its path to maturity. 'Meaning and purpose' is presumably found within the self, not in communities or traditions (religious, philosophical, social) which mediate meanings and locate people within them. Perhaps 'meaning and purpose' do not arrive in our lives as confusions which require the employment of the values-clarification school of moral philosophy, to assist us in the process of confusion-elimination.

The section on relationships glows with sentiments which Christians will want to affirm. Since capitalist societies manifestly do not 'value others for themselves' or 'respect the dignity of all people', one may want to know on what basis we are said to 'value others for themselves', since the reasons why we do (to the extent that we do) are not simply self-evident. How far is it possible to 'work co-operatively with others' when we are arranged in competition with them? The exhortation to 'respect the privacy and property of others' is a revision of the earlier 'respect the beliefs, life, privacy and property of others'. Presumably the point was taken that respecting the beliefs of others, if they were murderous or discriminatory, might not perhaps be appropriate. Yet what remains of this particular principle of action, respect for privacy and property, could be equally at home in a moral code for obedient serfs. We are to show others they are valued, even when they manifestly are not. 'Others' are valued without distinction. *All* others? Near and far, as long as they are not 'me'? And are *all* relationships to be valued, of all kinds? Even those in which we are victims of the misuse of power over us? Having begun the values statement with 'We value ourselves', the addition that we also 'value others' does nothing to remove the moral individualism that is overtly at work. The valued 'others' are next in the list of objects the transitive verb 'to value' takes. There is little recognition of the sociality of existence, of our already being persons-in-relation, already partly formed by particular 'others', in interrelation and interaction with them.

Is the unconditional valuation of 'truth' consistent with the instrumental purposes of these statements? Belief in God, central to any theistic account of something called 'truth', is clearly not valued (because it cannot be agreed); so theists are discouraged at the outset. Are we to 'respect the rule of law', even when laws are unjust? The institution of marriage is a late arrival to the statement, giving rise to the qualification that, 'reflecting the range of views in the wider community', support for marriage 'may legitimately be interpreted as giving rise to positive promotion of marriage as an ideal . . .'.[25] Accommodation for the counter-view is found in recognition of families of 'different kinds'. So what is advocated, after all? That marriage should be promoted if enough parents in the catchment area think so (whether or not they are married themselves)? And whether wives and children are thriving or suffering? Doesn't the inclusion of 'support' for 'the institution of marriage', however laudable, reveal how fragile any consensus about marriage is (if one exists at all)? Would not attention to the social disagreement about marriage promote real moral learning? Frankly, is there any commissive force at all to the exhortation 'On the basis of these values, we should . . .', when even verbal agreement about them is out of reach? How can we 'promote opportunities for all' when no possibility of agreement currently exists about the structural adjustments which would be necessary to bring this about? How far are social inequalities even acknowledged, still less addressed?

The section on the environment raises huge questions. One is grateful to find it at all, while suspecting that the impact of the environmental imperative upon standard ways of philosophizing about it has been underestimated. The earlier version, 'We value the natural world as a source of wonder and inspiration', left readers wondering whether the natural world was to be valued only because of the response it elicits in us. But now, since 'we value the environment, both natural and shaped by humanity', inclusiveness is taken to absurd lengths. Poisonous slagheaps, radioactive seas full of dead and deformed fish, polluted air, pesticide-sodden earth, etc., etc., have all been 'shaped by humanity' and may one day be 'the basis of life' no longer. This is also how humanity shapes the environment. Is there not more work to be done here in overcoming the centuries of anthropocentrism, perhaps hinted at by the ambiguous reference to the 'place of human beings within nature'? Doesn't this section connive with the pretence that with a few liberal reforms (which in any case are not happening) the environmental crisis can be cracked? Since most environmental disasters can be 'justified' in the name of 'development', an environmentally aware generation will be highly suspicious of such statements.

Beyond secular humanism

Perhaps enough has been done to demonstrate that the secular consensus is not straightforwardly unproblematic! There are insuperable difficulties in its method and its content, indeed in its claim to be a consensus. Members from faith-traditions on the National Forum have contributed to an experiment which has an outcome considerably more morally sensitive than earlier Government-sponsored efforts. Nonetheless the SCAA experiment is a perfect example of the claim reported by Grey that 'Without … resources of tradition, the rhetorics of tolerance and freedom may often retain their appeal and inspiration but their appeal and power to nurture the common good is likely to be short, like the life and beauty of a cut flower.'[26] The contrast between the two approaches is marked. One is 'embodied in the structures and lived experience of the learning community'. The other begins with the creation of meta-statements, earthed in nothing in particular, but supported by society in general, from which moral principles are expected to flow. One seeks a genuine praxis; the other, disclaimers notwithstanding, is clearly theoretical, whatever pragmatic outcomes may be thought to disguise it. One is the lively, inventive, self-critical product of Christian tradition: the other is the product of secular humanism, defensive, defective, and, as the Five Polarities indicates, dualistic. It is not at all obvious that the humanistic ethic is the superior product in the moral market place, even if it claims by a subtle tactic to have been desired and agreed in advance by all potential customers.

The commendation of the Christian message has to be critically achieved. That is because, as Grey reminds us, religion is implicated in misery, war, neurosis, extremism, alienation and oppression. One sometimes wishes, in the name of Christ, that Bonhoeffer's observation 'We are moving towards a completely religionless time'[27] were more advanced than it is. Taylor's trilemma[28] achieves this critical commendation because it shows that Christians can engage as critically with their faith as students are expected to engage with whatever they are studying. Why liberation, ecological and feminist theologies? Because, as a matter of strategy, they make connections with students who aren't exactly rushing to be connected up with religion. Resistance to oppression, including the oppression of the environment, may make the connection which something once called 'apologetics' once sought to do. Liberation theologies may enable a more sympathetic understanding of the transformative possibilities of religious traditions.

I have elsewhere advocated 'spirituality' as an 'achievement-word', and sought to ground it in the Gospel injunctions to love God with all our hearts, and our neighbours as ourselves.[29] There will not be consensus outside the churches about this. Mary Grey's recalling of 'Christian theology to its evangelical roots as counter-culture' is clearly inconsistent with consensus-seeking, for this 'prophetic alternative' is to rumble consensus and not to contribute to it.

'The first [commandment] is, "Hear, O Israel: the
Lord our God is the one Lord, and you must love the
Lord your God with all your heart, with all your
soul, with all your mind, and with all your strength."
The second is this: "You must love your neighbour
as yourself." No other commandment is greater than
these." ' (Mark 12:29–31)

Here is an approach that is genuinely dominical – it goes back
to Christ himself. It has the unanimous support of Christians.
While Christians disagree about many things, they agree about
the centrality of love for God and for neighbour. There is a real
consensus here, and one which need not be confined to the
traditions of Christianity and Judaism. A spiritually developed
person is one who has made some progress in the life-task of
loving God and one's neighbour.

There is surely advantage to be gained in deriving an
understanding of spirituality and spiritual development from
within a religious tradition. There are several kinds of spiritual
traditions in Christianity, but all of them are variations on the
basic love of God and neighbour. While Jesus did not use the
word, his teaching is 'holistic' because it summons all the
different dimensions of the human being (parts of the whole) to
the tasks of loving God and neighbour. The emotions,
personality, intellect and will-power are all involved, indeed
we might say, *balanced*. The European Enlightenment has
elevated the intellect above the other faculties of the person and
produced a fearful imbalance which successive generations of
university tutors faithfully reproduce. Perhaps in the practice of
the love of God and neighbour the balance of heart, soul, mind
and strength is best achieved.

Moral development is learning to love one's neighbour as
one's self. 'Neighbour' is a fundamental category – more
fundamental even than 'person'. Moral insight is solidarity
with the suffering neighbour. Moral maturity is acceptance of
responsibility for one's neighbour. There are 'near neighbours',
people with whom we have personal contact, and 'distant
neighbours', people whom we do not know directly, but whose
plight is known to us and moves us. When we love our
neighbours, we may even learn to follow Christ in loving our
enemies (Matthew 5:43).

Neighbour-love is the best way of introducing teaching about world faiths, and about all kinds of minorities: cultural, religious, sexual, disabled, etc. The lifting of the veil of ignorance makes love more possible and prejudice less possible. This is what education is able to make happen.

Beginning with the love commandments throws light on modern preoccupations with the individual self. The SCAA report is less individualistic than its predecessors, yet an obvious omission is the dialectic between self-love and neighbour-love that loving one's neighbour as one's self assumes. I am created by God as a person-in-relation; my being is constituted by others, and I help constitute the being of others reciprocally. This is how we are. Self-love, if it is not to become selfishness, must be balanced by neighbour-love: neighbour-love, if it is not to become a pitiable and oppressive self-emptying, must be balanced by a self-love which recognizes its own needs.

The love commandments enable a realistic and practical approach to each of the four SCAA areas: society, relationships, self and environment. How is the environment involved? A form of the love of God is the joyful recognition of God's creation, both as God's way of sustaining us and our children and as providing a home for all the living creatures God has also made. The poisoning of the earth is therefore a rebellion against God: the reckless misuse of the resources of creation is selfishness on a vast scale. The care of creation is the human vocation. The love of God and neighbour inevitably lead to the care of the earth.

The undoubted pluralism of the context for the commendation of the gospel is itself liberating. Christians do not have to perpetuate the old certainties and intolerances of Christendom with its decaying institutions and investments in a former age. Confidence in the gospel is far from the triumphalism of exclusivist and imperialist Christianity. The problems of operating from within a Christian theological framework, rooted in critically appropriated Christian traditions, are not obviously more daunting than the problems besetting the consensus-seekers. Church-related schools, colleges and universities have a heritage of faith which they will not confuse with the high-sounding moral sentiments of the present generation of curriculum-makers. The best contribution they can make to a pluralistic society is to remain faithful to the living Christian traditions which produced them.

Notes

1. National Curriculum Council, *Spiritual and Moral Development: A Discussion Paper* (London: NCC, April 1993). For a critical discussion of this document see Adrian Thatcher, ' "Policing the sublime": a wholly (holy?) ironic approach to the spiritual development of children' in Jeff Astley and Leslie J. Francis (eds), *Christian Theology and Religious Education: Connections and Contradictions* (London: SPCK, 1996), ch. 8. The NCC document was reissued by the School Curriculum And Assessment Authority as *Spiritual and Moral Development* (SCAA Discussion Papers, no. 3) (London: SCAA, September 1995). Given the influence these and subsequent 'discussion papers' were to have on teachers and inspectors, the tentative term 'discussion paper' is a misnomer.
2. Ofsted, *Framework for the Inspection of Schools* (London: HMSO, 1993), p. 21. The guidelines have since been revised several times. A further 'discussion paper' appeared: Ofsted, *Spiritual, Moral, Social and Cultural Development – an Ofsted Discussion Paper* (London: HMSO, February 1994).
3. Department for Education, *Religious Education and Collective Worship* (Circular 1/94; London: HMSO, January 1994), sections 1–2.
4. SCAA, *The National Forum for Values in Education and the Community: Final Report and Recommendations* (96/43; London: SCAA, September 1996) (emphasis added).
5. SCAA is now replaced by a successor body, the Qualifications and Curriculum Authority (QCA).
6. Alasdair MacIntyre, *After Virtue: A Study in Moral Theory* (London: Duckworth, 1981), p. 3.
7. Ibid., p. 2.
8. Arthur Marwick, *The Nature of History* (London and Basingstoke: Macmillan, 1970), p. 13.
9. Charles Dickens, *Hard Times* (first pub. 1854; Harmondsworth: Penguin, 1969), chs 1–2.
10. See e.g., John Milbank, *Theology and Social Theory* (Oxford: Blackwell, 1990), part 4.
11. Zygmunt Bauman, *Postmodern Ethics* (Oxford: Blackwell, 1993), p. 8.
12. SCAA *National Forum: Final Report*, para. 9.
13. Ibid., p. 4.

14. Ibid.
15. Thatcher, ' "Policing the Sublime" '.
16. Friedrich Nietzsche, *The Gay Science*, 125: in *Thus Spoke Zarathustra*, tr. R. J. Hollingdale (Harmondsworth: Penguin Books, 1961), Introduction, pp. 14–15.
17. National Curriculum Council, *Spiritual and Moral Development – a Discussion Paper*.
18. SCAA, *National Forum: Final Report*, para. 10.
19. From now on, the latest version of the Values Statement is used. It is the one sent to schools in *Guidance for Schools: The Promotion of Pupils' Spiritual, Moral, Social and Cultural Development* (undated), pp. 34–5.
20. Ibid., p. 33.
21. SCAA, *National Forum: Final Report*, para. 18.
22. Gilbert Ryle, *The Concept of Mind* (Harmondsworth: Penguin Books, 1976; first pub. 1949), p. 99.
23. *Guidance for Schools*, p. 33.
24. Ibid.
25. Ibid.
26. Mary Grey, pp. 15–16, above.
27. Dietrich Bonhoeffer, trans. R. Gregor Smith, *The World Come of Age* (London and Glasgow: Collins, 1967), p. 14.
28. See Mary Grey, p. 14 above.
29. Adrian Thatcher, ' "Policing the Sublime" ' and 'Spirituality without Inwardness', *Scottish Journal of Theology*, 46/2 (1993).

4

Spirituality as an Academic Discipline

Philip Sheldrake

Paradoxically, the progressive decline in religious practice in the West has been accompanied by an increasing hunger for spirituality.[1] One sign is the availability of an extraordinary variety of publications and courses on the so-called New Age, popular psychology, science and religion, mysticism, ritual and meditation. In general bookstores, popular editions of Christian mystics such as Meister Eckhart or *The Cloud of Unknowing* rub shoulders with Sufism and the occult. In the British Isles, Celtic spirituality (sometimes a rather uncritical pagan–Christian mix) has been enthusiastically 'rediscovered'. Music too plays its part in the spirituality boom as recordings of plainchant appear in CD best-seller lists.

Many people who are interested in spirituality are also suspicious of religious dogma. A coherent belief system is no longer assumed to be necessary for a fruitful spiritual journey. There has been a privatization of spirituality and a concentration on interiority. Eclecticism and anti-rationalism are two aspects of contemporary spiritual experience. This reflects a wider Western cultural fragmentation popularly known as postmodernity.

Alongside this cultural phenomenon there has been a second important development over the last fifteen years in the English-speaking world. Spirituality is slowly, and sometimes reluctantly, being accepted as a serious academic discipline that need not be confined to seminaries or other centres of Christian formation. This essay attempts to reflect on some of the issues that arise from this development. Although the field of spirituality is taught as frequently in a comparative as in a classically theological way, this study limits itself to spirituality as part of or, at least, in close relationship to Christian theology.[2]

The culture of postmodernity

Teachers and scholars are not protected from the popular interest in spirituality even if they have some misgivings about a number of its features. Equally, for better or for worse, the impact of postmodern culture (as well as theory) on the developing discipline of spirituality has been significant.[3]

Postmodernity is too complex to discuss fully but a summary is needed. The roots of postmodernity lie in the experience of loss that, theorists suggest, characterizes the last part of the second millennium. What has been lost is the spirit of optimism and certainty born of what, at the beginning of the twentieth century, appeared to be a stable social, religious, intellectual and moral order. The decisive breakpoint was the period of the two World Wars that reached an appalling climax in the Nazi extermination camps and the bombing of Hiroshima.[4]

Theorists seem to support broadly two versions of postmodernism. The first is essentially deconstructive. Its proponents are radically suspicious of attempts to defend the possibility of normative interpretations of culture. The second form of postmodernism is less extreme. It recognizes the reality of social and cultural fragmentation but seeks to reconstruct a strategy that will enable some kind of authoritative interpretation of events. However, both versions of postmodernism have something in common. They reject the epistemological optimism of 'modernity' or the Enlightenment. In other words, postmodernism criticizes the 'modernist' confidence in the powers of human reason to discover essential truths or to establish definitive meanings. Postmodernism recognizes that all interpretations of 'truth' are culturally-conditioned, contingent and morally flawed as well as intellectually partial. Contemporary culture is suspicious of total systems, whether philosophical or theological, that seek to escape from the limitations of context. It is a short step from this suspicion to a rejection of conventional religious institutions.

Spirituality in the academy

'Spirituality' is a word that is sometimes difficult to pin down. There have been attempts to offer generic definitions that transcend the assumptions of specific religious traditions. However, a number of writers question the validity and coherence of this process.[5] In Christian terms, a working definition might be that 'spirituality' is the study of how individuals and groups appropriate traditional Christian beliefs about God, the human person, creation, and their interrelationship, and then express these in worship, fundamental values and life-style. Thus, spirituality is the whole of life viewed in terms of a conscious relationship with God, in Jesus Christ, through the indwelling of the Spirit and within the community of believers.

An increasing number of universities and colleges on both sides of the Atlantic now offer spirituality in some shape or form within their theology and religious studies syllabuses. Some have developed separate graduate programmes in the field. The content of spirituality within a theology syllabus is usually multidisciplinary, involving the study of historical traditions, classic texts and the crucial theological issues that underlie these. Often the study of spirituality also overspills the confines of theology into an engagement with other areas of human knowledge such as anthropology, psychology or literature. New journals have appeared with the explicit aim of encouraging a scholarly approach to the field.[6] The last few years have also witnessed the birth of at least one scholarly society in the English-speaking world, the Society for the Study of Christian Spirituality. This is closely associated with the American Academy of Religion but has an increasingly international membership. The situation of spirituality as an academic discipline is less well-developed in the United Kingdom than in North America. With few academic posts in the field, no major centre of research or established scholarly network, spirituality lacks a high profile.

This lack of profile is partly associated with the fact that spirituality continues to be viewed with suspicion in academic circles. There are other contributory causes. For example, university theology departments (at least the English ones) often share a more widespread suspicion of so-called 'applied' or 'practical' subjects. Intellectual assumptions born of the Enlightenment still pervade the traditional universities and are not always at ease with the notion of 'experience' or 'praxis'. Such concepts seem to imply uncritical subjectivity or dangerous sectarianism. Spirituality has also suffered from a parallel decline in support for courses in 'Church theology', for example, ecclesiology, sacraments and liturgy.

Because the popular definition of 'spirituality' appears rather slippery it is perceived as an eclectic and intellectually shallow religiosity that borders on the superstitious.[7] Theologians have particular suspicions concerning its subject matter. Some of these are rooted in a long tradition of separation between theology and spirituality. This has led to the two words being interpreted as concerned, respectively, with the intellectual and devotional dimensions of Christian religion. Nowadays, however, spirituality demands to be taken seriously as a scholarly field in its own right. This raises difficulties for theologians especially when spirituality refuses to see itself simply as a subordinate discipline. Spirituality appears to want to cross all kinds of disciplinary boundaries that were previously considered as 'hard'. It also seems to lay claim to almost unlimited resources (for example, historical, theological, philosophical, psychological and anthropological). Spirituality has been accused of not defining its own methodology very precisely. As a matter of fact, significant attempts have been made by scholars in recent years to provide a coherent definition and methodology from both a theological and a historical standpoint.[8] Spirituality is beginning to take shape as a substantial field with a special, but not exclusive, relationship to theology.

Despite these considerable strides, the debate about the shape of the field has not yet reached a definitive conclusion even among scholars. There seem to be three points of consensus at present. First, in relationship to theology spirituality is multidisciplinary. It is also interdisciplinary and moves beyond theology into conversation with other disciplines. Second, in the study of spirituality there is a need for a proper understanding of context, the historical process and historical method. Third, scholars tend to adopt one of three different approaches to the field: historical-contextual, hermeneutical and theological. These should not claim to be exclusive but are mutually complementary. Having said this, views continue to differ sharply on the basic question of *how* spirituality relates to theology.

The great divorce

The history of the relationship between spirituality and theology is a complex one and, until recently, would best be described as a divorce. This division went deeper than method or content. It was, at heart, a separation of affectivity and conceptual knowledge. Further, 'spirituality' concentrated on subjectivity and interiority and became distanced from liturgy and ethics. The roots of these divisions go back to the Middle Ages and were further reinforced by the Reformation and the Enlightenment. To some extent, the whole community of believers internalized an opposition between subjective experience and reason and between the 'secular' and 'sacred' spheres of human life.

The consequence of the process was that the 'spiritual life' increasingly moved to the margins of theology and of culture in general. 'Spirituality' began to demand a new specialized language, distinct from theological discourse, capable of expressing its separate existence. The result was that what became known successively as 'ascetical and mystical theology', 'spiritual theology' and finally 'spirituality' tended to be confined to contexts of *Christian formation* as opposed to centres of academic study.[9]

Theology in practice

If we are to think of spirituality as an academic discipline in relation to theology it is necessary first of all to ask how we understand theology. Both theology and spirituality have changed greatly in the last thirty years. Each of them has moved away from abstract theory to a greater reflection on experience. Matters have progressed a great deal since the 1950s when Thomas Merton suggested that the technical language of theology, as opposed to poetry for example, failed to provide him with what he needed to articulate his understanding of contemplation.[10] In citing Merton's disquiet about theology, the American spirituality scholar Sandra Schneiders admits that our understanding of theology in the 1990s is unlikely to be Thomas Merton's. Yet she would still say that

> his insight into the fact that systematic theology, however precise and clear it might be, was not adequate to the concrete experience of the spiritual life which, as experience, is far more inclusive, was quite accurate. In other words, the task of spirituality as a discipline is to study Christian spiritual experience which, in our day, cannot be reduced to the exclusively Christian or the exclusively religious even when it is the experience of the committed Christian.[11]

Two issues are raised by this statement. First, it is possible to understand 'theology' in more inclusive ways that the one Schneiders criticizes. Second, while the spiritual experience of Christians is broadly-based, such experience raises specifically theological questions precisely because it is the experience of *committed Christians*. Schneiders is certainly correct in opposing the hegemony of *a priori*, abstract theology. Its ideological (as well as systematic) framework tended towards intellectual imperialism. This view of theology subordinates other disciplines, including spirituality, to its own method and denies them their integrity. We may accept Schneiders' statement that spirituality, as an area of study, tends to focus on the [Christian] spiritual life as experience.[12] Yet, contemporary *inductive* styles of theology also consider 'spiritual experience' as the legitimate starting point. Indeed, the approaches of liberation theology and feminist theology explicitly take the spiritual and experiential as their basis.

Theology that is fully alive is always grounded in spiritual experience. Theology needs to be *lived* out as much as it needs to be studied and expounded. Theology as a whole, not merely spirituality, has a necessary place for praxis. Praxis is broader than 'personal practices' such as devotions or rituals. In an academic context, this implies that what is sometimes called 'applied' or 'pastoral' theology is not an optional extra within the theological core curriculum. However, the place of praxis in theology means more than this. 'Doing theology' is much broader than traditional post-Enlightenment concepts of academic study.[13] Theology is not merely concerned with particular content or specific resources. It exists within every phase of examining and interpreting spiritual experience. This implies that the interpreter is a *theological person*, not merely that there is an explicit use of theological tools. For the Christian, personal faith is an irreducible horizon at every moment of experiencing and interpreting.

Being a theological person implies more than intellectual assumptions. *Theologia*, which may be distinguished in a certain sense from 'the theology of the academy', inevitably involves what Eastern Orthodox Christianity has termed *theoria*. To Westerners this word is misleading. It is more accurately translated as 'contemplation' rather than 'theory'.[14] The committed believer is one who *lives* theology rather than 'does' it as a detached activity. Sadly, Westerners still tend to think and act as if 'knowledge' is solely objective and rational. Theology is then understood as informative rather than performative; concerned with ideas rather than action. Consequently, the title of 'theologian' is limited to those who provide specialized analysis and information while standing at a personal distance from the object of reflection.

A broader approach understands 'being a theologian' as a quality of presence to the reality that is reflected upon. This raises challenging questions concerning the relationship between research or teaching and such 'applications' as prayer, preaching, pastoral care and evangelization. Are the latter optional extras for a theologian to be kept in a separate compartment of life lest they compromise 'objectivity'? Or are they important components of the theological life?

The more ancient meaning of a theologian is precisely a person who experiences the content of theological reflection. Contemporary Christian scholars of spirituality accept the self-implicating nature of the field. Theology in its proper sense is also self-implicating. This does not imply anti-intellectualism. The self-implicating nature of a discipline does not exclude a critical approach. The critical element is the servant of good theology but is not what theologians do or live theology for.

Philip Sheldrake

One may address the same question to both theology and spirituality. Why does anyone bother to study *this* area of knowledge and experience at all? The answer would seem to be that a kind of transformation is implied by the search for knowledge. Such a view is increasingly accepted by creative theologians such as the American David Tracy. ' "Saying the truth" is distinct from, although never separate from, "doing the truth" ... More concretely, there is never an authentic disclosure of truth which is not also transformative.'[15]

The problem is whether a faith-based understanding of theology will increasingly exclude it from colleges and universities that wish to espouse pluralism and avoid sectarianism. Whether it will or not, the fact is that if religions are not approached precisely as *faiths* we will not understand them at all. This does not imply that a person must be committed to a faith community before he or she can legitimately study theology. However it does imply that to study religious faith is to be confronted by the truth claims it embodies. The tradition of what might be called 'nonjudgemental neutrality' that sometimes characterizes university teaching of many disciplines, not merely theology, ultimately undermines intellectual ideals. In that sense, it is vital for the academic world to re-engage with matters of truth.[16]

Theologians and mysticism

Theologians such as the Roman Catholics Karl Rahner and David Tracy, the Anglican Rowan Williams and the Lutheran Paul Tillich have been fascinated by the theological possibilities of mystical writings. Recently, Tracy suggested that in our postmodern era 'we may now learn to drop earlier dismissals of "mysticism" and allow its uncanny negations to release us'.[17] This reflects his own movement towards a belief that the apophatic language of the mystics is where today's theologians must turn.

> As critical and speculative philosophical theologians and artists learn to let go into the sensed reality of some event of manifestation, some experience of releasement and primal thinking, a sense of the reality of mystical experience can begin to show

itself in itself. Even those with no explicit mystical experience, like myself, sense that thinking can become thanking, that silence does become, even for an Aquinas when he would 'write no more', the final form of speech possible to any authentic speaker.[18]

The hidden face of God plays a strong role in the Christian tradition of mysticism. The mystic is brought to the frontiers of language or conceptual thinking and to the edge of mystery – a Mystery which is, nonetheless, intensely present. One of the great post-war French intellectuals, the late Michel de Certeau, drew parallels between postmodernity and mysticism. Both the mystic and the postmodern person live in a movement of perpetual departure. They are wanderers and pilgrims lost in the 'totality of the immense'. Each of them 'with the certainty of what is lacking, knows of every place and object that it is *not that*, one cannot stay *there* nor be content with *that*'.[19]

Post-Enlightenment 'modernity' emphasized intelligibility, not least that of God language. Because of this, de Certeau saw those people whose lives affirmed the essential otherness of a mysterious God as outsiders to the 'modern' project.[20] More recently, Tracy has suggested that hope lies in the challenge to traditional power structures offered by the 'otherness' exemplified in marginal groups, particularly the mystics and the mad.[21]

Karl Rahner and Rowan Williams have affirmed that spirituality is integral to the theological enterprise.[22] It cannot be reduced to subjective affectivity. On the contrary, spirituality is another way of knowing and learning. In fact, the key to good theology is prayer, understood as a relationship with the divine rather than simply devotions and techniques of meditation. Perhaps we may go further and affirm that true prayer is true theology and vice versa. Certainly both are matters of the heart and the head that unify love and knowledge.

The problem with theological 'knowledge' is that while we may be impelled to speak of God, we cannot in the end speak definitively *about* God. The problem with a purely intellectual search is that it regards what is sought as an object and an objective that can be reached. The reality of 'God' is not of this kind. In so far as we can, in Christian terms, speak of the human search for God, it will be a search that involves a continuous failure to 'find' God in any definitive sense. Thus Gregory of Nyssa suggested that a 'true' vision of God always involves a movement onwards.

> This truly is the vision of God: never to be satisfied in the desire to see him. But one must always, by looking at what he can see, rekindle his desire to see more. Thus, no limit would interrupt growth in the ascent to God, since no limit to the Good can be found nor is the increasing of desire for the Good brought to an end because it is satisfied.[23]

The approach to systematic theology of the Lutheran Paul Tillich sought to rescue religious knowledge from a limited rationalist definition. Like Rahner and Williams, Tillich wished to bridge the gap between love and knowledge. 'Love includes the knowledge of the beloved. But it is not the knowledge of analysis and calculating manipulation.' Tillich coined the phrase 'participating knowledge' in contrast to objective analysis. 'Thus it is participating knowledge which changes both the knower and the known in the very act of knowledge.'[24]

In summary, personal and collective change is central to the theological enterprise. The paradox of human 'knowledge' of God is that it is not centred on the self or on self-possession. There is a self-emptying, kenotic, quality to it. As theologians seek to 'know' God, they are inevitably moved beyond a predetermined, fixed and autonomous sense of 'the self'. To risk entering into this way of knowing implies that they are prepared to be transformed.

How do theology and spirituality relate?

Nowadays, most scholars agree that it is important to overcome the division between the experience of faith and intellectual reflection upon it. What differences remain concern how, methodologically, theology and spirituality relate to each other as areas of study and teaching. A basic question is whether we think we are bringing together two realities that do not have an inherent connection or whether we are making explicit a relationship that is always present implicitly. However this question is resolved, it is unlikely to be that spirituality is no more than the practical expression of Christian doctrine. Any description of the current debate needs to be nuanced in reference to specific writers. However, there are broadly speaking two major schools of thought. The first defends spirituality as an autonomous discipline that is distinct from theology while related to it. The second wants to avoid the development of a separate discipline and prefers to treat spirituality either as a subdivision of theology or as a dimension (often implicit) of all 'good' theology.

The most significant English-speaking proponent of the first position is Sandra Schneiders. She has published several ground-breaking articles on the definition of spirituality as an academic discipline and its methodology.[25] Schneiders believes that spirituality and theology are close partners that mutually interact but respect each other's autonomy. Spirituality should not be conceived as a subdivision of systematics, historical theology or moral theology. Theology cannot ultimately *contain* spirituality because the latter is essentially interdisciplinary in nature and, even in a Christian context, is no longer limited to a practical outworking of doctrines. The dominance of a purely theological approach to spirituality tends to exclude proper study of those aspects of contemporary Christian spiritualities that move beyond traditional boundaries. Equally, such an approach tends to apply doctrinal norms as the exclusive criteria for evaluating spiritualities. The Canadian Church historian the late Walter Principe offered implicit support for aspects of Schneiders' analysis when he suggested that 'spirituality' is a particularly fruitful arena where Christian and non-Christian scholars can meet. Here, rather than in a narrowly-conceived theological context, non-Christian insights have a better chance of challenging Christian assumptions and of suggesting fruitful new lines of enquiry.[26]

The second viewpoint is represented by the outstanding American scholar of mysticism, Bernard McGinn. McGinn believes that spirituality is primary in its partnership with theology. In that sense he rejects the old-fashioned view that spirituality was simply a derivative of dogmatic theology. Nevertheless, because McGinn is concerned that religious experience should be the concern of the whole of theology, he believes that spirituality is best studied and taught within a combination of theological disciplines: systematics, historical theology, ethics and the history of Christianity. Following von Balthasar, he believes that the specificity of Christian experience demands that Christian theology be the primary criterion of interpretation.[27] Other scholars who defend a theological position describe 'spirituality' in terms closely related to what used to be known in Roman Catholic circles as 'spiritual theology'. This means that spirituality can be encompassed within a generously conceived theological framework as a distinct area or discipline similar to systematics or Church history. Interestingly, this is true of two contemporary writers who are not Roman Catholics, the American Lutheran Bradley Hanson and the British Anglican Kenneth Leech.[28]

More recently, a number of British and American scholars have tried to free themselves from the constraints imposed by the sharp juxtaposition of positions just outlined.[29] It is possible to argue that the relationship between spirituality and theology is central without suggesting that spirituality should not be seen as a distinct discipline. The important word is 'distinct'. In different ways, the new wave of writers reject attempts by systematic or fundamental theologians to squeeze spirituality into their own tidy systems. Some speak of the need for a 'turn to spirituality' within the overall theological enterprise.[30] Theology must come to realize more effectively its own spiritual core. It must also seek to enter into dialogue with spirituality in a way that is parallel to yet radically different from its more familiar conversation with philosophy. This allows the discourse of theology to be questioned by the insight that the reality of God is beyond the 'God' of conceptual exposition. The reality of God is more likely to be encountered by the way of 'knowing' espoused by mystical texts that are, from the perspective of conceptual thinking, ways of unknowing.[31]

The relationship of spirituality and theology is inherent and essential. A theology that is disconnected from spirituality becomes abstract and disengaged. On the other hand, spirituality cut adrift from theology risks losing touch with the broader 'Great Tradition' of faith that theology, at best, seeks to represent.[32] We are still left with a difficult question concerning the precise model for the spirituality–theology relationship.

Overall, the 'spiritual theology' model is unsatisfactory. This views spirituality as a segment, a slice of a larger theological cake. The contemporary interdisciplinary study of spirituality cannot be fully comprehended by theology or be reduced to a sub-discipline of it. For one thing, it is difficult to avoid the historical evidence that specific spiritual traditions arise from the concrete realities of human and Christian existence rather than from ideas and doctrines.[33] The suggestion that experience has priority over theory needs to be nuanced. It is impossible to break open the hermeneutical circle in such a way as to establish a straightforward pattern of cause and effect. Experience itself implies assumptions, theories and reflection. Yet the Christian way did not begin with a shift of theory born of intellectual speculation. The first followers of Jesus experienced their own lives and the nature of God's relationship with the world in a new way because of the impact upon them of the events of Jesus' life. In that sense, experience is fundamental. We may say that a Trinitarian understanding of God gives rise to specific attitudes to the Christian life. However, it is also possible to say that Trinitarian language gradually emerged as the only satisfactory way of speaking about the God who had been experienced in Jesus.

Another approach would be to visualize the relationship between theology and spirituality in terms of two overlapping but non-concentric circles. This would certainly leave us free to posit a necessary relationship between the disciplines without containing spirituality exclusively within theology. The weakness of the model is that it also suggests that there may be areas of theology untouched by spirituality. We cannot separate doctrine from spirituality without dismembering theology through neglecting its fundamental relationships.

Perhaps a more fruitful model might be portrayed rather like a wheel intersected by an axle. The 'wheel' of theology rotates around an axis that is spirituality. Yet, because the image is three-dimensional, it also suggests that spirituality reaches outwards beyond theology into another dimension.

Disciplines, boundaries and the interdisciplinary

Because both spirituality and theology have shifted their attention to human experience, they have entered into dialogue with other disciplines. The growth of fruitful encounters between disciplines in recent years owes something to the disconcerting theories of postmodernism that have already been mentioned. The rationalist approach to knowledge of 'modernism' tended to favour inwardly consistent but mutually exclusive disciplines. Specialization, purity and the isolation of specific areas of study was the predominant ethos in academic circles. This emphasis on the differences between disciplines discouraged interdisciplinary conversation. The assumptions behind these tendencies have recently been questioned and the mood has changed. This has its effect on theology as much as on any other field. The identity of an academic discipline is no longer to be found in maintaining 'hard' boundaries and sharp distinctions but in blurred edges and boundaries that are crossed. This shift has been characterized as 'a centrifugal, rather than a centripetal, sense of disciplinary identity'.[34] The word that best characterizes the new situation is 'conversation' between different perspectives, presuppositions and methods in the search for meaning.

One area where there is a fruitful dialogue is between spirituality and ethics or moral theology.[35] This is ironic, given that in old-style Roman Catholic theology, ascetical theology was merely a subdivision of moral theology. It could be argued that traditional moral theology reinforced the split between theology and spirituality. Both moral theology and ascetical theology were preoccupied with sinfulness and the enfeebled nature of the human condition. This overpowered any serious theological consideration of holiness and gave the impression that ascetical theology had very little if anything to say theologically in its own right. It appeared to deal merely with some subsidiary (even optional) aspects of the 'moral life'.[36]

Nowadays, moral theology has ceased to be concerned primarily with the quality of actions. There has been a shift from action to human agent. Spirituality and moral theology find a common language in a renewed theology of the human person and of grace. There is an increasing awareness of the basic unity between the moral and the spiritual life. A number of writers have suggested that the joint task of spirituality and moral theology is to explore renewed understandings of 'virtue' (that is, what enables a person to become truly human within a commitment to Christ and aided by the action of grace) and 'character' (or what we should *be*, rather than do, if we are to become fully human persons).[37] Moral theologians increasingly emphasize that our ultimate guide to goodness is not objective codes of behaviour or moral rules but the presence within us of the Holy Spirit. The indwelling of God focuses the recovery of a fruitful relationship between ethics and spirituality.

Some of the most fruitful reflection on the relationship between spirituality and ethics has been in the writings of Christian (particularly Roman Catholic) feminist theologians. Spirituality is, if you like, the main source of ethics just as it should be of theology as a whole. The traffic, however, cannot be one-way. Doctrinal theology and moral theory may act as vital critiques of spirituality in a way that may transform it.[38]

Context is an essential element of the study of spirituality. It is a concept imported from the disciplines of history and the social sciences. Attention to it in the study of spirituality demands a dialogue with those disciplines.[39] 'Context' has become a primary hermeneutical framework in the study of spiritual traditions. All experience, including spiritual experience, is determined to some degree by culture. Spirituality is never abstract or pure in form. The contextual approach to spirituality, in addition, seeks to address not merely explicitly religious issues but the situation of a spiritual tradition within the whole social context. 'Context' is not really a 'something' that is added to or subtracted from spiritual experience but, as Michel de Certeau showed, is the element within which experiences take their forms and expressions. Even though religions claim a transcendent dimension, all faiths have been embedded in specific cultures.[40]

De Certeau's assertions about culture and context in relation to spirituality would now be broadly accepted. However, the way in which contextual studies have developed raises serious questions for scholars of spirituality. Some have pointed out that the history of spirituality has come to mean the study of how religious attitudes and values are conditioned by surrounding culture and society. This brings historical spirituality close to the study of *mentalités*, or world-views, beloved of modern French historians. This 'social' version of history is itself informed by anthropology and sociology. The limitation is that such an approach to spirituality, if it is exclusive, tends to abandon theological sources and the questions raised by theological theory. We need a middle way between the older (exclusively theological) approach and the newer stress on social contexts.[41]

In the field of spirituality, the emphasis on context has also necessitated a conversation with the social and human sciences. The study of spirituality frequently includes historical, psychological, sociological and literary approaches. The absolute necessity of a sophisticated historical approach is now widely accepted and employed. A socio-political approach has been particularly noticeable in liberationist and feminist approaches to spirituality. It is gradually becoming common coinage as one aspect of more general studies in the field. One of the most recent 'conversations' is between spirituality and literature. Particularly in the English-speaking world, modern literature frequently addresses deep issues of meaning and belief. This 'unthematic', and even agnostic, spirituality is attracting increasing attention.[42]

Apart from a growing interest in the dialogue between spirituality and science,[43] one of the most striking and controversial interdisciplinary conversations is the one between spirituality and psychology. References are too numerous to list. While psychology is a legitimate and necessary dimension of an experiential approach to spirituality, it has distinct limitations if it is given disproportionate attention. For example, psychological terminology has at times become a substitute for serious engagement with the Christian theological and spiritual tradition. At other times it has encouraged a thoroughly *un*contextual approach to the wisdom of the past. Most worrying of all, the seriousness of spirituality as a field of study is undermined by books that blend a superficial approach to the great traditions with 'popular' psychology. At worst, some of this writing is dangerously naive. At best it perpetuates a theologically dubious, individualistic, self-help approach to the spiritual quest.[44]

The rise of a more interdisciplinary consciousness inhibits grand systems not least because the material that now has to be encompassed is so vast. In the field of spirituality some modesty may be appropriate. The nature of the discipline resists simple systematization – not least by single scholars. It is the age of collected papers, encyclopedia articles, limited focuses. The essay seems to be replacing architectonic structures. An essay, after all, is not merely a more informal, modest, limited and

open-ended piece of prose. It is appropriately, in its fundamental sense, an experiment, a trial, a first tentative attempt at
learning.

Theology and criteria of evaluation

Finally, what use are spirituality and theology to each other? A
number of writers have described how theology provides
criteria for evaluating spirituality. Spirituality obviously needs
tools to analyse and to evaluate different traditions, texts and
practices. Given the plurality of contemporary approaches to
spirituality, and the apparent novelty of some of them, the
question of criteria for assessing what is 'authentic' from a
Christian perspective takes on greater importance. Such criteria
will be based on the central theological principles developed
within the community of faith. From a theological perspective,
the process will address questions to spiritualities in order to
discern theological dimensions that are often only implicit.

Several Roman Catholic and Protestant theologians have
addressed the increasing role of experience in theology by
developing criteria for evaluating religious experience. These
criteria are also useful for evaluating different approaches to
spirituality. Such theologians as Schubert Ogden and David
Tracy agree that it is first of all important to show that
religious experience meets the basic demands of modern
'secular' knowledge and life. This approach is referred to as
'criteria of adequacy'. Beyond this basic, human level lies a
further dimension. This concerns the question of faithfulness to
a specifically Christian understanding of existence. This
approach is termed 'criteria of appropriateness'. The contemporary work of David Tracy may be taken as a typical
example.

The application of criteria of adequacy does not reduce
theology and spirituality to non-religious norms. It implies that
neither spirituality nor theology can be innocent of generally
accepted elements of human knowledge. Nor can they ignore
the ways in which previously over-confident views of human
progress have been undermined by recent, painful historical
events. To put it simply, we have to take into account the new
worlds opened up by cosmology, evolutionary theory, psychology and the social and political sciences.

Tracy suggests three broad criteria of adequacy. First, every religious interpretation of experience needs to be meaningful. What aspect of ordinary human experience, shared by many or all, is expressed in any given spiritual tradition? Does it relate to reality as commonly understood? Second, the specifically religious understanding of experience should be coherent. All spiritualities make cognitive claims because they seek to reveal meaning. Can these claims be expressed coherently? Do they fit with the generally accepted claims of responsible knowledge? Third, any spiritual tradition needs to throw light on the underlying conditions that make existence possible. Does it have anything to say about whether our confidence in life is actually worthwhile? Does it affirm that 'the good' will have the last word? Does it confirm the underlying conditions for living in the human world?[45]

When we turn to a specifically Christian perspective, David Tracy argues the need for criteria of appropriateness in general terms,[46] while other theologians such as Dermot Lane and Walter Principe have provided useful summaries of what these criteria might be. In general terms, every particular spirituality ought to relate us to a God worthy of our complete loving commitment. The vision of God needs to operate within the boundaries portrayed by the central doctrines of the Trinity and the Incarnation. It should bring about genuine conversion. Equally, a spirituality should not offer 'special' or purely individualistic experiences. It needs to open up connections to a wider community of experience. This criterion seems particularly important in a world where so-called New Age practices or new religious movements appear to offer experience detached from commitment or insights that are open only to special initiates.[47]

Spirituality evaluating theology

Interestingly, the way that spiritualities offer criteria for judging theology has received much less attention. One fundamental point must be borne in mind. This concerns whether particular theological perspectives offer not merely an attempt at describing the reality of God but a knowledge that enlivens the *practice* of the presence of God. Intellectual coherence is not sufficient.

Spirituality [is] that which keeps theology to its proper vocation, that which prevents theology from evading its own real object. Spirituality does not really answer the question, Who is God? but it preserves the orientation, the perspective, within which this question remains a question that is being evaded or chided.[48]

One of the main virtues of Karl Rahner's theology is that it consistently reminds us that spirituality provides solid foundations for judging the adequacy of theological explanations. For example, classical 'spiritual texts' frequently contain wisdom that philosophical theology has not taken seriously.[49] If we push Rahner's basic stance that theology arises from an experience of the Spirit to its logical conclusion, spirituality becomes *the* way of integrating the multiple disciplines of theology. Spirituality is the unifying factor that underlies all attempts to 'do' theology or, more properly, *be* a theologian. Scholars of spirituality tend to believe that it is a kind of Ricoeurian 'field-encompassing field'. This suggests that spirituality has a unique capacity to unite the theological enterprise which has become fragmented or even internally competitive.[50]

Spirituality does not merely unify our tentative attempts to approach the reality of God. It also offers a critique of any attempt by theology to launch itself into some stratosphere of timeless truth, abstract distinctions or ungrounded definition. The way that spirituality 'speaks' of God is radically different from systematics. If theology allows its explanations to be questioned it will find that spirituality recognizes that what is implied by the word 'God' cannot ultimately be spoken completely. In that way 'spirituality' prevents theology, particularly philosophical theology, from eluding the elusiveness that matters most – that of God. Spirituality ultimately drives theology beyond words into silence. This is not the silence of meaninglessness but one filled with infinite presence.

Notes

1. See Wade Roof's landmark study of the new generation of spiritual seekers in the USA, *A Generation of Seekers: The*

Spiritual Journey of the Baby Boom Generation (New York: Harper Collins, 1994).

2. The fact of different (though not mutually exclusive) approaches to the discipline was recognized by the Faculty of Theology and Religious Studies of the University of London in the early 1990s. It allowed the creation of two distinct MAs in spirituality, one comparative (at the School of Oriental and African Studies), the other theological (at Heythrop College).

3. See for example, Ann Astell, 'Postmodern christian spirituality: a *coincidentia oppositorum?*' and Philip Sheldrake, 'The crisis of postmodernity', *Christian Spirituality Bulletin*, 4/1 (Summer 1996), pp. 1–5 and 6–10 respectively; Veronica Brady, 'Postmodernism and the spiritual life', *The Way*, 36/3 (July 1996), pp. 179–87.

4. Among some theorists, 'Auschwitz' has become a paradigm of the postmodern experience. See, for example, Jean-François Lyotard, *The Postmodern Explained* (Minneapolis: University of Minnesota Press, 1993), pp. 18–19. Such a view has also been adopted in one recent work on the impact of postmodernity on Christian spirituality. See Ann W. Astell (ed.), *Divine Representations: Postmodernism and Spirituality* (New York: Paulist Press, 1994), pp. 2–3.

5. For example, see Jon Alexander, 'What do recent writers mean by spirituality?', *Spirituality Today*, 32 (1980), pp. 247–56.

6. For example, *Studies in Spirituality* (begun 1991 in Nijmegen, The Netherlands) and *Christian Spirituality Bulletin* (begun 1993 at Loyola Marymount University, Los Angeles, as the journal of the Society for the Study of Christian Spirituality). The older journal *The Way* (founded 1961) from Heythrop College, University of London, continues to bridge the gap between scholarship and a general readership and also produces scholarly *Supplements* three times a year.

7. See, for example, the strictures of Nicholas Lash in *The Beginning and the End of 'Religion'* (Cambridge: Cambridge University Press, 1996), pp. 17, 116, 165 and 174–75.

8. For example: Bradley Hanson (ed.), *Modern Christian Spirituality: Methodological and Historical Essays* (Atlanta: Scholars Press, 1990), Part One: 'What is spirituality' and 'Theological approaches to spirituality: a Lutheran perspective', *Christian Spirituality Bulletin*, 2/1 (Spring 1994), pp. 5–8; Edward Kinerk, 'Towards a method for the study of spirituality', *Review for Religious*, 40/1 (1981), pp. 3–19; Bernard McGinn, 'The letter and the spirit: spirituality as an academic discipline', *Christian Spirituality Bulletin*, 1/2 (Fall

1993), pp. 1–10; Walter Principe, 'Towards defining spirituality', *Sciences Religieuses*, 12/2 (1983), pp. 127–41; Sandra Schneiders, 'Theology and spirituality: strangers, rivals or partners?', *Horizons*, 13/2 (1986), pp. 253–74, 'Spirituality in the academy', *Theological Studies*, 50 (1989), pp. 676–97, 'A hermeneutical approach to the study of Christian spirituality', *Christian Spirituality Bulletin*, 2/1 (Spring 1994), pp. 9–14, and 'Spirituality as an academic discipline: reflections from experience', *Christian Spirituality Bulletin*, 1/2 (Fall 1993), pp. 10–15; Philip Sheldrake, *Spirituality and History: Questions of Interpretation and Method* (2nd revised edn, London: SPCK, 1995/ Maryknoll, NY: Orbis Books, 1998), ch. 2; Otger Steggink, 'Study in spirituality in retrospect', *Studies in Spirituality*, 1 (1991), pp. 5–23; Kees Waaijman, 'Toward a phenomenological definition of spirituality', *Studies in Spirituality*, 3 (1993), pp. 5–57.

9. For a summary of this separation, see Philip Sheldrake, 'Spirituality and theology' in Peter Byrne and Leslie Houlden (eds), *Companion Encyclopedia of Theology* (London: Routledge, 1995), especially pp. 516–19.

10. Thomas Merton, *Sign of Jonah* (Cambridge, MA: Harvard University Press, 1953), pp. 8–9. Merton attempted to use theological categories to approach the teachings of John of the Cross in his unsuccessful book *The Ascent to Truth* (Cambridge, MA: Harvard University Press, 1951).

11. Sandra Schneiders, 'A hermeneutical approach to the study of Christian spirituality', p. 11.

12. See Schneiders, 'A hermeneutical approach', p. 11.

13. On the relation of praxis to the theological enterprise, see for example, David Tracy, *The Analogical Imagination: Christian Theology and the Culture of Pluralism* (New York: Crossroad, 1991 edn), ch. 2, 'A theological portrait of the theologian'.

14. See John Meyendorff, *Byzantine Theology* (London: Mowbray, 1974), Introduction; Vladimir Lossky, *The Mystical Theology of the Eastern Church* (London: James Clarke, 1973), ch. 1.

15. Tracy, *Analogical Imagination*, pp. 77–8.

16. An important response to this dilemma is offered by Edward Farley, the author of a number of works on theological education. See 'The structure of theological study' in Robin Gill (ed.), *Readings in Modern Theology* (London: SPCK, 1995), pp. 255–66, reprinted from Farley's highly influential book, *The Fragility of Knowledge: Theological Education in the Church and the University* (Philadelphia: Fortress, 1988).

17. Tracy, *Analogical Imagination*, p. 360.

18. Tracy, *Analogical Imagination*, p. 385.

Philip Sheldrake

19. Michel de Certeau, *The Mystic Fable*, vol. 1 (ET; Chicago: University of Chicago Press, 1992), p. 299. The emphases are the author's.
20. De Certeau, *Mystic Fable*, especially 'Introduction', pp. 1–26.
21. David Tracy, *On Naming the Present* (Maryknoll, NY.: Orbis Books/London: SCM Press, 1994) pp. 3–6.
22. See, for example, Karl Rahner, 'The theology of mysticism' in K. Lehmann and L. Raffelt (eds), *The Practice of Faith: A Handbook of Contemporary Spirituality* (New York: Crossroad, 1986), pp. 70–7; Rowan Williams, *Teresa of Avila* (London: Geoffrey Chapman, 1991), ch. 5 'Mysticism and incarnation'.
23. See the modern English translation of Gregory of Nyssa, *The Life of Moses* (New York: Paulist Press, 1978), Book 2.239.
24. Paul Tillich, *Systematic Theology*, vol. 3 (London: Nisbet, 1963), p. 137.
25. Sandra Schneiders 'Theology and spirituality: strangers, rivals or partners?', 'Spirituality in the academy', 'Spirituality as an academic discipline: reflections from experience' and 'A hermeneutical approach to the study of Christian spirituality' (see above, note 8).
26. Walter Principe, 'Spirituality, Christian' in Michael Downey (ed.), *A New Dictionary of Catholic Spirituality* (Collegeville, MN: The Liturgical Press, 1993), pp. 931–8.
27. Bernard McGinn, 'The letter and the spirit' (see note 8 above).
28. See Bradley Hanson, 'Spirituality as spiritual theology' in *Modern Christian Spirituality*, pp. 45–51, and 'Theological approaches to spirituality' (note 8 above); also Kenneth Leech, *True God: An Exploration in Spiritual Theology* (London: Sheldon Press, 1985).
29. See the articles in *Christian Spirituality Bulletin*, 3/2 (Fall 1995): Philip Endean, 'Theology out of spirituality: the approach of Karl Rahner', pp. 6–8; Mark McIntosh, 'Lover without a name: spirituality and constructive Christology today', pp. 9–12; J. Matthew Ashley, 'The turn to spirituality? The relationship between theology and spirituality', pp. 13–18; Anne M. Clifford, 'Re-membering the spiritual core of theology: a response', pp. 19–21.
30. For example, Ashley, 'The turn to spirituality', *passim*.
31. See McIntosh, 'Lover without a name', pp. 9–10 and Clifford, 'Re-membering the spiritual core of theology', p. 19.
32. See, for example, Lash, *The Beginning and the End of 'Religion'*, ch. 9, *passim*.
33. See, for example, Josef Sudbrack, 'Spirituality' in Karl Rahner, Cornelius Ernst and Kevin Smyth (eds), *Sacramentum Mundi:*

An Encyclopedia of Theology, vol. 6 (ET; New York: Herder & Herder/London: Burns & Oates, 1970), p. 151.

34. See Jamie Scott and Paul Simpson-Housley (eds), *Sacred Places and Profane Spaces: Essays in the Geographics of Judaism, Christianity and Islam* (Westport; CT: Greenwood Press, 1991), p. 178.

35. See a recent collection of essays edited by Michael Barnes, *The Way Supplement*, 88 (Spring1997): *Spirituality and Ethics*.

36. See, for example, Keith Egan, 'The divorce of spirituality from theology' in Patrick Carey and Earl Muller (eds), *Theological Education in the Catholic Tradition* (New York: Crossroad, 1997), pp. 296–307, especially 301–4.

37. An accessible overview of these shifts of perspective in moral theology is Kevin Kelly, *New Directions in Moral Theology: The Challenge of Being Human* (London: Geoffrey Chapman, 1992), especially ch. 2. See also James M. Gustafson, 'The idea of Christian ethics' in Byrne and Houlden (eds), *Companion Encyclopedia of Theology*, pp. 691–715.

38. For example Ann E. Patrick, *Liberating conscience: Feminist Explorations in Catholic Moral Theology* (New York: Continuum, 1996), ch. 6, 'Toward liberating conscience: spirituality and moral responsibility', and 'Ethics and spirituality: the social justice connection', *The Way Supplement*, 63 (1998), pp. 103–16. See also Anne E. Carr, *Transforming Grace* (San Francisco: Harper & Row, 1988), ch. 10.

39. On the contextual nature of the study of spirituality, see Steggink, 'Study in spirituality', pp. 12–14; Waaijman, 'Toward a phenomenological definition', pp. 39–42; and Philip Sheldrake, *Spirituality and History: Questions of Interpretation and Method* (London: SPCK, 2nd edn, 1995), pp. 58, 84–6, 167–8.

40. The seminal study was the article by Michel de Certeau, 'Culture and spiritual experience', *Concilium*, 19: *Spirituality in the Secular City* (1966), pp. 3–31.

41. See Caroline Walker Bynum, *Jesus as Mother: Studies in the Spirituality of the High Middle Ages* (Berkeley: University of California Press, 1982), pp. 3–6; also Columba Stewart, 'Asceticism and spirituality in late antiquity: new vision, impasse or hiatus?', *Christian Spirituality Bulletin*, 4/1 (Summer 1996), pp. 11–15: a review of Vincent Wimbush and Richard Valantasis (eds), *Asceticism* (New York: Oxford University Press, 1995).

42. See, for example, the collection of essays published by *The Way Supplement*, 81: *Spirituality, Imagination and Contemporary Literature* (Autumn 1994).

Philip Sheldrake

43. For example, *The Way*, 32/4: *Mysticism, Spirituality and Science* (October 1992).
44. This relationship was examined more critically in a collection of essays published by *The Way Supplement*, 69: *Spirituality and Psychology* (Autumn 1990).
45. David Tracy, *Blessed Rage for Order* (New York: The Seabury Press, 1975), pp. 64–71; see also Schubert Ogden, *The Reality of God* (New York: Harper & Row, 1963), pp. 122 and 190–2.
46. Tracy, *Blessed Rage for Order*, pp. 72–9.
47. Dermot Lane, *The Experience of God* (Dublin: Veritas, 1985), p. 26; Walter Principe, 'Pluralism in Christian spirituality', *The Way*, 32/1 (January 1992), pp. 58–60.
48. Andrew Louth, *Theology and Spirituality* (Fairacres Publications 55; Oxford: SLG Press, 1978), p. 4.
49. See, for example, Karl Rahner, *The Dynamic Element in the Church* (ET; New York: Herder & Herder/London: Burns & Oates, 1964). Rahner had in mind the 'rules for discernment of spirits', in *The Spiritual Exercises* of Ignatius Loyola, but the point is important more generally.
50. Implicitly in Alan Jones, 'Spirituality and theology', *Review for Religious*, 39/2 (March 1980), pp. 161–76, and explicitly in Sandra Schneiders, 'Spirituality in the academy'.

5

Educators as Mystics:
Resurrecting the Contemplative

David Nixon and Vanessa Parffrey

> In order to play the prophetic role which education
> for liberation desperately needs, educators first need
> to become mystics, to recover their own potential for
> contemplation, wonder, stillness, relationship with
> the natural world, and a thirst for learning which
> transcends narrow curriculum limits.[1]

T o resurrect the contemplative is not only to find again a
stance in which contemplation may take place with all its
implications for stillness and wonder, but to bring back to life
and revalue the women and men engaged in contemplative
activity before they are entombed in ignorance or antipathy. By
examining some aspects of contemplation it may be possible to
reinvest this activity with a language and action appropriate for
the future and thereby to rejuvenate our curricular definitions.
We will look firstly at the traditional language of contemplation and find that it rests uneasily with the language of the
curriculum; however it has much to offer our contemporary
culture and some aspects of this will be touched upon. Lastly
we will ask whether two apparently different forms of language
have points of convergence and where some of these may be
found.

By language for contemplation we mean two things: how we
engage in contemplative activity, for example, body posture,

David Nixon and Vanessa Parffrey

silence and so on; and secondly, how we describe the activity both as we are in the midst of it and subsequently. A key feature of this language of engagement is our initial disposition for wonder and stillness. If we are seekers for a 'path with heart and meaning'[2] then we will approach such activity with openness and generosity – the kind of grace which Ignatius Loyola has us ask for in the *Spiritual Exercises*. He also talks to us of 'indifference', bidding us 'want not health rather than sickness, riches rather than poverty, honour rather than dishonour, long rather than short life, and so on in all the rest ...'.[3] This bears comparison with the Buddhist notion of detachment. So we have here an intentionality which may be the distinguishing feature which gently separates a random and unexpected spiritual experience (a beautiful sunset, a mathematical formula, an animal dissection, a beggar on the streets) from our process of contemplation. Of course the sunset or the formula may enter our contemplative moment but it will be of a different order as memory to be reflected upon.

There are four classic preparatory stances for contemplation: body posture, focus, mantra and silence. Some of our more recent concern with the importance of body posture stems from an increasing interest in Eastern meditation, especially yoga.[4] Experience will soon tell us that certain positions of the body lend themselves more naturally to recollection and that other postures may express our inner feelings – humility, awe, fear and so on. We are reminded that our contemplation includes our bodies in their fullest sensory capacity; any denial of this is unhelpfully dualistic and may lead us to be distracted by the same bodily aspects we are trying to deny. Within this realm, too, we take note of our breathing pattern, fast or slow, traditionally breathing in the Spirit and breathing out our anxieties.

Secondly, it is common as we prepare to be still to focus our attention internally and externally. Internally we may 'centre' ourselves by focusing on body posture, then on breathing, acknowledging the surroundings in terms of noise, light etc, but not being distracted by them, looking within our beings for a still point where we are truly ourselves, without pretence, without mask, naked to ourselves. Externally it may be helpful to focus on a candle, an icon, something out of the natural world – plant or stone; something which allows the conscious mind a point of attention without itself distracting from the inwardness. It is the mirror through which we see darkly.

Thirdly, in both Eastern and Christian traditions the use of a mantra has been common but not essential practice to approach a contemplative stance. One of the best-known mantras of the Christian tradition is the Jesus prayer: the constant repetition of a phrase or part of a phrase including 'Jesus, Son of the living God, have mercy on me, a sinner'. Sometimes it is enough simply to repeat the divine name over and over again. The conscious, busy mind is thereby occupied, letting the imaginative and contemplative part of us be open, generous and free. The prayers 'Our Father' and 'Hail Mary' may also be regarded as mantras. The power of the mantra in the modern world is perhaps reflected in the catch-phrases of comedy shows, advertising jingles and the signature tunes of TV soaps.

Lastly, we prepare for contemplation by being still and silent. If we are using a mantra this may persuade our minds to be quiet, to press the pause button on the endless internal monologue of conscious beings. How we express the mantra may indicate the depth of our silence: if we pray aloud with our lips our mind is still quite active; if we pray silently in our minds we are stiller; if we are 'repeating' the mantra in our hearts, that is where our silence is beginning to lie. It is towards the silence of the heart or soul that we are aiming.[5]

We turn now to some examples of the language we use to describe our prayer or contemplation, drawn mainly from the Ignatian tradition. Ignatius almost always writes in the context of long retreats with the guidance of a spiritual director. His insights have been widely developed over the last fifty years in particular to include short retreats and the life of contemplation in the middle of a busy day. Contemplation or meditation is for him a process in which we are moved both spiritually and emotionally towards or away from God. That which moves us towards God, where our emotions are engaged, perhaps very strongly, when we feel a deep sense of peace with self and God, he calls *consolation*. When we are dry, when 'nothing happens', when we are distracted badly, when the experience is like a desert, when we are on the verge of despair, this for Ignatius is *desolation*.[6] An important insight here is to reckon that many different emotions may lead us to God. We may normally associate ideas of tranquillity or happiness with the Divine, but

Ignatius reminds us that tears, anger or other so-called 'negative emotions' may equally well be a step towards God. This takes us a little beyond trying to inspire 'awe and wonder', which itself seems to have become a source of dryness!

For Ignatius it is important that we feel something, and then determine to what extent it comes from God. This is based on a somewhat medieval concept of *discernment of spirits* – that around us are a host of different spirits which touch us and move us, not all of which come from God. There is some excellent writing here on the *enemy* (the evil spirit) behaving like a spoiled child, a false lover, a shrewd army commander.[7] We may recoil at the supernaturalism of this, but as we prepare to engage with the world of contemplation and encourage others to do so, it is well to remember that others have been there before and have understood some of the pitfalls. This also takes us firmly away from sentimentality and pious optimism, setting us in the context of a whole life: body, mind and spirit.

How then does any of this discussion relate to the 'real' world of schools, colleges and universities? It may be pertinent to observe that this world is termed 'real' in distinction from what at first glimpse may be irrelevant or esoteric. One of the reasons for writing with specialized terminology is to contrast the two worlds in which we operate.

In England and Wales, the 1988 Education Reform Act thrust schools into a competitive market-place, a change constituting no less than a paradigmatic leap; schools in Scotland and in other countries are in a similar situation. The vocabulary of utilitarianism and an excessively focused curriculum, together with its concentration upon targets and performance data, all conspire against notions of breadth and balance. Both in the curriculum itself and in the process of management, there is the risk of neglecting the broader curricular needs of the child, including spiritual development. This, together with the generally confused thinking by the British Government and by Ofsted (Office for Standards in Education) about definitions and distinctions between spirituality, morality and RE, leads us to reflect both on the need for a language of spirituality within the curriculum and, at one and the same time, on the inauspicious circumstances in which we must conduct this debate.

From the world of meditation we have seen the importance

of relationship, with self, others and the Divine, centred primarily on the notion of feelings – the heart. With this in mind, the mythical shaman Don Juan suggests the following advice to one seeking the 'right' path:

> Look at every path closely and deliberately. Try it as many times as you think necessary. Then ask yourself and yourself alone one question. This question is one that only a very old man asks. My benefactor told me about it once when I was young and my blood was too vigorous to understand it. Now I do understand it. I will tell you what it is: Does this path have a heart? If it does, the path is good. If it doesn't, the path is of no use.[8]

If we believe our language reflects a deeper reality, then we are forced to conclude that two world views exist from which we draw separate and distinct inspiration. It may be that these world views are irreconcilable – indeed there is a tendency for the predominant one (the mechanical) to belittle and devalue the weaker one (the spiritual). Interestingly, this tendency occurred when the power relation was in reverse, and the 'spiritual world-view' held sway.[9] In the second part of this chapter we wish firstly to examine some general characteristics of the 'model of the heart' and show that its language offers a positive contribution to our present culture, and secondly to consider whether there are some points of convergence for these two apparently discrete worlds.

We hear constant criticism that our contemporary culture is selfish, individualistic and conformist. The language of spirituality and contemplation offers an alternative by putting in place notions of the corporate, the other (or perhaps the Other) and of real transformation. When we talk of our spiritual experience with another, be it soul friend or director, we are inviting another person to accompany us on the journey, during our search for heart and meaning. We go beyond self to the other, possibly invoking too the presence of the Other, in a move which takes us out of self, beyond the downward spiral of self-reference. In this movement outwards we encounter the reality of transformation, a change of heart. We are empowered to say that things can be altered and for the better, for us personally and for us as a society. Mary Grey talks about the possibility of dangerous memory[10] as part of the liberation process which may apply both to individuals and to groups. We may dimly remember a time when language expressed the future of the heart and the opportunities for the growth of human potential, instead of simply desiring to measure our output. It is not a language which is always rational either in its mode of expression or in what it attempts to describe. It may be down-graded by those who wish to quantify and prescribe, and be an irritant to those who cannot pin down its mercurial quality, but it does express a valid aspect of human existence.

Such language has to sail between a rock and a hard place: it is dismissed as irrelevant to serious academic study because it is not quantitative but it loses much of its force if it takes on the mantle of rationality in order to be taken seriously. Its phraseology may appear muddled and imprecise, but that is because the Spirit blows where it wills. However when we broaden our definition of language to include the means of expression beyond words – silence, focal point, body posture and so on – then we may be able to find a way to authorize the heart and at the same time find links between these two worlds.

The Spirit may well blow where it wills, but as we have already seen it may be possible to describe its traces. It may be difficult to use quantitative language, but this does not mean that no language is possible. Such descriptive terms as *consolation* or *desolation* confront the notion that we cannot and should not name these things. Further, the failure to name has inherent dangers: that spirituality becomes sentimentality (nice, warm feelings to each other); that it is reduced to the domain of a few specialists; that a potential 'dark' side is ignored. The real insight of Ignatius' suggestions for prayer lies in the realm of reflection and analysis. When we have followed his guidelines, however loosely, we are instructed to find a different place or posture and ask some basic questions – what did I do? how did it feel? where was God in this experience or this prayer? We begin to look as objectively as possible at our spiritual experience, not within a rational, scientific context, but in the context of our reflective activity. George Ashenbrenner of the American College in Rome suggests this modern-language interpretation of Ignatius to his seminarians:

I am present to God my creator, who has today been
continuing my own history of salvation; present to
Jesus, the Christ of whom I am a member; present to
the Spirit, who dwells in me.
In the light of that presence, let me ask –
What am I thankful for tonight?
What movements or feelings am I aware have been
present in me?
What have been my relationships today – with
others, with God?
How have I responded to these movements?
I – along with all that I have done today – am present
to God ...
my Father who has been and is present to me in his
mercy,
Christ who wants to change me still more and to
help me give myself more to the people around me,
the Spirit who is prodding me to open myself more
fully to his action.
How will I respond totally with my heart to God's
invitation?

This reflection has parallels with the discipline of teacher
education. Teaching for 'continual professional development' is
a continual cycle of reflective learning. The teacher, or indeed
any other professional practitioner, is invited to reflect alone,
with others, and in engagement with the literature, on an
experience, a relationship, a piece of 'practice'. In the light of
these dialogues, meanings – nuggets of learning – are crystal-
lized and then, through further deliberation, are translated into
new action that flows from these insights and new meanings.
The ensuing action brings the individual back again to the
beginning of the cycle but with a different locus or path.[11]

This cyclical path of reflection – the 'experiential learning
cycle' – can be envisaged as the path of spiritual development.
The experiences and relationship are, of course, pertaining to
things of God, but the systematic and disciplined examination
of that relationship is identical and both serve to ensure that
praxis and reflection are combined: not only the contemplative,
not only the actor, but the two together in prayerful action.

Two useful insights may be introduced here from different

disciplines. Firstly, Philip Endean in his article 'Spirituality and the university' begins by describing two contrasting areas of study. There is traditional theology approached with the academic rigour of Enlightenment ideas about objectivity and then, quite separate, there is the study of spirituality, often based on founders of religious movements or orders (Benedictine or Ignatian spirituality, for example). This second area of study uses a different kind of language (which Endean finds appropriate) and may draw different kinds of conclusions about issues on which theology is much more precise, especially in the moral or ethical field (which Endean finds uncomfortable). The result of this is that theology fails to influence spirituality and, vice versa, spirituality fails to influence theology. It may seem that this method of writing on spirituality gives full weight to religious experience, but on further reflection it will be found that it is not really allowed to influence or change our self-perception or our understanding of God.

Happily, Endean is able to point to some new developments in spirituality which, recognizing these weaknesses, hope to find a way of bringing these two disciplines closer together. In the light of our deepening knowledge of both natural and human sciences, he is able to describe a modern study of spirituality:

> Contemporary academic spirituality, then, represents an attempt to take seriously ongoing religious experience as a source for intellectual reflection, largely in reaction against approaches to theology which excluded experience. The agenda is one of overcoming the marginalisation of human experience from the religious academy, of submitting religious experience to critical scrutiny and allowing that experience to enrich our reflective self-understanding.[12]

Although the remainder of Endean's article points up some of the difficulties involved in carrying out this task, he has no doubt that there is a consensus about the need to bring theology and spirituality closer together. Ultimately he feels that, for the Christian at any rate, any divergence of method will be short-lived because there is only God-with-us, Emmanuel, 'there is no human experience except that which is shot through with God's presence'.[13]

This is a useful example because it indicates the way in which specifically spiritual or religious experience becomes subject to the disciplines of academic enquiry while maintaining its own cohesion and value. A second insight which gives similar value to experience, situated equally within the academy, is drawn from another discipline, sociology. In *Habits of the Heart* Robert Bellah and his associates examine the problem of how to create a morally coherent life within contemporary American society.[14] They ask questions like 'How ought we to live?', 'How do we think about how to live?', 'Who are we as Americans?', 'What is our character?' They interview and engage with Americans from a wide background and geographical spread. The writers reflect upon the life-stories they have heard and the way in which they are drawn into and involved with those stories. Their results are presented in terms of essays around themes, individuals and community concepts. Avoiding tables, graphs and other mechanistic devices invites the reader more easily to look at her own experiences and reactions within an established framework. This kind of investigative technique honours experience and allows it to shape the way we perceive ourselves.

> A study of the mores ['habits of the heart'] gives us insight into the state of society, its coherence and long-term viability. Secondly, it is in the sphere of mores, and the climates of opinion they express, that we are apt to discern incipient changes of vision – those new flights of social imagination that may indicate where society is heading.[15]

The conclusions of this American study point broadly in the same direction that we are advocating here: in both cases a transformation involving the convergence of apparently discrete elements. In their case it is greater convergence of the private and public domains, of the rich with the poor; in our case, within education, an attempt to draw together values and language from two conflicting world views.

The purpose of this chapter so far has been to revisit the

traditional language of contemplation, to uncover its riches for us, and to use its method to suggest further avenues for exploration. In identifying two worlds and their associated models of language we have seen how there are points both of divergence and of convergence. We may wish to say that it is the challenge and duty of serious spiritual people, especially Christians, to seek to enhance points of convergence and work to minimize difference.

The traditional language of prayer with which we began this chapter may not be easily accessible. Some people may find that reflection upon, and reactions to, poetry, music, paintings or sculpture provide the open door to contemplation which previous generations uncovered in the practice of prayer. In this, we are suggesting that the language we use for contemplation needs to be stretched.

The genius of contemplation is that it is a 'being' and not a 'doing': it may lead to action which is apostolic or simply to more of the same. It challenges because it does not attempt to justify itself – it simply *is* and requires that others *are*, in the midst of a world and a curriculum which chases its own tail of busy-ness. Even as a community of Christian enquirers, we are still so often hooked into the issue of discussing and defining the mystery rather than entering into it. But to discover real being and help others to do the same is a gift without price, it is a bloom of lotus ...

> On the day when the lotus bloomed, alas my mind was straying, and I knew it not. My basket was empty and the flower remained unheeded. Only now and again a sadness fell upon me, and I started up from my dream and felt a sweet trace of a strange fragrance in the south wind. That vague sweetness made my heart ache with longing and it seemed to me that it was the eager breath of the summer seeking for its completion. I knew not then that it was so near, that it was mine, and that this perfect sweetness had blossomed in the depth of my own heart.[16]

Notes

1. Mary Grey, p. 27 above.
2. Janet Ruffing, 'Look at every path closely and deliberately', *The Way Supplement*, 84 (Autumn 1995), p. 3.
3. David Fleming (ed.), *The Spiritual Exercises of St Ignatius* (St Louis: Institute of Jesuit Sources, 1978), no. 23.
4. See *Some Aspects of Christian Meditation* (Rome: Congregation for the Doctrine of the Faith, 1989).
5. For more detailed discussion of these aspects of contemplation, see Robert Faricy, *Praying* (London: SCM Press, 1983) and Mother Mary Clare, *Encountering the Depths* (Oxford: SLG Press, 1993).
6. *Spiritual Exercises*, nos 316 and 317.
7. *Spiritual Exercises*, nos 325, 326 and 327.
8. Carlos Castaneda, cited by Ruffing, 'Look at every path', p. 4, quoting Jack Kornfield, *A Path with Heart: A Guide Through the Perils and Promises of Spiritual Life* (New York: Bantam, 1993), p. 12.
9. I am grateful to Dr Jack Priestley in a recent lecture for a story told by Francis Bacon about the number of teeth in a horse's mouth. Eminent scholars examined all the texts of Church and Scripture to find the answer. A young adventurous cleric suggested they look in the mouth and count them. This was too much; they dismissed him and concluded that since the texts said nothing about the number of teeth it was therefore a mystery and impossible to know.
10. Mary Grey in Chapter 2 above, p. 19.
11. As Eliot famously describes it in *East Coker*: T. S. Eliot, *Collected Poems 1909 – 1962* (London: Faber, 1974), p. 203.
12. Philip Endean, 'Spirituality and the university', *The Way Supplement*, 84 (Autumn 1995), p. 91.
13. Ibid., p. 98.
14. Robert Bellah, Richard Madsen, William Sullivan, Ann Swidler and Steven Tipton, *Habits of the Heart* (Berkeley: University of California Press, 1985), p. vii.
15. Ibid., p. 275.
16. Rabindranath Tagore, *Gitanjali* (London: Macmillan, 1913), p. 16.

6

Non-conformist Approaches to Spiritual and Moral Development

Andrew Bolton

Introduction

Since the 1988 Education Reform Act the central purpose of the school curriculum in England and Wales has been to promote the development of the whole child, including the spiritual and moral. Religious education, affirmed by the same Act, is undergoing a major revival. Collective worship, although more problematic, is having to be taken seriously. In British society there is a continuing vigorous debate about values, begun in the early 1990s after the killing of James Bulger and then reinforced in the middle of the decade by the killings of the London headteacher Philip Lawrence and of the children and their teacher at Dunblane. Similar events in the USA have posed similar questions. Reflecting unease in the general population, there is continuing talk by politicians and religious leaders of a moral crisis and a desire to make schools more effective in transmitting moral values. In 1996 the School Curriculum and Assessment Authority (SCAA) initiated a major project to develop a values statement with a broad consensus of support in schools and society (SCAA, 1996, pp. 5, 17). SCAA's efforts were applauded by the Archbishop of Canterbury (Carey, 1996, p. 4) and subsequently endorsed by the Chief Rabbi and other faith leaders including Catholic, Free

Church, Hindu and Muslim (SCAA, 1997). In 1998 the Qualifications and Curriculum Authority (QCA), having replaced SCAA, carried out a pilot project on spiritual, moral, social and cultural development with about fifty schools as a prelude for revision of the national curriculum in the year 2000 (QCA, 1998). In English and Welsh schools, spiritual, moral, social and cultural development is going to be more important in the new millennium, not less.

Suddenly, the religious traditions of Church colleges and the theological skills of many of their staff look like an important educational resource for our troubled times – particularly when most such colleges are involved in teacher training and have the resources of theological departments.

It is undeniable that there is a spiritual and moral crisis in society. At the same time one could also say that this is true of British churches and their colleges. Unremitting secularization in the wider society, declining church attendance and the fashion of postmodern perspectives are some indicators suggesting that we are living in a post-Christendom Europe. Do churches and their colleges have themselves the spiritual and ethical resources to be prophetic, or will we simply seek to survive by being an agent of the state – seduced by government enthusiasm for spiritual and moral development through a centralized school curriculum?

Mary Grey has challenged us with three examples of transformational theologies: liberation theology, ecological theology and feminist liberation theology. In describing a non-conformist approach I provide further examples, those of home-grown British transformational theologies, with a significant history going back before the Reformation. These can, I believe, furnish us with courageous examples that have been genuinely prophetic and counter-cultural in the past and with a timely relevance today. The Dissenters can provide resources both for questioning teachers, suspicious of government enthusiasm for spiritual and moral development, and for Christians from traditions outside the Protestant dissenting traditions.

It is important to stress that historic non-conformity can provide a resource for all Christians. There are, after all, Anglican non-conformists and Baptist conformists. Alan Wilkinson (1986) has shown that in terms of World War I and II it was Anglicans who sometimes showed more prophetic insight and courage in confronting unjust acts by the British government. The Anglican Desmond Tutu in South Africa has also been of the non-conformist spirit in questioning governmental injustice whether the government was white or black. Archbishops Runcie and Carey both upset Conservative governments by questioning their treatment of the poor. John Wesley, after all, was a non-conformist who died an Anglican.

Therefore, I want to define religious non-conformity as a questioning of corrupt authority, refusing to be obedient to it on the grounds of conscience, and with a radical vision of a better and more humane society reflecting the Kingdom of God. This is not an attempt to perpetuate historical sectarian issues. However, in a post-Christian society we need to consider very seriously whether we all should become self-conscious non-conformists. If so, I suggest we will be helped by drawing on the historical experience of those who have pioneered this way within our own culture as indigenous prophets. This chapter is therefore an attempt to remind non-conformists of their heritage, to respectfully help Anglicans to see how they can be freed from their establishment past to be more effectively prophetic, and to provide a more radical view of spiritual and moral development for teachers.

This chapter builds on my experience of developing a successful child-centred approach to religious education in a state comprehensive in multi-cultural Leicester (Bolton, 1993), recent tutoring in religious education at Westminster College, Oxford, and current work as a Religious Education adviser in Leicester, a city where 50 per cent of children come from ethnic minority backgrounds. I ought also to mention my interest in Judaism and in Anabaptism and Quakerism as particular non-conformist influences, and my continuing membership of the Reorganized Church of Jesus Christ of Latter Day Saints that gives me daily a sense of non-conformity and almost the feeling of belonging to an ethnic minority. This paper, one in a series advocating a more radically humane purpose for religious education and moral development (see Bolton, 1996a, b; 1997a, b), makes more explicit my underlying non-conformist theological assumptions.

Non-conformists have seen the defining moment for the beginning of an establishment, and therefore compromised, Christianity as the fourth-century reign of the Roman Emperor

Constantine the Great. The central thrust of this paper is a non-conformist critique of developments in English and Welsh education, since 1988, in terms of a new 'Constantinian shift'. This is followed by proposals for a counter-cultural contribution from Church colleges. In preparation, however, it is important to clarify two important distinctions: first between society and the state, and second between dissenting and establishment Christianity.

Society versus the state

Chief Rabbi Jonathan Sacks (1996) distinguishes between two fundamentally different views of human beings. One, Greek, is Aristotle's description of human beings as political animals, rational self-interested individuals whose conflict with each other is contained by state power. The other, Hebrew, expressed by Maimonides, describes human beings as social animals. The political human being develops the coercive state through a Hobbesian contract. The social human being creates the institutions of civil society – families, communities, voluntary associations and moral traditions – based on social covenant, a moral commitment, a bond of love which expresses 'we' and depends on an internalized sense of identity rather than coercion.

Martin Buber (1957, pp. 161ff.) expressed the same distinction before Sacks in terms of the social principle and the political principle. In the political principle, *I–It* relationships predominate between people where some exploit, oppress and coerce others. In the social principle the relationship is more frequently *I–Thou*, as people choose to work together for some common need or interest. In the social principle we are persons known by name, interdependent with others. The state, by contrast, reduces our humanity to a statistic, a number, to be sacrificed, if necessary, on the altar of either war or global capitalism. What is important, argues Buber, is that the social principle is not supplanted by the political principle, fellowship by domination, the horizontal by the vertical.

Progressively in recent centuries it is the political principle, with a Hobbesian flavour, which has increasingly dominated our society. The Hebrew story of covenant community is eclipsed by the discourse of the political arena as liberal individualism and capitalism have eroded the bonds of covenant community, whether of marriage, neighbourhood, religious congregation or college. Yet it is something we have chosen or allowed, and with it our capacity to live inter-dependent and self-determined lives has diminished.

Education was once entirely an expression of voluntary covenanted communities: family with synagogue, mosque or church school. The state, through Education Acts from 1870 onwards, has increased its control of schools. Education is now dominated by a centralized national curriculum with league tables of competing schools. It is now politicized, with the social principle subordinated to the state. In the nineteenth century Dissenters were very suspicious of state involvement in education (Cruickshank, 1963). Now that the state has almost complete control of the curriculum, where are the Dissenters today?

The state is not child-centred. Its ethic is frequently Machiavellian. The teacher must choose whether s/he is contributing to an educational experience which strengthens the social principle or the state. An important purpose of education is not to serve the state but to create cohesive local communities where children flourish. To simply acquiesce in the politicization of education is morally bankrupt. At the very least, we should be living interdependent and self-determined lives and enabling the children we teach to do the same.

Dissenting versus establishment Christianity

Some forms of religion, however, betray or compromise the social principle and serve the state. Thus we must distinguish between dissenting and establishment Christianity.

Alistair Kee (1982, pp. 306ff.) is one of many who argue that the Roman Emperor Constantine the Great (306–337 CE) transformed and corrupted Christianity: 'Christ remains at the centre of Christianity, but the values of the historical Jesus are now replaced by the values of Constantine' (Kee, 1982, p. 153). Discipleship had previously required the surrender of all wealth to the poor, acceptance of the suffering of the cross rather than inflicting the sword of suffering on others, and servanthood rather than Lordship. Now under Constantine the church welcomed the rich, enemies were to be smitten rather than loved, and bishops moved into palaces and became known as

'princes of the church'. The ideology of Constantine transformed Christianity into an imperial cult. Within a century of
Constantine's death Christianity had become the state religion,
non-Christians could not hold public worship nor be in the
army, and with infant baptism of everyone, the church ceased
to be a voluntary community of those who had made an adult
existential decision to follow the Nazarene.

In the English Reformation the formation of the Church of
England continued the Constantinian legacy. The monarch is
the head of the church and today the Prime Minister makes the
final choice of those to be bishop or archbishop before seeking
the Queen's approval. It is interesting to note that behind the
religious education and worship clauses of the 1988 Education
Reform Act were two members of the House of Lords,
Baroness Cox and Baroness Blatch. Baroness Cox declared her
purpose as being 'to restore in our schools the centrality of
Christianity as the major spiritual tradition of this land' (cited
in Bates, 1996, p. 96). Jesus, it seems, continues to have friends
in high places. But has he again been betrayed by a kiss?

There is another kind of English Christianity which is a
significant alternative to establishment Christianity, that of
non-conformity. To be non-conformist historically in England
was to be first of all Protestant. Protestantism was born as an
ethical act: that of questioning and challenging corrupt
authority. Whilst beginning with the questioning of Catholi-
cism, Protestants went on quickly to question each other and
themselves. Non-conformists could be described as radical
Protestants. Watts (1978, p. 3) observes 'A consistent thread
none the less links the Tudor Anabaptists with the twentieth-
century Free Churchman, a refusal to accept the dictates of the
state in matters of conscience. The refusal to render to Caesar
the things that are God's is of the very essence of dissent.'
Macaulay put it more bluntly: the Dissenter 'prostrated himself
in the dust before his Maker, but set his foot on the neck of his
king' (cited in Watts, 1978, p. 5).

In practice, non-conformity meant refusing to conform to the
Church of England. The grounds for dissenting were either the
authority of the Spirit in the life of the individual or group or the
authority of the biblical witness. Both were ways of rejecting the
Constantinian shift and its subsequent tradition, by appealing to
the spirit and letter of the New Testament church.

In gathering as covenanted fellowships of voluntary believers the Non-conformists emphasized conversion through personal religious experience and freely taken existential decision. Spirit and ethics were intimately connected and 'Dissent taught the value of devotion, discipline, personal probity and responsibility' (Watts, 1978, p. 5). Relationships between believers tended to be horizontal – a 'priesthood of all believers' – rather than a hierarchy going from lay person to archbishop. The non-conformist model of discerning truth and righteousness is that of Rabbinic argument, one with another and with past tradition, but with no central authority. In contrast, the Catholic model can be traced back to the hierarchy and bureaucracy needed for the functioning of imperial Rome.

Non-conformity in about pluralism based on individual freedom of conscience. Thomas Helwys (1612, p. 3), for example, one of the persecuted founders of the Baptists, argued thus: 'Men's religion to God is betwixt God and themselves; the king shall not answer for it, neither may the king be judge between God and man. Let them be heretics, Turks, Jews or whatsoever, it appertains not to the earthly powers to punish them in the least measure.'

It has been argued that the non-conformists, in their resistance to a persecuting state church, enabled pluralism to develop in England centuries earlier than elsewhere in Europe (Watts, 1978: p. 4). It is perhaps no accident that it was not until 1656, during the time of Cromwell and a flourishing of radical dissent, that Jews were allowed quietly back in England for the first time since their expulsion in 1290. Anabaptist groups like the Mennonites, Hutterites and later the Amish, together with Quakers, take their commitment to pluralism even further in their renunciation of violence.

The relationship between men and women could be radically equal. For instance:

> ... in their attitude to women the Levellers were ahead of their time. They encouraged women to play their part in politics side by side with their husbands and brothers, because they believed in the equality of all 'made in the image of God'. This was indeed an article of their religious creed, which reflected the

influence of the Anabaptists among them. Everyone knows that however low the position of women sank around them, the Quakers always preached and practised equality. But few of us remember that they were following the example which their forerunners the Anabaptists had set from the early days of the sixteenth century onward. In their community women had an equal standing, an equal right to pray and speak at its meetings. So many of the Levellers were members of this sect that it must have seemed natural to practise on weekdays what they taught on Sundays. (Brailsford, 1976, pp. 316–17)

'The world is my parish', argued John Wesley as he justified going beyond normal ecclesiastical boundaries. But others thought this also, like William Carey, the Baptist missionary. Early Anabaptists went all over Europe at considerable risk preaching and witnessing, as early accounts like the *Chronicle of the Hutterian Brethren* show. North America became a dissenters' refuge where Puritans, Quakers, Anabaptists and Baptists might flee and in so doing become international movements. They were proclaiming what they felt to be a universal rather than an ethnic or nationalistic message.

Many dissenting groups were also radical politically, from pre-Reformation Lollards and seventeenth-century Levellers to nineteenth- and early twentieth-century social gospellers. The Anabaptist sense of economic solidarity, combined with their refusal to fight or pay war taxes, was subversive of the state. Quakers in like manner were ethically subversive whilst clearly not violent revolutionaries. Among these radicals there can be a very vivid vision of the Kingdom of God on earth. Consider for example the words of Gerrard Winstanley, leader of the Digger community:

> This great Leveller, Christ our King of Righteousness in us, shall cause men to beat their swords into ploughshares and spears into pruning hooks, and nations shall learn war no more; and every one shall delight to let each other enjoy the pleasures of the earth, and shall hold each other no longer in bondage. (Cited in Rowland, 1988, p. 114)

Whilst the Digger community was short-lived, it remains a very powerful symbol. A longer-lived example is that of the Quakers in Pennsylvania (1682–1756), portrayed vividly in Edward Hicks's art inspired by Isaiah 11 (Mather, 1973). Among the Anabaptists Hutterians lived all things in common for most of the movement's 460 years. Hutterian communities flourish today in the prairie states and provinces of North America. Related Bruderhof communities prosper in Pennsylvania, New York and in Britain in Kent and Sussex. It could be argued that Marxism, as a secularized vision of a realized Kingdom of God, arose because much of Christianity was establishment rather than dissenting. Another way of describing non-conformists is to say that they had a 'bottom-up' view of society rather than a 'top-down' establishment view. They knew what it was to be marginal, persecuted, slandered and poor.

Some non-conformists, especially among Anabaptists, had a much more positive view of children, some even denying original sin. That perhaps enabled them to take more seriously Jesus' words that to be humble like a child is to be greatest in the kingdom of heaven (Matthew 18:1–11). Quakers argued for 'that of God in every man', including children. If to be a Christian was an adult choice, then children could be children and educated to read the Bible, learn a trade, and be prepared to make their own existential decision. All Hutterian children in the sixteenth century were taught to read, write and learn a trade whilst having their freedom of will respected (Gross, 1980, pp. 179–81). Education was more than indoctrination for conformity.

Non-conformists have always been a minority in Britain and usually with little power except in the time of Cromwell and in the late nineteenth and early twentieth century. However, their influence has been very significant. An ethical, dissenting, minority can leaven the whole lump.

Non-conformity can be extended beyond Free Church Christianity to include all who on grounds of conscience are non-conformists: Humanists, Hindus, Muslims, Sikhs and Jews, radical Anglicans and Catholics. All these groups are able to be non-conformist, that is, asking critical questions of unjust authority. The flourishing, or not, of a Christian non-conformist perspective will depend on an individual's courage, a non-conformist supporting community, a reading of history from 'below', a willingness to identify with the contemporary poor and the New Testament witness.

A typology for non-conformist and establishment Christianities

Whilst recognizing that non-conformity is very varied, I use Table 6.1 to summarize the differences between non-conformist and establishment Christianity by developing an ideal typology to clarify our thinking. It is recognized that both can exist in tension pyschologically within each of us.

Table 6.1

Non-conformist Christianity	Establishment Christianity
church as a gathered, covenant fellowship: a believers' church	church as a territorial parish
every one their own priest (priesthood of all believers) who can come directly to God and to the King	priestly mediation of state to people and sometimes of people to state
non-hierarchical	hierarchical
women equal to men	women subservient to men
government of the church lay controlled	government of the church controlled by clergy together with the state
worship spontaneous, free and participatory	worship formal, liturgical and clergy dominated
non-credal	credal
suspicious of the state; a 'bottom-up' perspective	an arm of the state; a 'top-down' perspective
return to New Testament Christianity; church corrupted by wealth and power after Constantine	continuation of Constantinian tradition
emphasis on religious experience, conversion or 'awakening' and existential commitment	baptism and confirmation more rite of passage than decision based on conviction

Table 6.1 cont.

Non-conformist Christianity	Establishment Christianity
radical questioning	conformity
advocacy of pluralism	advocacy of uniformity
international perspective, although in wartime (e.g. World War I) can also become nationalistic	nationalistic
tendency to radical pacifism	just war theology but frequently betrayed by nationalism
witness	coercion
stewardship	private property
a clear vision of the Kingdom of God on earth, a social gospel of transforming all things	peace and justice after this life
associated with radical politics from Lollards, Diggers to social gospellers	conservative politically although notable exceptions

The new Constantinian shift

Since 1988 Britain has been witnessing a new Constantinian shift, a new Establishmentarianism, a new 'Church of Education' to unify the fragmenting British kingdom. The actions of Constantine in the fourth century and Henry VIII in the sixteenth century have been simultaneously carried out by the secular state, this time on education rather than Christianity. Education has been stolen from local education authorities and local democracy, brought under state control and nationalized. The school is the new parish church. The new prayer book, designed to bring national uniformity to education, is the holy national curriculum, but without Cranmer's beauty of language. The Chief Executive of the Qualifications and Curriculum Authority is our new Archbishop – as subservient to government as any Erastian Anglican. Inquisition-like Ofsted inspections, the equivalent of sixteenth-century Ecclesiastical Commissioners, are carried out to make sure that teachers, the new state clergy, are complying. Influential dissenters in teacher training colleges and departments of education are reported and pilloried. Child-centred approaches and group work are considered heresy and are being suppressed through a national curriculum for teacher training. It is rumoured that teachers will soon have to wear correct vestments or uniform. How Constantine would have congratulated those in power today in seizing such an opportunity to control the thinking of the people through the centralized control of children's education! It is interesting to note that 'New Labour' has carried on where the 'Old Conservatives' left off.

For centuries we have had establishment Christianity. Now we have establishment education. But where are the Latter Day Dissenters? Ironically, only religious education remains under local control – a legacy of the Dissenting tradition which in the last century refused to have Anglicanism paid for by the rates. Only in religious education are teachers free to teach a non-conformist spirituality and ethic. RE thus has the opportunity to be the chapel of non-conformity amidst the national curriculum.

A non-conformist approach to spiritual and moral development in schools

However, Church colleges in their training of teachers also have opportunities, if they do not lose courage. What might a non-conformist approach to spiritual and moral development in schools look like?

Non-conformity, like twentieth-century liberation theology, has continually been renewed by a reading of the Bible by the poor, oppressed and marginalized. What might we find if we were to begin with the biblical witness in today's current educational context from the point of view of children?

In the New Testament Spirit and Kingdom ethics are inseparably connected. The Sermon on the Mount, taken seriously by radical non-conformists like the Anabaptists, follows Jesus' own baptism of water and spirit. In Luke Jesus is portrayed, after his baptism and time in the wilderness, returning in the power of the Spirit to Galilee (Luke 4:14) to read that famous passage from Isaiah before his home synagogue of Nazareth. Jesus read it as a Rabbi, a teacher, on his first teaching practice. Let me alter it slightly for teachers today:

> The Spirit of the Lord is upon me
>> because he has anointed me to be good news
>> to the children of the poor.
>
> He has sent me to proclaim release to the excluded
>> and to those with special needs,
>
> To set at liberty those children who are oppressed by their economic and social conditions,
>
> To proclaim the acceptable year of the Lord.
>> Luke 4:18–19 (RSV adapted)

Acts, chapter 2 begins with Pentecostal filling of the disciples by the Holy Spirit and ends with disciples living 'all things in common', i.e. the voluntary redistribution of wealth. Acts 2 is very much a fulfilment of Luke 4:18–19 and has strong echoes of the Jubilee year in Leviticus 25. Non-conformity is the continuation of an ancient radical tradition. I must confess that talk about spiritual development leaves me very impatient if it remains individualistic and disconnected from the achievement of social and economic justice. In the Bible, Spirit is always communal, an inspiration to live for others.

A non-conformist approach to spiritual and moral development is holistic and about the quality of human relationships provided for the child by the school. The onus here is on teachers, parents and other adults in society. The problems of society should not be blamed on children but on the adults around them. A child is fallen only to the degree that it is corrupted or betrayed by adults. We forget the high view that Jesus had of children and his desire for their unrestrained access to himself. The concept of original sin in children, together with their damnation as unbaptized infants, does not begin with the teaching of Jesus. Interestingly, the blessing of children in Mark 10 comes directly after Jesus' condemnation of divorce. Jesus when asked who is the greatest in the Kingdom of Heaven puts a child in the centre of the disciples (Matthew 18:1–5). Who is greatest in a school? The head or a child? Who is the greatest in society? The Prime Minister, the monarch, the

Archbishop, the business man, the general? Or a child? Does the child exist to serve the state, or does the state exist to serve the child? Not to be child-centred is to betray the gospel.

What if classrooms were places of fellowship, participation and a sense of joy? Different giftedness would be accepted and nurtured but in a co-operative rather than a competitive and elitist way. Children would experience the gospel implicitly in the quality of relationships surrounding them. Children's freedom to discover and learn the skills of research in order to answer their own critical questions would be more important than 'learning' lots of factual content. There would also be more room for the spontaneous.

Individual conscience and personal experience would be respected in each child. To become committed in faith, or not, is a decision for the adult. So children should be equipped to make adult decisions responsibly rather than learn to carry out obediently the decisions made for them by others. Pluralism of views and traditions, including the secular, would be respected. Children would be encouraged to understand their own tradition and that of others with empathy and respect. Children would gain the confidence to protest assertively, but non-violently, against bullying, injustice, unfaithfulness, inequality and violence and be helped to develop a global rather than an ethnic, national or sectarian ethic, using the resources from within their family tradition.

Practical skills would be as important as intellectual skills. Jesus was a carpenter as well as a Rabbi; both manual and intellectual work are noble. Finally, the RE department would be a 'chapel of non-conformity' amidst the establishment religion of the national curriculum.

Implications for pursuing a non-conformist stance by Church colleges of higher education

Mary Grey challenges Church colleges to be genuinely counter-cultural. To be counter-cultural is to be non-conformist, to have the ethical integrity of a dissenter with all the vulnerability that involves. In order to be this, Church colleges will be helped by drawing on the theological resources of historic and contemporary non-conformity. At Westminster College in 1997, as part of a college-wide review including that of mission statement and vision, a working party identified the principles outlined in Table 6.2. It was very helpful to rediscover our roots as a college, to know who we are, and seek to be faithful to that, in a contemporary world with many pressures simply to conform to government and society. The quotation 'Where there is no vision, the people perish' (Proverbs 29:18, AV) is a timely reminder.

Besides identifying biblical roots and a contemporary vision of purpose, what are some other implications for Church colleges if they are, in Mary Grey's terms, to be prophetically counter-cultural?

In order to be able to maintain a prophetic stance in relationship to the state, it is important that Church colleges work so as not to be completely dependent on state funding. Otherwise, they cannot dissent at injustice or the increasing power and control of the state over education. If 'power corrupts and utter power corrupts utterly' then the independence and strength of the churches and their colleges is important for the political health of a nation – whether the government is right- or left-wing. Church colleges are to be part of Buber's social principle rather than the political principle.

Non-conformity is about questioning and being disobedient to corrupt authority, being willing to 'obey God rather than man' as Peter put it (Acts 5:29). Several Church colleges, like Westminster College, were founded to train teachers for the inner-city poor. They should also ask 'Why are there inner-city poor?' and rigorously inform their teaching and witness by thorough research about injustice, poverty and violence in society and understand the impact of these on children, particularly the children of the poor, whether in British inner cities or in Third World slums. Our students, whether they are going to become teachers or not, should have a passion for justice and truth provoked as they better understand social and economic systems and the possibilities of things being different. John Hull (1996) has talked of the spirituality of money. One could also talk in a similar way about the spirituality of nationalism. The idolatrous nature of money and nationalism should be understood critically and contrasted with the spirituality of 'persons in community'. The central question should be 'What blesses or harms the child?' Asking such a question is a very powerful tool for discerning what is really

Table 6.2 Spiritual, moral, social and cultural

Read horizontally across. What is attempted below is to show how Westminster College, as an institution of higher education founded by the Methodist Church, can contribute to the current focus on the spiritual, moral, social and cultural dimensions in schools and society in a way that is faithful to its distinctive foundation and biblical roots. This attempt also helped clarify the college's sense of purpose formulated in a mission statement.

	Spiritual	Moral	Social	Cultural
Biblical roots e.g. text of Wesley's first open-air preaching (Luke 4:18)	'The Spirit is upon me because he has anointed me to …	preach good news to the poor.…	He has sent me to proclaim release to the captives and recovering of sight to the blind, to set at liberty those who are oppressed.'	Interpretation and application of texts and revelation in diverse cultures
Methodist foundation	Wesley's heart 'strangely warmed'. A quest for social and personal holiness. Conversion	Ministry to poor; social gospel tradition; non-conformity	Fellowship. Quest for holiness supported by discipline of the class meeting and congregational 'societal' life	'The world is my parish.' Valuing diversity and meeting the challenges offered in a pluralistic society

	Spiritual	Moral	Social	Cultural
Westminster College	Witness to Spirit through the religious life, academic teaching and all human relationships in the college. Discovering what it means to be human and for that to thrive	Education in service of the disadvantaged. Teaching informed by research into the causes of disadvantage. Foster life-long ethical enquiry which is relational and global and is informed by the dissenting tradition	Mutual responsibility and interactive learning encouraged and supported by the small class and tutorial	An open, inclusive, collegiate community with local, national and international outreach
Working in schools	Create an ethos which is open to the spiritual dimension of life that transcends self	Working in partnership with school communities to reflect upon the nature and outcomes of the educational activities of teaching and learning	Professionally committed to developing positive self-esteem, confidence in learning, and good relationships with others	Celebration of the richness of diverse cultures and peoples through partnership with different learning communities
Serving society locally, nationally and internationally	Inspiring a vision of a new humanity in a new society	Developing a capacity for a critical understanding of a just order	Enabling communities to flourish with social justice, sustainable development, stewardship of the environment and global citizenship	Engaging with the concerns of different communities to promote goodness, truth and beauty

going on in the world. Whilst not all trainee teachers have a faith, nearly all are committed to children. Asking such a question can enable students to see whether the fruits of an ideological or religious view are humanizing or dehumanizing.

It is also at a Church college that students can be challenged to consider what is entailed in making life-long commitments to children, whether in their own marriages or in their future careers.

Theological and philosophical resources for the training of all student teachers should be pluralistic. It is not just non-conformist Christianity that connects Spirit with justice for the poor. Judaism, Islam and Sikhism, for instance, connect the two with boldness. Humanism and philosophy can also make their contribution to critical thinking. For some, faith and questioning are mutually exclusive, but for the non-conformist faith provokes questions about poverty, violence, injustice and personal existential questions like 'What should I do?'

Teacher-training students with a religious studies specialism are privileged in their courses to learn how to contribute intelligently and critically to the spiritual and moral development of children. However, the principle of the 'priesthood of all believers' means that all BEd students should have these opportunities through their specialist subject and through other courses. In fact the spiritual and moral enlargement of all people in the college should flow explicitly from the institution's mission statement rooted in a reclamation of the radical Christian tradition. Students should know clearly before they come that they will be imaginatively and creatively challenged to think for themselves and to be critical of establishment spirituality and morality in so far as it reflects the interests of the rich, powerful and unjust. In other words, to be able to question and to disobey corrupt authority, to be people of integrity, to develop their own critical valuing process in dialogue with others, to have the spiritual and moral resources to be non-conformist.

It is important that a Church college should demonstrate in its own structures and fellowship a glimpse of the Kingdom way of life on earth. At the very least, ethical non-conformity should be fostered among staff and students. If it is not, then staff with non-conformist consciences should regularly and quietly gather in support of each other and at appropriate times make their views clearly known and stand together in support of each other. The sense of community, caring and support, with 'I–Thou' relationships flourishing, should be clearly sensed by students and cleaners, gardeners and porters. To empower staff to contribute to such an environment might include converting from hierarchical structures to a collegial fellowship to facilitate dissent with responsibility. Payment of principals, for example, should not tend in the same direction as the greed of chairpersons of privatized utilities.

In conclusion

A new establishment religion, the 'Church of Education', needs the challenge of a new form of critical and ethical dissent, drawing on the radical English tradition of non-conformity. However, a non-conformist who subserviently fulfils the aims of government and the rich and powerful in society has become a Judas and betrayed the Master by selling out for pieces of silver or a continuing salary.

It is thus important to distinguish between a non-conformist and an establishment view of children's spiritual and moral development. One liberates and empowers, the other oppresses. One is leaven and salt, the other is the opiate of the people. One strengthens community and 'I–Thou' relationships, the other the state and 'I–It'. One is about voluntary federation, the other about centralized control. One is about human equality, the other is about hierarchical status, power and wealth. One is about co-operation and service, the other about competition and individualism. One is about witness, the other about coercion and violence. One is about stewardship, the other is about private wealth. One celebrates diversity of races, cultures, and perspectives, the other presses for conformity. One has the mood of joy and critical thinking, the other has the mood of obedience, sorrow and guilt. One is informed by the Spirit of Christ, the other, for all its glitter, is in the end demonic and a betrayal of children and their future. We need to remember that spiritual and moral development in the 'Church of Education' can legally be the following:

> All German young people ... will be educated in the
> Hitler Youth physically, intellectually, and morally

in the spirit of National Socialism to serve the nation and the community. (Law passed 1 December 1936: cited in Burleigh and Wippermann, 1991, p. 229)

Note

I am grateful to Tim Macquiban for a sheet left on the photocopier about the non-conformist conscience that launched me on the line of thought developed in this chapter and supported more recently by a helpful clarifying discussion. Thanks to Susan Hector for the final quotation above and to a college environment that nourished the radical in me. I am also grateful to participants in the conference session on 14 December 1996 at La Sainte Union, Southampton at which I gave the first draft of this chapter, whose kindly dissent helped clarify my thinking on a number of points. The Spiritual, Moral, Social and Cultural Working Party at Westminster College was a very stimulating group from which Table 6.2 emerged through numerous drafts. Finally, it is important to stress that the views expressed in this paper are my own and not necessarily those of Westminster College or of any other colleague past or present.

References and further reading

D. Bates (1996) 'Christianity, culture and other religions (Part 2): F. H. Hilliard, Ninian Smart and the 1988 Education Reform Act', *British Journal of Religious Education*, 18/2, pp. 85–102.

A. Bolton (1993) 'An approach to World Religions through beliefs and values in Years 10 and 11 in a Leicestershire upper school' in C. Erricker, A. Brown, M. Hayward, D. Kadodwala and P. Williams (eds), *Teaching World Religions* (Oxford: Heinemann), pp. 12–18.

A. Bolton (1996a) 'A developing vision for Religious Education', *Resource*, 18/2 (Spring 1996), pp. 3–7.

A. Bolton (1996b) 'RE and values: key questions for the next 5-10 years', *Journal of Beliefs and Values*, 17/2, pp. 8–11.

A. Bolton (1997a) 'Moral development: whose ethics in the teaching of Religious Education?', *Journal of Moral Development*, 26/2, pp. 197–210.

A. Bolton (1997b) 'Should Religious Education foster national consciousness?', *British Journal of Religious Education*, 19/3, pp. 134–42.

H. N. Brailsford (1976) *The Levellers and the English Revolution* (Nottingham: Spokesman).

M. Buber (1957) *Pointing the Way* (London: Routledge and Kegan Paul).

M. Burleigh and W. Wippermann (1991) *The Racial State: Germany 1933–1945* (Cambridge: Cambridge University Press).

G. Carey (1996) Speech in the House of Lords by the Archbishop of Canterbury. Friday 5 July.

M. Cruickshank (1963) *Church and State in English Education, 1870 to the Present Day* (London: Macmillan).

M. Grey (1996) 'Christian theology, spirituality and the curriculum' address to 'Engaging the Curriculum, Spirituality and Moral Development Forum', Southampton (13–14 December) (ch. 2 above, pp. 12–32).

L. Gross (1980) *The Golden Years of the Hutterites* (Scottdale, PA: Herald).

T. Helwys (1612) *The Mistery of Inquity* (London).

J. Hull (1996) 'God, money and the spirituality of education', *British Journal of Religious Education* 18/2, pp. 66–8.

Hutterian Brethren (eds) (1987) *The Chronicle of the Hutterian Brethren*, vol. 1 (Rifton, NY: Plough).

A. Kee (1982) *Constantine Versus Christ: The Triumph of Ideology* (London: SCM).

E. J. Mather (1973) *Edward Hicks: A Peaceable Season* (Princeton, NJ: Pyne Press).

K. Patel (1996) 'Moral lessons for teachers', *The Times Higher Education Supplement* (1 November), p. 1.

QCA (Qualifications and Curriculum Authority) (1998) *Guidelines for Schools: The Promotion of Pupils' Spiritual, Moral, Social and Cultural Development* (London: QCA).

C. Rowland (1988) *Radical Christianity: Reading of Recovery* (Oxford: Blackwell).

J. Sacks (1996) 'Renewing civil society' (Millennium Lecture, given at Manchester Business School, 20 March).

SCAA (School Curriculum and Assessment Authority) (1996) *Education for Adult Life: The Spiritual and Moral Development Of Young People* (SCAA Discussion Papers, no. 6; London: SCAA).

SCAA (1997) 'Work on values gets go-ahead – support from faith groups', news release at conference 'Making Sense of Values in Learning', Great Western Royal Hotel, London (22 May).

N. Tate (1996) SCAA news release (30 October).

M. R. Watts (1978) *The Dissenters* (Oxford: Oxford University Press).

A. Wilkinson (1986) *Dissent or Conform? War, Peace and the English Churches 1900–1945* (London: SCM).

7

Poor in Spirit? The Child's World, the Curriculum and 'Spirituality'

A. Elizabeth Ramsey

T here are various perspectives on the recent explosion of interest in the so-called 'spiritual' dimension to human experience and the ways in which this is reflected in the school curriculum. Each new tragic occurrence to hit the headlines, particularly those incidents in which children are either the victims or the perpetrators of crimes, provokes a fresh outcry and renewed attempts to identify the sources of disaffection and rootlessness in society. Whatever is understood by the word 'spirituality', there seems to be a general consensus of opinion that society somehow lacks an ingredient that is implied by the term. In this so-called 'postmodern' era, in which change is the norm and signposts are often more permanent than the destinations to which they point, beliefs and traditions which have undergirded our thinking about ourselves as 'persons' and ourselves in relation to society and other persons have become marginalized.

A cursory glance at the bookshelves of any well-stocked bookshop confirms the challenge to European and North American patterns of rationality. A decline in confidence in belief systems purporting to give over-arching meanings to society in general has led to a focus on self-identity, self-realization and the quest for personal fulfilment. This includes holistic approaches to health and well-being. Shelf space labelled 'Spirituality and New Age' often exceeds the space designated for 'Religion', and the two areas are no longer seen to be connected.

After openly accepting the risk of being labelled a traditionalist, which indeed he is, David Carr proceeds to argue that 'the only way to make much sense of spiritual education ... is via the engagement of young people with some serious tradition of spiritual reflection or enquiry through which they might come to appreciate the nature of genuine spiritual concerns and questions'.[1] He condemns what he calls 'promiscuous postmodern cavorting with essentially disinherited and disjointed fragments of the life of different and diverse human cultures'. Expressed like this, there is a point to Carr's concerns. Of course educators, on the whole, wish their students to engage with the beliefs and theories that underpin feelings and opinions. But is it possible to define what is meant by a 'serious' tradition, even within the context of spirituality itself?

Certainly the promoters of the 'World Spirituality' series[2] decided that they needed to use a 'working hypothesis' in order to make initial headway with the project. Ewert Cousins, the General Editor, points out in his preface to the series that 'no attempt was made to arrive at a common definition of spirituality that would be accepted by all in precisely the same way', adding that 'the term "spirituality", or an equivalent, is not found in a number of the traditions'. The 'working hypothesis' which found consensus among the editors was as follows: 'The series focuses on that inner dimension of the person called by certain traditions the spirit. This spiritual core is the deepest centre of the person. It is here that the person is open to the transcendent dimension; it is here that the person experiences ultimate reality.'[3]

Schools are equipping children, or arguably should be doing so, with the knowledge, understanding and skills for living in a pluralistic and multi-faith society. Any success in this area must hinge on the provision of opportunities to explore *difference*, using learning and teaching strategies which enable children to engage with the appropriate issues and relate them to their own experiences of life and relationships. This necessitates an understanding of spirituality which takes into account the total reality of the child's experience and which will enable children to harness their spiritual development to their experiences of life and relationships.

The situation in England and Wales is that schools are receiving official inspection reports which comment on their ability to promote the spiritual, moral, social and cultural development of pupils. This implies that there are commonly agreed criteria with regard to measuring development in these areas. But reflective teachers in schools receiving good overall inspection reports, with these areas favourably highlighted, often comment that they feel no clearer about the underlying justification of the criteria being used.

Inspection reports typically include statements which refer to 'caring and supportive' communities, 'where pupils' spiritual, moral, social and cultural development is successfully promoted'. Daily acts of worship 'where pupils are given opportunities for reflection and prayer' are considered to 'promote spiritual awareness'. It seems to be important for children to be encouraged 'to make sense of their personal experiences and feelings through planned, thoughtful discussions in the classroom'. Reference is made to the observation that pupils 'demonstrate excitement and wonder in their learning', and opportunities for spiritual development are seen to be provided 'across the curriculum, especially in religious education, story time and music lessons'. The ethos of a school in itself is thought to 'provide strong moral guidance for the pupils', and pupils are described as having 'a clear sense of right and wrong' and showing 'a well developed sense of fair play and honesty'.[4]

We find here a loose connection between spirituality and 'acts of worship', including the suggestion that there is a link between spirituality, reflection and prayer. The connection, however, is by no means made explicit. One significant underlying assumption in the statements just cited seems to be that 'the turn to the self' is, to some extent at least, a *fait accompli*. In his book *The Ethics of Authenticity*,[5] Charles Taylor describes this 'turn to the self' as 'a form of individualism' which is accepted as an important aspect of Western culture. Children, for example, 'are encouraged to make sense of their *personal* experiences and feelings'. Taylor expands the 'turn to the self' by stating it assumes that 'everyone has a right to develop their own form of life, grounded on their own sense of what is really important or of value' adding, 'people are called upon to be true to themselves and to seek their own self-fulfillment'.[6] The postmodernity debate has yet to be overtly and rigorously applied with any seriousness to religious education in primary schools. It would seem, however, that postmodernity is already shaping educational practice. In other words, culture is influencing education more than education is influencing culture.

The official Ofsted Frameworks for Inspection in England and Wales also reflect a shift of focus away from religious education as having the major role in children's personal, social, spiritual and moral development. This partly reflects the wish of Her Majesty's Inspectors and others to ensure that the sole responsibility for pupils' development in these areas does not rest with the religious educators. ' "Spiritual" is not synonymous with "religious" ', states the 1994 Framework; 'all areas of the curriculum may contribute to pupils' spiritual development', and this is most certainly the case. However, it is possible to take a more cynical view. Educators need to take action to ensure that religious education does not become primarily a descriptive activity. The acceptance of the view that religion is necessarily encapsulated within a few major traditions may mean a denial of the dynamic potential of religion to be an innovatory force, particularly through its spiritual dimensions.

So my argument begins to turn on the dangers of the spiritual and the religious becoming disentangled from the political. How is Mary Grey's vision of the 'once and future child' to be realized unless the boundaries of the 'traditions' are overstepped? Yet in overstepping these boundaries, how are we to avoid the dangers of Carr's 'promiscuous postmodern cavorting'? Part of the answer must surely lie in having both the insight and the courage to view change positively and not, necessarily, as the negation of all that is best in our traditions. The need for further debate about 'postmodernity' and spiritual and religious development is urgent. Even 'The New Age' itself is arguably not postmodern but rather, according to Paul Heelas, 'exemplifies most of those (traditional) processes widespread within religion in the West'.[7]

The appropriateness of seeking to identify models of spirituality and guidelines for moral behaviour within the context of an education suitable for all children has to be rigorously questioned and challenged. Indeed, the more rigorous the search for a working definition of spirituality in a broad educational context, the more the search itself begins to seem something of a luxury. The crucial point at issue is the reality of the child's world. As John Hull has claimed, 'spirituality [can be] the high-sounding rhetoric that disguises the reality'.[8] Unfortunately, the reality that is Liverpool, where most of my work in schools takes place, may not be accepted as 'typical' by those who know Liverpool only through media representation. I therefore approached the headteacher of a church school in Cheshire and suggested she might provide a selection of case studies which illustrate the reality of the world experienced by some of her children. Details of the case studies have been changed in order to respect confidentiality and protect identity.[9] The reality remains typical. The subject of the first case study is Rick, aged 10.

The headteacher writes: 'I have no watch with which to tell the time tonight because I lent it to Rick. Rick had to come to see me on the hour every hour today because I wanted to make sure he was still smiling.' She goes on to describe his attractive features including large brown eyes, but concludes 'he doesn't know how to smile'. She describes his behaviour as gradually becoming more and more disturbed. 'Today he crawled under a table in his class and stayed there making strange sounds. He has begun to kick out at other children without any provocation, and to use foul language. Our discipline system is very precise and structured and after a fourth misdemeanour a letter is generally sent to the child's home. However, in Rick's case our worry is that if we send a letter home, his mother will threaten to put Rick into care.'

She suggested to Rick that he and she had a talk and continues: 'Rick was able to share the fact that he felt very angry inside, not with me or with his teacher but with his mum and that he also was really angry with his new "dad". I asked whether he felt mainly happy or unhappy inside. His reply was "unhappy most of the time".' The headteacher decided to ask the mother to come to school. They spoke for about three hours. Rick's mother told her that her three children have different fathers. She described her present partner as not being very sensitive and having little patience with Rick. Her previous partner was sectioned under the Mental Health Act. Before him, there was Rick's father. The headteacher's account continues: 'Rick's mother said, "I want to tell you something but I don't have the words". She continued to talk and it was a long time before I said, "Are you trying to tell me you were raped?" "Yes, but that's a word I can't use." ' The headteacher concluded her account with the question, asked from within the context of a church school, 'How do you teach Rick that God is his loving Father and that he must love others as he loves himself? You see he doesn't love himself and has never had a father's love.'

It is here we find the clash of two different modes of discourse. A theoretical affirmation of a vague spirituality is clashing with the political reality of a child grappling with hurt and pain. Couple this with the existing problems of spirituality in a pluralist culture and we find ourselves with a crisis. How can Rick be enabled to develop his 'own form of life, grounded on [his] own sense of what is really important or of value' in the fashion suggested by Taylor? Herein lies a major educational challenge of our time, reflecting the whole crisis of Western culture. Rick is by no means exceptional in his background. It seems clear that teachers are often unwilling, for various reasons, to admit the full nature and scale of the emotional and social problems of the children in their schools. Jane Erricker, on the basis of her involvement with the 'Children and Worldviews' project, strongly underlines the significance of the children's experiences and the fact that these examples from Cheshire typify the experiences of many children throughout the country.

In her second case study, the headteacher from Cheshire focused on Sadie, aged 5. 'Whenever she sees me in school she takes a flying jump and tries to cling to me as though she will never let go.' Sadie lives with her mother now but when she first came to school she lived with her grandmother. Mother was in the de-tox unit. Mother's partner was dealing in drugs and was Mother's supplier. When Mother's money ran out she sold her furniture, cooker etc. to raise money. Sadie no longer received cooked meals at home. When Mother could not raise the money she was beaten up. Sadie was present on those occasions. The headteacher continues: 'On my desk for the weekend is a bead necklace which Sadie made for me. She wore the bracelet which matched it. Her bracelet broke, so I offered her my necklace. She refused it. She gave me all she had to give.'

The final case study to be selected relates to Ste. The partner of Ste's mother had taken pornographic photographs of Ste when he was a baby which had been traced by the police. Because Mother consequently threw out her partner, she was persecuted and a knife was held to Ste's throat. He was still a baby in a pram. Burning rags were put through the letter box and the house was set alight. Eventually the family managed to move away from the area and so Ste arrived at his new school. Mother is now agoraphobic. The headteacher describes the first time Ste took Holy Communion as one of the most meaningful celebrations of Eucharist she has experienced. 'Ste's school sweatshirt had a hole in the front. His pyjamas stuck out through the hole. It is a way of keeping warm when you don't have underclothes. The priest sat at a table in school with Ste on his knee. Ste helped with the bread and the chalice at the consecration.' How Ste felt is not recorded.

John Hull has depicted 'the reality' which may be disguised by 'the high-sounding rhetoric' which can pass for spirituality as 'that which inspires young people to live for others'.[10] The headteacher in Cheshire is doing what she can to develop the capacity for response which she recognizes in Rick, Sadie and Ste. Hence we move through the reality of the child's world to the demands and possibilities of the curriculum. The criteria suggested in an influential Ofsted document include 'becoming aware of and reflecting on experience', 'developing personal views and insights', and 'understanding and evaluating a range of possible responses and interpretations'.[11] Under the specific heading 'Aspects of spiritual development' the document lists 'Beliefs', a 'Sense of awe, wonder and mystery', and 'Experiencing feelings of transcendence'.[12]

In efforts to apply the suggested criteria, teachers are aware of the importance of beginning with the children's own experiences of life and relationships and can find the use of stories to be a useful strategy. One teacher whom I worked alongside, now herself an Ofsted inspector, made a collection over a number of years of questions which in her experience with young children had promoted interesting reflection and discussion, often in the context of a story. The questions included the following:

If you were making a new world to live in, what would you
put in it? What would you leave out?
What do we really need? What could we manage without?
What kind of people would you want in your world?
What is important to you?
What makes you happy? sad? angry? frightened?
Are you ever lonely? Who might be lonely?
What do you wonder about?
What is time?
What is love? peace? Why do people fight and quarrel?
How clever are people? What can they make? What can't
they make?

After a discussion about 'Time', the following poems were
produced by children on the subject:

> Time is all around us.
> It is a bud opening.
> People walking along the street.
> It is listening to your friend shouting
> Across the road.
> Each day is time.
> Time surrounds us.
> Living creatures live in time.
> Time is the sky changing its colours blue to grey.
> Time is the sun moving behind the clouds.
> The world is spinning through time.
> (Alison, aged 10)

> You could describe time as a weapon which after so
> long kills and destroys all the world.
> Time is like a tree that blossoms and dies again in
> winter.
> You can spend it.
> You can waste it and so kill it.
> Time is forever.
> We all need time.
> Time is alive.
> Time is a ball of fire spinning across earth.
> When we are at the end of ours, we cool down.
> Time measures our lives.

Time is like a flower opening.
We are born in time, we live in time, we die in time.
Time takes us through our lives.
We depend on time.
Time streaks like lightning across the sky when we
are enjoying ourselves.
Time shoots through the sky like a comet before the
human.
Time can sometimes plod on as slowly as a snail.
Time can bring sadness and time can bring joy.
(Steven, aged 10)[13]

Within the dynamic of the relationship between children, the
curriculum and spirituality, it is possible to interpret official
criteria in ways which not only seem to allow for, but positively
facilitate, both Taylor's 'turn to the self' and Carr's exploration
of experience within a specifically religious tradition. If
spirituality means anything in an educational context, whether
in church schools or otherwise, then it must relate to the very
foundation of our humanity and be in response to the
fundamental question of what it is that makes, and, perhaps
more importantly keeps, people human. Potentially, theology
has a unique response to make to these fundamental questions.

An excellent starting point in the Hebrew Scriptures lies in the
book of Job, which tells of Job's struggle to preserve his belief in
humanity, as well as God, in the face of well-nigh intolerable
suffering. The book of Job raises questions about human
responsibility and blame as well as questions concerning possible
ultimate meaning and purpose. The questions provoked by Job's
story are as relevant today as they ever were for Jews. Christians
increasingly recognize the relevance of the implications not only
of this book but of the whole of the Hebrew Scriptures as they
read and interpret them in their own right and not merely as the
'old' Testament superseded by the new. A re-discovery of
Christianity's Jewish roots and consequent reappraisals of
traditional Christian theology may encourage, among other
things, a much more rigorous questioning on the part of
Christians, and those educated within a broadly Christian
framework, of possible meanings to human existence. This in
turn may result in an increased willingness on the part of
teachers and other adults to explore alongside children as they

try to make sense of their experiences.

Jacob Neusner has disputed, with good reason considering the historical track record, the whole validity of what has commonly been called 'the Judaeo-Christian tradition'.[14] What we need to do is to grapple with the conflicts found in Christian–Jewish relations and find constructive ways of coping with them. For too long, the followers of the so-called 'new' way of Love have persecuted the followers of the way they have perceived as the 'old' way of the Law. This misunderstanding of Jewish Torah has been almost inextricably bound up with Christianity's self-understanding. The entreaty to love our neighbour is to be found of course in Leviticus 19. The overcoming of the binary Law/Gospel motif may bring us closer to realizing John Hull's goal of 'living for others'. With increasing willingness on the part of Jewish and Christian scholars to work together, a common spiritual and moral inheritance may be re-discovered which may yet have something life-enhancing and creative to offer to wider society and which, potentially, could span the divide between the 'secular' world and the so-called traditional religious stances or, to put it in another way, which may resolve the conflict between vague spirituality and political tragedy.

The turning point in relations between Christians and Jews was the 'interruption' of the Holocaust event. As Elisabeth Schüssler Fiorenza and David Tracy summarize it, 'If Christian theology is to enter history, then surely this interruption of the Holocaust is a frightening disclosure of the real history within which we have lived. The theological fact is that Christian theology cannot fully return to history until it faces the Holocaust.'[15] The twentieth century has been a century of genocides and each genocide has had its particular examples of horror, reflecting the seemingly unending capacity of human beings to inflict the grossest acts of inhumanity upon one another. The Jewish Holocaust is, arguably, unique for Christians – and certainly in the eyes of many Jews – because it not only has a historical dimension but also a deeply theological significance. Even more important than the shared questions concerning theodicy are the questions surrounding the implications of the Holocaust's having occurred in the heart of so-called Christian Europe.

The novelist Elie Wiesel faces the depths of depraved humanity as experienced in Auschwitz in his book *Night*.[16] He writes starkly 'Never shall I forget that night, the first night in the camp, which has turned my life into one long night, seven times cursed and seven times sealed. Never shall I forget that smoke. Never shall I forget the little faces of the children, whose bodies I saw turned into wreaths of smoke beneath a silent blue sky. Never shall I forget those flames which consumed my faith forever ... Never shall I forget those moments which murdered my God and my soul, and turned my dreams to dust.' Another novelist and Auschwitz survivor, Primo Levi in his book, *If This Is a Man*, has raised, with astounding clarity and gentleness, similar questions to those raised in the book of Job. Philip Roth regards the book as 'one of the century's truly necessary books', and describes Primo Levi as being 'profoundly in touch with the minutest workings of the most endearing human events and with the most contemptible. What has survived in Levi's writing isn't just his memory of the unbearable, but also ... his delight in what made the world *exquisite* to him.'[17]

I wish to suggest that the implications of the Holocaust and a whole re-discovered, mutually tolerant Jewish–Christian tradition are pertinent to educationalists working with children from all kinds of backgrounds, including the most negative social and emotional experiences. How can a teacher recover the 'exquisite' for the child who tries not to feel at all because his/her feelings are too raw and damaged? One Holocaust survivor, Haim Ginott, entreats teachers with these words: 'My eyes saw what no [one] should witness: Gas chambers built by *learned* engineers, children poisoned by *educated* physicians, infants killed by *trained* nurses, women and babies shot and burned by High School and College *graduates*. So I am suspicious of education. My request is: Help your children become human. Your efforts must never produce learned monsters, skilled psychopaths, educated Eichmanns. Reading, writing, and arithmetic are important only if they serve to make our children more humane.'[18]

The task of the educator must be to ensure that 'spirituality' meets the often ugly reality of the child's world. I have attempted to show that we need to emphasize the importance of the children's experiences of life in general and relationships in particular. Unless their humanity is touched, the whole process of education may be deemed to have failed. Providing opportunities for this *touching* of humanity is a vital task for schools in 'postmodern' society. Dialogue between Jews and Christians, combined with a re-interpretation and new understanding of the Judaeo-Christian traditions, could, potentially, underpin and provide inspiration for re-discoveries of the interface between beliefs and values. This would in no way be to encourage any new attitude of supremacy, but rather a renewed humility and willingness to re-discover, which could, by implication, extend to the possibilities of learning from all the major world religions. The sequence, creation–revelation–redemption, 'the theological centre of the Jewish Prayer Book',[19] arguably not only forms the essential theological drama of Judaism and then Christianity, but reflects and sustains the life experiences of all human beings.

What have been isolated and set apart as traditions may re-enter history and transform the child's world through the engaging of the curriculum, inspiring young people, as John Hull suggests, 'to live for others' and to realize what enables a person to become fully human. The story of Passover, for example, gives a context for exploration of the fundamental issues of freedom and slavery, with the accompanying themes of risk, choice, hope, disappointment, leadership, hardship, sacrifice and so on. The theme of Creation may not only initiate discussion and thinking about how the world came into being but can inspire visions of 'making all things new', of new worlds, of creating a better world, of a Messianic age when justice and peace will prevail over all the world. The 'poor in spirit', including the children facing the crisis of the reality of their world, may surely he redeemed: 'at last the clouds cleared and the new sun shone for the first time on the new lakes and rivers and seas' (Stephen, aged 10).

Notes

Gratitude is expressed to Professor Ian Markham for his active support and encouragement in the producing of this article.

1. David Carr, 'Rival conceptions of spiritual education', *Journal of Philosophy of Education*, 30/2 (1996), p. 173.
2. A major series published by the Crossroad Publishing Company, New York.
3. Arthur Green (ed.), *Jewish Spirituality: From the Bible Through the Middle Ages* (New York: Crossroad/London: SCM Press, 1989 paperback), p. xii.

4. Gratitude is expressed to the headteachers who provided copies of their inspection reports for inclusion in this chapter.

5. Charles Taylor, *The Ethics of Authenticity* (London: Harvard University Press, 1991), p. 14.

6. Ibid.

7. Paul Heelas, 'De-traditionalisation of religion and self: the New Age and postmodernity' in Kieran Flanagan and Peter C. Jupp (eds), *Postmodernity, Sociology and Religion* (Basingstoke: Macmillan Press, 1996).

8. John Hull, 'Spiritual and moral development – the role of RE', paper given at a Christian Education Movement Conference (June 1994).

9. Gratitude is expressed to the headteacher for her contribution to the discussion.

10. John Hull, 'Spiritual and moral development – the role of RE', paper given at a Christian Education Movement conference (June 1994).

11. National Curriculum Council, *Spiritual and Moral Development: A Discussion Paper* (London: NCC, 1993).

12. It is of interest to note that this document was re-published in September 1995 by the School Curriculum and Assessment Authority soon after the killing of the child James Bulger by two older children. Sir Ron Dearing stated in his Foreword that 'as a society we need to be much concerned for the moral and spiritual dimension of our civilisation'. A revised document was issued in May 1996.

13. Gratitude is expressed to this teacher and the children's parents for permission to use these poems.

14. Jacob Neusner, *Jews and Christians: The Myth of a Common Tradition* (London: SCM, 1991).

15. Elisabeth Schüssler Fiorenza and David Tracy, 'The Holocaust as interruption and the Christian return into history' in Schüssler Fiorenza and Tracy (eds), *Concilium*, 175: *The Holocaust As Interruption* (1984), pp. 83–6.

16. Elie Wiesel, *Night* (London: Penguin, 1981), p. 45.

17. Philip Roth, quoted on the cover of Primo Levi, *If This Is a Man: The Truce* (London: Abacus, re-printed 1995).

18. Haim Ginott, *Teacher and Child* (London: Macmillan, 1972/ First Collier Books, 1993).

19. See Alan Mintz, 'Prayer and the Prayerbook' in Barry W. Holtz (ed.), *Back to the Sources: Reading the Classic Jewish Texts* (New York: Summit Books, 1984).

8

Spiritual and Moral Development: A Suitable Case for Treatment

Clive and Jane Erricker

A storm is blowing from Paradise: it has got caught in his wings with such violence that the angel [of history] can no longer close them. This storm irresistibly propels him into the future to which his back is turned, while the pile of debris before him grows skyward. This storm is what we call progress.[1]

Addressing the context

C hildren growing up in today's world have inherited a process of rapid change in which the sense of community and belonging is varied and fluid. Their situation may be compared to that of the angel in the quotation from Walter Benjamin above. As adults concerned with their education, we must take account of this phenomenon when we seek to construct a school curriculum that will enable them to gain a measure of confidence in becoming future adults in our societies. With this in mind, we cannot regard spiritual and moral development as marginal issues. Nevertheless we find that addressing these issues raises a great deal of uncertainty in the minds of teachers. Whey should this be so? We offer three hypotheses:

1. We no longer have a clear sense of what spiritual and moral development mean in the context of education.
2. We do not know to what 'authorities' or consensus we can turn to provide us with a framework for development in these areas.
3. We are unsure as to what structures and strategies we should employ to implement spiritual and moral development.

Before seeking to address this state of affairs we must ask how it has come about. Here we wish to identify two influences:

1. That it is a result of increasing pluralism;
2. That it is a result of increasing secularization.

In this context, as a working definition, we take pluralism to refer to the presence of different ethnic and faith communities, and secularization to refer to the decline in institutionalized religious adherence and specifically Christian commitment. But pluralism and secularization do not have to be seen as enemies of society. They do not necessarily lead to social disintegration, and to assume they do will simply add to the conflict in social attitudes, ranging different interest groups against one another. A different approach would be to ask how accepting and addressing the presence of these two factors in a constructive way might develop more suitable provision for children and engage more positively with experience.

Recent research, especially that carried out by David Hay,[2] suggests that the significance of spirituality, in a religious sense, has not diminished in our contemporary world. Amongst adults and children alike the importance of the Transcendent remains as a matter of individual experience, even if it is not derived from commitment to a religious institution. Indeed, Hay goes further to suggest that it is a biological phenomenon. This raises the question of the relationship between institutionalized religion and experiences that could be defined as 'spiritual'. One way of resolving this relationship is to identify 'God', or the Transcendent, understood as 'God', as the common denominator. Spirituality then becomes 'the experience of God in one's life,' however broadly the term is interpreted. This identification represents a move away from doctrical definition towards a more inclusive understanding of 'spiritual' experience.

The knock-on effect in curriculum terms would be to embrace a broader acceptance of what spiritual experience might mean for children and what our educational agenda might be. Nevertheless, even given Hay's model, the term is still wedded to a traditional understanding of the religious and to that extent is still exclusivist. We should like to go further, in suggesting that the term 'spirituality' can encompass learning experiences that develop an individual's sense of self-under-standing and his or her awareness of the nature of human existence in a way that can affirm or deny the sense of the Transcendent. We advocate drawing a line between a positive sense of spirituality and its opposite; this would constitute a distinction between life-affirmation and life-negation. If this distinction were accepted, three curriculum consequences would follow:

1. Children who find a lack of meaning in life would be helped to affirm the value of their existence and that of others;
2. Children whose negative experiences have left them without a sense of hope or direction would be helped to construct a positive future;
3. Children would be offered alternative visions of positive human spirituality and values.

It is clear that such an inclusive definition begs many questions in relation to more traditional understandings and that it does not advertise particular doctrinal solution to existential problems. This chapter advocates this definition as the ground on which a pragmatic policy and programme of spiritual development can be based, by elaborating on the three areas of obstacles, affirmation and process identified above.

Obstacles to spiritual development: the threat of the 'other'

Mary Grey begins her chapter by addressing the challenges presented to theology and spirituality, amongst which she identifies postmodernism, the marginalization of Christian theology, and disaffection with regard to all the main denominations of the institutional church. Given this situation, the response of the churches, their theologians and their educational institutions, such as church colleges and church schools, is critical. They can entrench themselves against a society perceived as morally fragmenting in consequence of the influence of relativisim, and affirm the exclusive uniqueness of the truth of Christianity; or they can affirm the need for change and renewal by entering into what Richard Rorty has termed 'conversation' with others.[3] Professor Grey's chapter outlines the possibility of such a 'conversation', and our chapter is a further contribution to it. However, there are risks in taking this path, and we have to be sure we are willing to take them for any meaningful 'conversation' to take place and any progress to ensue.

The first, psychological, risk is that of self-transformation. We can use this term positively if we have a sense of the outcome resulting. But 'listening' to others challenges the very sense of our self-definition. Language is both the key to understanding and the barrier to it. The concepts we use have to be understood as vehicles towards this purpose rather than principally the way in which we claim our own truth or even the truth. Theologies become attempts to seek new understandings. The implication of this is the acknowledgement that the truth, in any final sense of the term, is not known but still being pursued (here we posit a distinction between the present understanding and the future vision) and that our goal is not the discovery of this 'truth' *per se* but the greater discernment of what it means to construct a more humane and 'spiritual' world. As such, the metaphorical utterances formulated in doctrinal statements constitute both the significant constructions of reality of particular theologies and the vehicles for growth. They are, however, significant in two particular ways, which are in tension with one another. For some they are significant as constructions which are immutable; for others they are reference points, or points of navigation. As the first, we may be loath to lose them; as the second, we must, inevitably, allow that we may move on from them. Amongst the implications we suggest follow from this distinction is the understanding, implicit in the view of those holding the second position, that values and the implementation of specific ethical principles are the real goal. The notion of truth in some transcendent sense can actually be an impediment to this goal, much as nirvana, for Buddhists, can act as a new form of attachment. The mythologies we bring to this endeavour, whilst crucially important, must be open to transformation;

127

they are not sacred. Jeffrey Kane's message is particularly apt in this respect:

> Each culture offers a unique and incomplete spectrum of metaphors for understanding ourselves and the world around us. As such, they enable us to encounter the world and ourselves only partially. Although each culture provides a generative context for creating our individuality and identifying ourselves it also limits the spectrum of light available to us.[4]

The second, political, risk is the transformation of power structures. Any mission to engage the curriculum from the perspective of the church and its educational institutions must acknowledge that such a venture has to scrutinize the value and purpose of its own institutions and their curricula. Put bluntly, what do these institutions stand for and what power structures do they serve and wish to preserve? To exemplify the problem, it is salutary to survey the way in which a particular curriculum provision in religious education was arrived at, and its relevance to spiritual and moral development. To take a British example, the parliamentary debate that resulted in the 1988 Education Reform Act, as far as RE provision was concerned, highlighted the division over the subject's purpose. The outcome was a compromise that affirmed the primacy of Christianity as the main religious tradition of England and Wales and referred to the importance of the Christian heritage, but also recognized the contribution and representation of other faiths in society. Ensuing debate surrounded the question of just what percentage of the curriculum should focus on Christianity, the present mandatory 51 per cent (i.e. more than half), or a greater and more precise amount (70 per cent or even 90 per cent were two further figures quoted). The nature of such a debate is problematic for two reasons. The first is that it suggests religious education is concerned primarily with content, not with children's development. The second is that, by implication, Christianity, or more precisely the Christian church, appears as a self-serving institution. The view that Christianity is taught for the purposes of children's moral development also persists despite there being no reference to this in the Act. Indeed such a view is held to be appropriate by many educators, governors, parents, teachers and student teachers concerned with religious education.

Additionally, the omission of humanism from the RE curriculum has added to the sense of division between religious, especially Christian, and 'secular' world-views which has been present since the Enlightenment and which isolates RE in the curriculum as something apart and devalued, in educational terms. An example of the problems this omission raises relates to the mistrust of RE that teachers involved in multi-cultural and anti-racist education often have, because they identify it as having a different agenda, in terms of values. The persistence of the opposition of secular and religious frameworks of meaning is unhelpful to the whole educational enterprise and creates very real difficulties as far as agreeing an understanding of spiritual development is concerned.

This situation, both historically formed and compounded by the legacy of recent legislation, is the context in which we are addressing spiritual and moral development. As a result, we must give a clear message as to what meanings these terms can be given and how such meanings can operate in an educational context.

At this point it is worth considering the recent initiatives of the School Curriculum and Assessment Authority (SCAA, now QCA – the Qualifications and Curriculum Authority). The conference on Education for Adult Life[5] specifically addressed spiritual and moral development, and was accompanied by the re-issuing of the SCAA Discussion Paper[6] on the same theme and a subsequent document emphasizing family values.[7] The tenor of debate was set by its chief executive, Nicholas Tate, in his opening address. In this he pointed to the need for children to know right from wrong; the importance of the deep, residual belief in God; the need to slay the dragon of relativisim; and his reservations over too much emphasis being placed on the development of children's self-esteem. Although these statements are now a part of recent history, their impact has been considerable in shaping the debate that has followed and the voices that have been considered worthy of attention in that debate. Unfortunately, one effect of this message was to confirm much of what needed to be undone. Spiritual development was linked to traditional religious nurture;

morality was a matter of instruction and appeared to be the prime justification for considering spiritual development, in any sense; materialism, the bedfellow of relativism and individualism, was implicitly aligned with secularity. Additionally, the competences and capacities of teachers and children were both left unacknowledged. The results of such rhetoric are most likely to reinforce the very divisions we need to reconcile, and will do so by seeking to affirm power structures based on those divisions, within which children and teachers are at the bottom and traditional authorities, within which the established churches will be included, are at the top. Such inequality does not invite participation in 'conversation'. One cannot, therefore, expect much enthusiasm for spiritual and moral development, understood in this way, within the classroom or the school. The notion of 'otherness' is simply reinforced.

Common affirmation: an inclusivist understanding of development

Howard Gardner reminds us that 'bringing the pedagogical means and the educational goals together will be a time consuming process, and there will be many mistakes along the way. But the effort is a critical one, one worth undertaking, and one worth doing right.[8] He goes on to state how important partnership with colleges and universities is in this endeavour. Although he is not talking specifically about spiritual and moral development, his point remains relevant. 'The signals sent by colleges concerning the kind of learning they value and the kind of students they welcome are enormously important.'[9]

Here we make the case for the kind of learning, and the attitudes that underpin that learning, that church colleges and other higher education institutions should encourage.

1. Church colleges are serving an increasingly plural, regional, national and global society. It is a society in which spiritual and material concerns are often opposed. The danger is that the churches' educational institutions will seek to re-establish a Christian hegemony rather than serve the cause of an inclusive spiritual enterprise. Historically, the Christian tradition has been best represented and most positively acknowledged when it has served the interests of

justice and equality in society, rather than extending its own interests through colonization and conversion. This has been true from its inception, when the early church debated its mission, through to the present dilemmas about its role in the contemporary world. Accordingly, the value of Church colleges, and Church schools, in the state educational system is valued according to the emphasis they place on addressing spiritual and moral concerns in education, as a foundation for learning and development, without sectarian interest.

2. Such a mission demands holistic definitions of 'spiritual' and 'moral' to which others who are not committed Christians can subscribe. Since this cannot be based on exclusivity and doctrinal formulae, it has to be focused on a sense of what it means to be fully human, from an inclusivist perspective. With this in mind, we have to find a vocabulary to which we can subscribe which is not in conflict with the exclusivist language we might still wish to own, by virtue of belonging to a particular faith tradition. In effect this means being able to acknowledge the meaning of the word 'faith' in two distinct but complementary senses. As we see it this can only be possible by affirming the following:

- that faith traditions are processes;
- that their narratives and vocabularies are the vehicles for expressing and evolving their spiritual progress.

Here Wilfred Cantwell Smith's observations can give us hope:

> The Christian tradition is still in process. The Islamic has not ceased to evolve. Nor the Jewish, nor the Buddhist. The Hindu's is always in transition. The only traditions that are not changing before our eyes are those that have ceased to exist ...[10]

This statement prefaces his judgement that there is a need for new conceptual patterns in the contemporary world in its plurality, and that religion as a conceptual term is effectively obsolete and unhelpful. Cantwell Smith offers this idea 'to fellow human beings throughout the world, including those whose faith is derived from other traditions and also those whose faith is not religious, in the hopes that it might contributed to the intellectual aspect of our new task of together constructing a brotherhood on earth deserving the loyalty of all our groups'. Such aspirations, he continues 'would seem fantastical and pretentious, were it not that today surely no man's faith is finally legitimate unless it can so aspire'.[11]

Cantwell Smith first published this (in the United States) in 1963. This accounts for the unconscious sexism in his terminology, but also makes us aware that attempting to make such a vision a practical reality has to take account of the difficulties in discourse and understanding that have subsequently emerged. Two of the main writers who have addressed these difficulties have been Edward Said and Richard Rorty. Edward Said's comment that all academic knowledge is 'tinged and impressed with, violated by, the gross political fact'[12] exemplifies the need to understand the difficulty of retaining a notion of pristine doctrinal truth, which espouses consistent values, in the context of social and political expediency. Rorty identifies the need to recognize that 'we no longer worship *anything*, where we treat *nothing* as a quasi divinity, where we treat *everything* – our language, our conscience, our community – as a product of time and chance.[13] Here we can identify two influential criticisms of religious understanding. In both of these criticisms the notion of religious truth is seen as being in opposition to the realities of human experience, and consequently obscures our understanding of the latter. Taking account of the force of such criticisms, and responding to them, presents the situation, with its possibilities and pitfalls, in which we have to find the intellectual and educational will and practical resolve to construct an outline of what spiritual and moral education could be, and what provision it would require in schools and colleges.

The 'spiritual' can be distinguished from the moral domain insofar as it pays attention to those motivations, or what we might call inherent qualities, that constitute our highest aspirations in being human. At the heart of these, or indeed their foundation, must be what Paddy Walsh has called a 'love of humanity'.[14] Mike Newby's article 'Spiritual development and love of the world' can be read as an interesting commentary on this.[15] From what source this 'love' is derived and how we give it substantive definition is not the paramount issue: that is for particular 'faith' groups to debate amongst themselves. The significant event is the palpable practice of such a motivation, the way it informs and makes possible a more harmonious and moral society which values equality, respect for persons and a sense of justice and worth in relationships. We may wish to extend the notion of 'humanity' or 'world' to attempt an even more inclusivist term, such as 'persons' (including all life-forms). Walsh and Newby both pursue a concern for the development of the human spirit rather than a concern for the human relationship with the Transcendent, understood as God.

It is instructive to compare this approach with the references made in Mary Grey's chapter to Newman's *The Idea of a University*.[16] Newman was much concerned with what he understood to be the fragmentation of learning that occurred through the influence of secularization in higher education. As a result he saw Christian humanism as providing a focus for the ethos that was required for academic study to cohere in a social vision. This can be understood as a proper and pertinent nineteenth-century reaction to the times in which he lived but needs to be expanded into a late twentieth-century context which takes account of the diversification of society that he could not have imagined. The significant issue is to retain his notion of an overall vision without constricting it by a doctrinal definition that others would find alienating. At the same time we must not allow this to dissolve into no vision at all: what Newman calls 'navigating the ocean of interminable scepticism'. We must retain and re-assert Newman's idea that knowledge amounts to a unity of head and heart and that all knowledge is a part of one whole whilst acknowledging the new social context which we occupy.

What matters is to start with an inclusivist attitude towards progress within which all worthy action can be identified as approximate to the goal but not likely to be wholly illustrative of it. Faith, in this context, represents the acknowledgement that the established aspiration is appropriate as a willed intention that can provide spiritual progress, if pursued in a disciplined way. So much for the aspiration; however, whether it be love of the world, the imitation of Christ or nirvana (which, as the Dalai Lama said, was much too big an ambition), it should not be overemphasized. The Dalai Lama was more concerned with the development of patience, and his comments in this respect are salutary.

> Now I am talking as a human being, not as a Buddhist. This, I think, is very important, because ideology and religion is for human beings, not the other way around ... Emphasis should be on humanity ... Many are making a great effort to control external things – like arms control. But without being able to control inner things, how can you control external arms? Real arms control is to control anger ... People think patience is weakness. But I think not. Anger comes from fear, and fear from weakness. So, if you have strength then you have more courage. This is where patience comes from.[17]

Grand aims can be both slogans behind which those with power and authority can hide and whips with which they can beat others. There is no spiritual or moral integrity in that. Exploring inner space and, in a societal sense, outer space is where spiritual and moral education conjoin. What are the practicalities of the development we envisage towards an inclusive understanding? Here we come up against the inadequacies of our present educational system and, in the specific example of the research of the Children and World-views Project we wish to cite, the way in which children's spiritual and moral development is inadequately served.

Research properly starts by investigating and assessing the present state of affairs. Our research was based on asking the question 'What, in terms of their experience, are the significant issues that children feel confront them in their lives?' A further question that followed from this was 'In what ways and by employing what strategies did they think they could deal with these issues?' We also hoped to be able to determine, by pursuing these research questions, what relationships and advice had served children well and resulted in empowerment, through enabling them to construct their own sense of spiritual and moral development identified in the values they espoused, the sentiments they expressed and justifications they employed. The outcome of this was, of course, to identify the 'road they travelled'. We were constructing an empirical investigation into the territory of children on the basis that real conversation, speaking *and* listening, only occurs when you understand the concerns of the other party and how they construct their sense of identity and world-view. The outcomes, so far, have been illuminating and are treated in the final section of this chapter, but the replies did not pay particular attention to the notions of awe and wonder. These we are tempted to regard as constructions that adults provide as part of the spiritual landscape that children should imbibe and inhabit, though by saying that we do not mean that children do not have their own sense of what these terms refer to in their own experience, but rather that there is a tendency for adults to solicit from children the answers they want to hear. We are aware of the way in which a misplaced sense of 'awe and wonder' can act as a protection against hearing what children actually want to say and contribute to a culture of sentimentality in which the statements of children are accorded a recognition which is only commensurate with their assumed immaturity and naiveté.[18]

In contrast with this sense of adult self-interest, we can approach teaching and learning with what might be called an understanding of the pragmatics or praxis of love or (to use a more graspable concept) concern. Jeffrey Kane comments: 'A loving teacher is one who acts as the child asks ... approaches his/her task with the question "What do these children ask of me?" ... guided by a disciplined sense of responsibility to the child as a human being evolving in the world.'[19] Since children are not all immediately lovable human beings, it would be well to qualify this statement with Rorty's comment on the 'imaginative ability to see strange people as fellow sufferers'.[20] This indicates the sort of professional capacity that teachers are required to develop to fulfil any worthwhile provision for spiritual and moral education. Rorty also allows us to be released from the burden of thinking that our task is beyond us by placing the emphasis on some realizable progress, rather than on achieving a distant, ideal goal as the necessary aim. The point is that when we feel the need to achieve unrealistic goals we resort to unhelpful moral rhetoric rather than consider the agonizing but realistic small steps forward that each of us has to make in attaining spiritual progress. He states that: 'the realisation of utopias, and the envisaging of still further utopias, as an endless process' is appropriate 'rather than a convergence toward an already existing Truth'.[21] Such a process would recognize also the need for 'a general turn against theory and towards narrative'.[22] However, in following Rorty's understanding of process it is not necessary or appropriate to assume his anti-religious stance. In fact, such a stance is divisive and unhelpful, but it should alert religious institutions to the need to recognize voices other than their own as being of value rather than retreat into a marginalized position or respond to such voices either aggressively or dismissively.

To examine what such an approach would mean in practice we return to the research of the Children and Worldviews Project which constitutes the third and last section of this chapter.

The process of spiritual and moral education

Children live in real worlds. That means that they experience pain, adversity, fragmentation of experience, and the awareness of mortality. If we seek to ignore this we simply ignore them. Our starting point must be to take what they have to say about their experience seriously, and not convert their understanding to ours, to what we would like it to be. This means that we must be able to acknowledge them as 'fellow travellers' and confer the rights that this entails.

Unfortunately, there are two obvious barriers we erect against such acknowledgement: that our greater experience provides us with better judgement and that, as a consequence, their immaturity can only be advanced by our wisdom. Our research supports neither of these attitudes. We may compare such arguments to those which underpin opposition to the liberation theology that Mary Grey espouses. For example, the poor and uneducated cannot possibly take part in the debate of theologians about the mission of the church, because they lack the requisite understanding. Equally, children lack the requisite understanding to participate in and influence their own education. Paulo Freire had much to say about the assumptions upon which such arguments were based in what he termed 'narration sickness' in education.[23]

But what about the evidence for the argument that children have a central and mature role to play in their spiritual and moral education? Consider the following.

When children speak about what matters to them most they most often cite the importance of their mother, as in the case of the following example from one child.

> 'I really care about my mum because she gave me birth and gave me everything and she never ignores me.'

This child continues by identifying an ordering of significant relationships as follows.

> 'I really care about my family because they are my blood.'

Perhaps this is an unconscious use of metaphor, as he clearly uses the term in more than a literalistic way, yet is unable to fully articulate the use he applies to it.

> 'I really care about my pets and one of them is a dog and his name is Tommy. I really care about my world because people smoke and pollute. I really get worried when people knock on my door and run away. I really care for trees because they give us fresh air and keep the air clean. I really care about people when they hurt themselves. I was really worried when my grandad was hurt and in hospital.'

What follows this litany is both highly reflective and typical in that he then reveals the important effect of these loving relationships in his life and on his behaviour, especially in the face of conflict:

> 'I don't do bad things it's like people do bad things to me, so I feel like doing bad things back to them and then my mum comes sometimes when people do bad things to me. Sometimes I really want to get out of this school, break everything, but I can't 'cos then somebody just makes me stop, stops me. My mum

and dad calm me down, so does my sister. I go home,
I have a bit of a drink and I talk to my mum.'

This child is also well aware of the importance of his religion to
him; he says:

> 'Sikh, we are all Sikh ... My religion is very
> important to me because God is always in front of
> us, we might not see him but he's always in our
> hearts.'

These spiritual and moral concerns, patterned in a network of
supportive relationships, are echoed by children in different
situations and communities.

Another child explains how the fragmentation of his family
has created a spiritual vacuum but left him with a sense of
moral obligation or duty, because of his concern for his mother.
He lives with his father but sees his mother infrequently, about
twice a year. He pictures her alone in front of the television at
night. He explains that she tries to phone frequently but his dad
doesn't want her to. This situation results in creating specific
anxieties.

> 'But when we don't hear from her we think maybe
> she doesn't live any more, so we don't know where
> to go if we want to go and see her. Once we didn't
> know but she was in hospital 'cos she had very bad
> things, she forgot our phone number and she went
> up there and she wasn't in and we, I got really
> worried 'cos my mum wasn't there and found out
> that night, my nan phoned up and said she's in
> hospital.'

Other children's stories of their memories, experiences and
situations reiterate similar themes. Though in different cases
the person over whom they exhibit concern may vary, the issue
is invariable Where supportive adult relationships are present,
the children find the means to deal with the unavoidable
existential dilemmas that constitute the human condition, and
develop as a result of their experience. Where this support is
not present, the child may not develop and often, though not

always, their future development is blocked as a result of the trauma involved. In the second case, however, there appears always to be a lack of resolution to the significant event; in other words a sense of loss and fragmentation of meaning that has no obvious means of repair. This situation is not marginal or uncommon in children's lives, it does not exist only in economically deprived families or those with only one parent. It amounts to a matter of loving relationships and time spent listening and responding to children or the absence of these. Normative structures such as having two parents living together, one of each gender, are not, of themselves, the answer to deprivation. What matters is listening adults who are trusted, and positively bring their human qualities to having conversations with children in a nurturing and open relationship. When this is absent children will take the opportunity of talking to anyone who advertises themselves as acting in this role, provided the children can identify them as possessing the necessary qualities to inspire trust and confidence, such is their need. As a result, our research has led us to believe that the heart of spiritual and moral education is the taking-on of this task in schools. Yet, of necessity, attempting to offer such provision radically alters the educational agenda in the following ways.

1. There is no way forward without the involvement of parents, despite and because of the fact that parents are both the major providers of spiritual and moral nurture and the inhibitors of it.
2. Schools, teachers and those concerned with educational development have to make time for engagement with children's spiritual and moral experience and ideas. Without this, no satisfactory educational and social provision can be implemented.
3. An inclusivist definition of spiritual and moral education is the only way to properly address the concerns of children, according to their own agenda, despite the fact that our own definitions might betray different sectarian interests.

This does not mean going down the same road as Rorty in his alienated reference to worship.[24] Indeed, our studies with children have affirmed the significance of metaphor, image and ritual – the constituents of worship – in their meaning-making.[25] Without these constituents they are bereft of understanding. However, to claim that this expressive language is only effective in the context of Christian understanding is to debilitate children's development. The purpose of Christian mission must be to see God in the Other and attempt to establish a loving relationship on that basis, across the barriers of language. This is our understanding of the aim that pertains to Church colleges and Christian educational institutions generally, with regard to spiritual and moral development. When you see into children's minds you are looking at the state of society, or, if you prefer, the condition of creation. Enabling children and older students to 'weather the storms' in their own lives thus becomes part of our personal and professional responsibility.

Notes

1. Walter Benjamin in P. Berry and A. Wernick, *Shadow of Spirit: Postmodernism and Religion* (London: Routledge, 1992), preface.
2. D. Hay, *Exploring Inner Space* (London: John Murray, 1987) and 'Children and God', *The Tablet* (7 October 1995), pp. 1270–1; D. Hay, R. Nye and R. Murphy, 'Thinking about childhood spirituality: review of research and current directions' in L. Francis, W. Kay and W. Campbell (eds), *Research in Religious Education* (Leominster: Gracewing, 1996), pp. 47–71.
3. R. Rorty, *Philosophy and the Mirror of Nature* (Princeton, NJ: Princeton University Press, 1980), pp. 389ff.
4. J. Kane, Editorial, *Holistic Education Review*, 8/2 (Summer 1995). See also his editorial in *Holistic Education Review* 8/4 (Winter 1995).
5. 'Education for Adult Life: Spiritual and Moral Aspects of the Curriculum' (London, January 1996).
6. *Spiritual and Moral Development* (SCAA Discussion Paper no. 3; London: SCAA, January 1996).
7. *Education for Adult Life* (SCAA Discussion Paper no. 6; London: SCAA, November 1996).
8. H. Gardner, *The Unschooled Mind* (London: Fontana, 1991), p. 261.
9. Ibid., p. 262.
10. W. Cantwell Smith, *The Meaning and End of Religion* (London: SPCK, 1978), pp. 199–202.

11. Ibid., p. 202.
12. E. Said, *Orientalism* (London: Routledge and Kegan Paul, 1978).
13. R. Rorty, *Contingency, Irony and Solidarity* (Cambridge: Cambridge University Press, 1989), p. 22.
14. P. Walsh, *Education and Meaning: Philosophy in Practice* (London: Cassell, 1993).
15. M. Newby, 'Spiritual development and love of the world', *The International Journal of Children's Spirituality*, 1/1 (1996), pp. 44–51.
16. J. H. Newman, *The Idea of a University* (London: Longmans, Green and Co., 1910).
17. Dalai Lama, *Kindness, Clarity and Insight* (New York: Snow Lion, 1984), pp. 45–50, 64.
18. C. Erricker, 'Journeys through the heart: the effect of death, loss and conflict on children's worldviews', paper given at the International Seminar on Religious Education and Values, Los Angeles (August 1996).
19. J. Kane, Editorial, *Holistic Education Review*, 8/2.
20. R. Rorty, *Contingency, Irony and Solidarity*. p. xvi.
21. Ibid.
22. Ibid.
23. P. Freire, *Pedagogy of the Oppressed* (Harmondsworth: Penguin Books, 1972), p. 45.
24. R. Rorty, *Contingency, Irony and Solidarity*, p. 22.
25. C. Erricker and J. Erricker, 'Metaphorical awareness and the methodology of religious education', *British Journal of Religious Education*, 16/3 (Summer 1994), pp 164–84; J. Erricker and C. Erricker, 'Children speaking their minds', *Panorama*, 7/1 (Summer 1995), pp. 96–109.

9

Response to Clive and Jane Erricker

Ian Markham

T he Errickers have a vision: they want to celebrate the 'spirituality' of children in a way that accepts the realities of modernity. Modernity, for them, involves (a) the fact of pluralism and (b) the fact of secularization. By secularization, the Errickers mean the 'decline in institutionalized religious adherence and specifically Christian commitment'. They treat as a given that traditional forms of religions are in terminal decline. Fewer people go to church, therefore fewer and fewer people will use Christian terminology to describe their spirituality. Coupled with the increasing pluralism, by which the Errickers mean the 'presence of different ethnic and faith communities' in Britain, the Errickers believe a neutral way forward needs to be found for children to express their spirituality.

The Errickers are important because they are an extreme example (and, as a result, clearer) of the way that many talk about spirituality in our culture. Not only is the concept important in schools, it is also important in healthcare. The insight underpinning much of the debate is a sense that people are not simply bundles of atoms, explicable entirely in terms of a reductionist scientific account, but more than that. And this 'more than atoms' is the space occupied by the word 'spiritual'. The Errickers are more extreme in that they challenge this model. They do not want the spiritual necessarily to be opposed to the scientific. They write: 'We should like to go further, in suggesting that the term "spirituality" can encompass learning experiences that develop an individual's sense of self-understanding and his or her awareness of the nature of human existence in a way that can affirm or deny the sense of the Transcendent.' So, for the Errickers, spirituality cannot be linked to any particular religious narrative; instead it needs to be filled by the strategies suggested in the Errickers' article: a combination of exercises that encourage children to think about their values and lives in the widest possible context.

The Errickers, in my judgement, are pushing the debate in the wrong direction. In an attempt to become all-inclusive, the word 'spirituality' is in danger of becoming meaningless, or if it does not become meaningless, then at the very least utterly uninteresting. My difficulties with the Errickers' argument operate at several levels. On the first level I want to modify the Errickers' assumptions. It is increasingly agreed by sociologists that the secularization thesis is in trouble. The story that decline in church attendance means that fewer and fewer people think in Christian or religious ways is just not true. Grace Davie has made the case convincingly. The 'folk religion' phenomena and the widespread 'nominal' allegiance to Christian denominations should not be dismissed as a symptom of the decline. The truth is that people 'believe but do not belong'. Consider the following: millions watch *Songs of Praise* every week; *Thought for the Day* on Radio 4 survives endless change and reorganization; Princess Diana dies and thousands gather at churches; attendance at Christmas and Easter remains strong; and even baptisms remain very popular. As Grace Davie puts it:

> For most, if not all, of the British retain some sort of religious belief even if they do not see the need to attend their churches on a regular basis ... In contrast, secularism – at least in any developed sense – remains the creed of a relatively small minority.[1]

The fact is that we are still religious and for most people in Britain this takes a Christian form.

This leads to the Errickers' perception of pluralism. It is certainly true that significant religious minorities are a feature of British cultural life. It is also appropriate to take this

143

pluralism (or the term I prefer is plurality) into account when reflecting on spirituality. However, the Errickers' vision of spirituality would appal other faith communities. For a devout Jew or Muslim, there is a much more robust account of spirituality operating in their traditions. They would not recognize the illustrations provided by the Errickers of 'spirituality' as 'spiritual'.

The Errickers seem to assume that the only solution to the fact of plurality is neutrality. Spirituality cannot be couched in Christian terms because the Muslim and Hindu would find it unintelligible. Oddly, the Errickers entirely ignore the fact that their 'neutral' approach is also unintelligible to the Muslim or Hindu. The Errickers concede that it is grounded in a secular world-view. It avoids any overt mention of 'God' or the 'Bible'; this very absence is, itself, indicative of a certain world-view. Instead of imposing a Christian world-view, they are now imposing a God-absent, non-religious world-view. Neutrality, as many have observed, is impossible. We are all tradition-constituted. In opting for a non-religious spirituality, the Errickers are suggesting a certain world-view that all religious people would find problematic.

One must concede that the problem driving the Errickers to this rather unsatisfactory position is real enough. In a plural society where the different faith traditions have different accounts of spirituality, how do we handle this diversity? The Errickers can see only three options: first, the one they prefer, a traditionless model (i.e. the quest for a neutral account of spirituality). The second is the common denominator model. This involves finding an account of spirituality that most religious traditions could share. Naturally it will be very minimal, but at least it avoids disagreement. I suspect the Errickers hope that their traditionless model will be recognized as a partial account that many religious people will be able to embrace. In actual fact, as I shall show later in this article, the quest for a common denominator is doomed to failure. The third is simply to stand in a tradition and advocate that account of spirituality. The Errickers do not like this option because it is obviously imperalistic. Advocates of this position can retort quite legitimately that this approach is no more imperialist than the Errickers standing in the tradition of secularism and imposing their account of spirituality on everyone else.

However, let us for now agree that imperialism is unsatisfactory in any form.

It is true that these three models have tended to dominate the spirituality debate. However, there is, in fact, a fourth model, which I shall show avoids some of the main pitfalls in this debate. This is called the 'engaged diversity' model.

The fact of plurality is the fact of disagreement. All the other models want to avoid disagreement: the first *evades* by stepping outside; the second *avoids* by suggesting that there is really agreement; and the third *imposes* by insisting on the rightness of one tradition. None of these models tries to grapple and enjoy the disagreement. The sad thing is that the disagreement is very interesting.

It is obviously impossible to describe the hundreds, possibly thousands, of different accounts of spirituality found across and within different faiths. However, allow me to describe four contrasting accounts of spirituality, which are found within strands of each faith.

The first is the Sufi account of spirituality as extinction of the self. Traditionally there is some suspicion about 'spiritual' in Islam; it was felt to conflict with the traditional Islamic stress on community. However, since Ghazali (d. 1111), Muslims have stressed the mystical life of the Prophet and, indeed, much of the Qur'an is an eloquent tribute to the Prophet's sense of God. So:

> God is the Light of the heavens and the earth; the likeness of His Light is as a niche wherein is a lamp (the lamp in a glass, the glass as it were a glittering star) kindled from a Blessed Tree, an olive that is neither of the East nor of the West whose oil well-nigh would shine, even if no fire touched it; Light upon Light. (Qur'an 24:35)[2]

However, instead of the Errickers' suggestion that children should be taught to affirm the 'self', you find in the Sufi strand an account of spirituality that suggests one should eliminate the self. The reason for this is that the central belief of Islam is the oneness and unity of God. The first pillar – the *Shahadah* – simply states 'There is no God but God, and Muhammad is his

Ian Markham

prophet'. Monotheism cannot be compromised, hence the Islamic hostility to the Christian doctrines of the Trinity and Incarnation. For the Sufi, this central belief meant that there is no reality apart from God; it becomes 'the means of integration of the human being in the light of the Oneness which belongs to God alone'.[3] For those submitting to God (the literal meaning of 'Islam'), the ultimate state is the extinction of the self in God. As the Qur'an puts it:

> And call not upon another god with God; there is no god save He. All things perish, except His Face. His is the Judgement, and unto Him you shall be returned. (Qur'an 28:88)

And later:

> All that dwells upon the earth is perishing, yet still abides the Face of thy Lord, majesty, splendid. (Qur'an 55:26–27)

These verses are responsible for the Sufi doctrine of survival after extinction. One popular image to make sense of this paradox is the unborn child, totally dependent and part of the mother, yet surviving. Other Sufis seem to go further in understanding the doctrine and seem to talk about their own identification with God himself. Much depends on what is meant when the Qur'an talks about the 'Face of thy Lord'. Seyyed Hossein Nasr explains: 'On the highest level, the realisation of this Face through "self-effacement" – or annihilation, as the Sufis have called it – means to be already resurrected in God while in this life and to see God "wherever one turns" ... Through this self-effacement or annihilation, which represents the highest possibility of the human state, the spiritual masters of Islam came to realise the ultimate meaning of the *Shahadah*, which is not only that God is One but also that he is the only Reality in the absolute sense ... He sees God everywhere ... He already lives in Allah's Sacred Name, having died to his passionate self.'[4] In this strand of Islam, we find the 'spiritual' (i.e. God) is the only reality; and the true Muslim aspires to live in that state which involves the extinction of the self. One can imagine a session that encourages children on

Response to Clive and Jane Erricker

what this might mean and how this attitude contrasts with the Errickers' secular account.

In Judaism one finds an account of spirituality that suggest that the mundane and normal should become spiritual through ritual. Arthur Green writes: 'Life in the presence of God – or the cultivation of a life in the ordinary world bearing the holiness once associated with sacred space and time, with Temple and with holy days – is perhaps as close as one can come to a definition of "spirituality" that is native to the Jewish tradition and indeed faithful to its Semitic roots.'[5] He goes on to bring out the contrast with Western spiritualities: 'Spirituality in the Western sense, inevitably opposed in some degree to "corporeality" or "worldliness", ... is unknown to the religious world view of ancient Israel.'[6] Although an ascetic – world-renouncing – strand did develop, Green correctly emphasizes that it is a late, and, in some respects, alien arrival.

Biblical spirituality is a very 'earthy' phenomenon. The presence of God, for much of the Bible, is located in a 'tent' (a portable temple) and then in the actual temple built in Jerusalem. God encounters his people in a place:

> There I will meet with the people of Israel, and it shall be sanctified by my glory; I will consecrate the tent of meeting and the altar; Aaron also and his sons I will consecrate, to serve me as priests. And I will dwell among the people of Israel, and will be their God. And they shall know that I am the LORD their god, who brought them forth out of the land of Egypt that I might dwell among them; I am the LORD their God. (Exodus 29:43-46)[7]

This sense of encountering God in a place at a certain time within the world lies at the heart of much Jewish ritual. The obligation to observe 613 commandments (many to do with diet and time) ensures that the spiritual becomes part of normal everyday life. Harold Kushner completely understands why, to the non-Jew, food laws seem so pointless. Because 'there is nothing intrinsically wicked about eating pork or lobster, and there is nothing intrinsically moral about eating cheese or chicken instead. But what the Jewish way of life does by imposing rules on our eating, sleeping, and working habits is to take the most common and mundane activities and invest them with deeper meaning, turning every one of them into an occasion for obeying (or disobeying) God.'[8] The normal takes on a transcendent significance: it ensures one becomes completely human. Harold Kushner puts it rather well when he writes:

> Judaism has the power to save your life from being wasted, from being spent on the trivial ... Judaism is a way of making sure that you don't spend your whole life, with its potential for holiness, on eating, sleeping, and paying your bills. It is a guide to investing your life in things that really matter, so that your life will matter. It comes to teach you how to transform pleasure into joy and celebration, how to feel like an extension of God by doing what God does, taking the ordinary and making it holy.[9]

This then is the heart of Jewish spirituality. It is located in the here and now; it stresses certain dispositions and values in this light. Imagine describing this account of spirituality to children. Imagine listening to them grapple with the ways in which the normal could, by certain rituals, become spiritual.

In Hinduism, the spiritual is found by discovering the self – the stillness beyond the conscious. The crucial Western illusion is to imagine that the individual ego is the 'real self'. The human ego is entrapped in the world, preoccupied with the trivial, and living for the moment. Krishna Sivaraman writes: 'The religious literature of India, in effect, acclaims with a striking unanimity that the actor who dominates the stage of life is a "person," but in the etymological sense of one wearing a mask, a false self. I, as the person (the first person as grammar sanctifies it), is not the real "I" and much less the immortal spirit which I truly am by essence or affinity behind the veil of my nature.'[10] The entanglement with the world (i.e. the immediate activities of human community) leaves the real self undiscovered. The truth about each person is that our real self – the *atman* – is part of Brahman – the cosmic self – on which everything depends.

Response to Clive and Jane Erricker

Spirituality, then, does involve a renunciation or (the term preferred by Sivaraman) 'worldlessness'.[11] 'Worldlessness, then, is not "life-and-world negation" but reflects a spiritual mood and a sense of orientation that includes a positive and negative disposition. Worldlessness is a disposition to live in the world singly or as a sufficient "human end," but as a means or medium to life "in God," as a condition of life in the spirit.'[12]

Instead of directing one's spirituality up and outward towards a transcendent God, in Hinduism you move down and inward. One discovers the true nature of oneself and in doing that one discovers Brahman. The methods by which this is attained vary from tradition to tradition. For many the opportunities of realizing this true self-awareness are very limited. Therefore for such people their main responsibility is to play their part in society. (Traditionally, the caste system meant that for many in society, their role was to serve the rest of society, in the hope that higher castes might be given more opportunity to realize *moksha* – release – and simply hope for a better opportunity in the next life.) For those influenced by Ramanuja, the heart of spirituality is *bhakti* (devotion); this is the way of love enabled by God.

In Buddhism, spirituality depends on the cultivation of certain ethical dispositions. Despite emerging from, and sharing many of the assumptions of, Hinduism, it has attracted all those who are deeply sceptical about metaphysical beliefs. Jane Compson, a Western convert to Buddhism, finds this element the most attractive when she writes:

> Christianity seems to be inextricably bound up with metaphysics and objective truth, but it seems to me that Hume, Kant, Nietzsche and Wittgenstein completely undermined metaphysics ... In contrast, the beauty of Buddhism is its simplicity. You need take nothing on authority, and metaphysical beliefs are not a pre-requisite. The Buddha said that he taught only two things, suffering and the end of suffering.[13]

It is true that the Four Noble Truths, which are at the heart of the Buddha's discovery, do not mention God or a divine being.

149

Instead we have: first, the truth of suffering; second, the truth of the cause of suffering; third, the truth of the cessation of suffering; and fourth, the eightfold Path.

Suffering does not simply describe actual pain but rather extends out to all the frustrations of being human. Everything changes: even pleasurable moments are marred by the realization that they will end; and every human person is a bundle of anxieties about appearance and status amongst our families, friends and communities. The solution to this suffering is the cultivation of certain attitudes and dispositions. Heinrich Zimmer explains:

> The craving of nescience, not-knowing-better, is the problem – nothing less and nothing more. Such ignorance is a natural function of the life-process, yet not necessarily ineradicable; no more ineradicable than the innocence of a child. It is simply that we do not know that we are moving in a world of mere conventions and that our feelings, thoughts, and acts are determined by these. We imagine that our ideas about things represent their ultimate reality, and so we are bound by them as by the meshes of a net. They are rooted in our own consciousness and attitudes; mere creations of the mind; conventional, involuntary patterns of seeing things; judging and behaving; yet our ignorance accepts them in every detail, without question, regarding them and their contents as the facts of existence. This – this mistake about the true essence of reality – is the cause of all the sufferings that constitute our lives.[14] Becoming aware of the transient nature of everything (even the sense of one's own self), one ceases to suffer. If everything is transient, then desire and clinging become inappropriate. You will cease expecting a perfectly stable environment, which will mean that all those inevitable disruptions will cease to concern you.

Spirituality, then, is the cultivation of certain dispositions that integrate this awareness of the transient nature of all things into your life. These are: Right Ideas (the knowledge of the four noble truths); Right Resolution (a commitment to realize the Noble Path in one's life); Right Speech (the means of communication, which should be characterized by wisdom and compassion); Right Behaviour (ensure that the mind is in control in everything you do); Right Vocation (one's occupation should be compatible with one's commitment not to harm others); Right Effort (to ensure that motives, attitudes and dispositions in the mind are compatible with the actions you are required to express); Right Mindfulness (the ability to see things truthfully); Right Dhyana (the capacity to meditate and concentrate the mind).[15]

The heart of Buddhist spirituality is a life lived compatible with the truth discovered by the Buddha in the Four Noble Truths. In the main it is the cultivation of certain ethical dispositions. In this respect it compares very markedly with the forms of spirituality found in other religious traditions. But it does not start with an engagement or encounter with a divine, transcendent reality. Although it is true that in Mahayana Buddhism 'worship' of Bodhisattvas (those about to attain Buddhahood) arose, this was a significant development of the Buddha's original teaching.

The point of this exercise is to illustrate that there is considerable disagreement between certain strands of each major religious tradition in the way that 'spirituality' is understood. My argument is that this disagreement should not be feared. Instead, it can make children think about the nature of human life in striking and interesting ways. In addition, it would cultivate a growing appreciation of other faith traditions and enable them to be authentic partners in the conversation.

Given that secularization is an illusion, then this is a much more appropriate response to the fact of plurality than the Errickers provide. Disagreement in any other branch of education is normally an aid to learning. For example, two economists disagree about the value of interest rates as a tool to control inflation. It would be absurd to evade, avoid or impose in this case. Instead the disagreement is introduced. Children are encouraged to listen and learn from it. My hope is that we learn to do the same with respect to spirituality.

Ian Markham

Notes

1. Grace Davie, *Religion in Britain Since 1945* (Oxford: Blackwell, 1994), p. 69.
2. All quotations from the Qur'an are taken from Arthur J. Arberry, *The Koran* (Oxford: Oxford University Press, 1964).
3. Seyyed Hossein Nasr, 'God' in Seyyed Hossein Nasr (ed.), *Islamic Spirituality: Foundations* (vol. 19 of 'World Spirituality' series; New York: Crossroad/London: Routledge and Kegan Paul, 1987), p. 312.
4. Ibid., p. 322.
5. Introduction in Arthur Green (ed.), *Jewish Spirituality: From the Bible Through the Middle Ages* (vol. 13 of 'World Spirituality' series; New York: Crossroad/London: Routledge and Kegan Paul, 1986), p. xiii.
6. Ibid., p. xiv.
7. All quotations from the Hebrew Bible taken from the Revised Standard Version of the Bible.
8. Harold Kushner, *To Life: A Celebration of Jewish Being and Thinking* (London: Little, Brown and Co., 1993), p. 54.
9. Ibid., p. 293.
10. 'Introduction' in Krishna Sivaraman (ed.), *Hindu Spirituality: Vedas Through Vedanta* (vol. 7 of 'World Spirituality' series; New York: Crossroad/London: Routledge and Kegan Paul, 1989), p. xvii.
11. Ibid., p. xvi.
12. Ibid.
13. Jane Compson, 'Why Buddhism makes sense' in Ian Markham (ed.), *A World Religions Reader* (Oxford: Blackwell, 1996), p. 148.
14. Heinrich Zimmer, 'Buddhahood' in Roger Eastman (ed.), *The Ways of Religion* (Oxford: Oxford University Press, 1993), p. 66.
15. The list given here is taken from Dwight Goddard, *A Buddhist Bible* (Boston: Beacon Press, 1966), pp. 646–53.

10

'Spiritual and Moral Development' and Religious Education*

John Beck

Mixed messages: the conflation of religion, 'the spiritual' and 'the moral'

Although many accept that truth in moral matters can be independent of God, the loss of the religious basis for morality has weakened its credibility. As the Archbishop of Canterbury has recently said, people ever since the Enlightenment 'have been living off the legacy of a deep, residual belief in God. But as people move further away from that, they find it more and more difficult to give a substantial basis for why they should be good'. This is one reason why religious education must continue to be a vital part of every child's curriculum ... It is also a reason why children's spiritual development is so important, as the origin of the will to do what is right. (Tate, 1996a, para. 23).

---

* An earlier version of this chapter was published in John Beck, *Morality and Citizenship in Education* (London: Cassell, 1998), ch. 3.

John Beck

Dr Nicholas Tate, at that time chief executive of the British School Curriculum and Assessment Authority, can serve here as a representative spokesperson of one particular approach to the contested question of what contemporary schools should do about transmitting moral values and promoting moral development in the young. The essentials of the traditionalist position are all there (either explicitly or implicitly) in this brief quotation:

- a somewhat reluctant recognition that for many people in contemporary society, questions of morality and moral truth are regarded as separate (or certainly separable) from questions of religion and religious truth;
- an unsubstantiated claim that, as a result of the decline of religious belief, more people now find it more difficult than in the past to find reasons for conducting themselves morally;
- a partially contradictory assertion that religious education is therefore vital for all children (and this turns out to be a kind of RE which gives priority to a traditional form of Christianity, whilst ostensibly acknowledging the value of other world faiths);
- a question-begging statement about the importance of something called 'spiritual development' as a fundamental source of 'the will to do what is right'.

Two essential assumptions are involved in maintaining this stance: first, a privileging of a particular kind of religiously based understanding of the term 'spiritual' (and 'spiritual development'); secondly, a reluctance, at least in the last instance, to accept that the religious/spiritual and the moral domains are, for many people, separable. Moreover, certain sorts of Christian conservatives have long seen it as their business (and indeed their responsibility) to fight to preserve such assumptions and also the language and the institutional arrangements that have embodied these assumptions in official educational discourse. (In part this has been a specifically *Anglican* concern.) As is well known, a successful campaign of this kind was conducted by Baroness Cox and Graham Leonard, the then Bishop of London, in their successful efforts to amend the 1988 Education Reform Bill so as secure a more prominent position for RE as a formally designated 'basic subject' within the National Curriculum, and to require that new 'agreed syllabuses' should 'reflect the fact that the religious traditions in Great Britain are in the main Christian whilst taking account of the teaching and practices of the other principal religions represented in Great Britain'. The amendments also, of course, included the specification of the requirement for daily acts of collective worship 'wholly or mainly of a broadly Christian character' (HM Government, 1988, pp. 4–6).

It is perhaps less widely known that the 1944 Education Act was the focus of similar interventionist efforts to secure official recognition for the category 'the spiritual'. Section 7 of the Act includes the statement:

> ... and it shall be the duty of the local education authority for every area, as far as their powers extend, to contribute to the spiritual, moral, mental and physical development of the community by securing that efficient education ... shall be available to meet the needs of the population of their area ... (HM Government, 1944, p. 4)[1]

However, as Peter Gilliat has pointed out, the term 'spiritual' was not part of the original draft of the 1944 legislation, being introduced in committee stage – again in the House of Lords. Viscount Bledisloe, proposing the amendment, argued that in view of the fact that, for the first time, both religious education and an act of worship were to become obligatory, 'surely we ought to incorporate in the Bill words which indicate our conviction that it is the Christian ethic and that it is spirituality which we want to advance in every stage of our national education if we want to promote morality as well as the other virtues of our race' (quoted in Gilliat, 1996, p. 162).

Significantly, we find here once again precisely the same conjunction we have previously encountered – of doctrinal Christianity, 'the spiritual' and the use of education to promote both 'spiritual development' and national moral virtue. The *locus classicus* for this kind of position is, probably, Matthew Arnold's *Culture and Anarchy* (Arnold, 1869). It is well worth taking a little time to consider Arnold's famous essay here – not least because certain phrases from it are so frequently cited by neo-conservative writers as a key legitimizing source for their overall vision of national cultural restoration. Nicholas Tate, for example, in a SCAA discussion paper on 'Curriculum, culture and society', cites Arnold in just this way:

> I am not suggesting that young people should spend all their time studying Jane Austen and Shakespeare or listening to Bach and Mozart. Far from it. What I am suggesting is that we (their educators) should give these things their proper value as (in the words of Matthew Arnold) 'the best that has been known and thought'. (Tate, 1996b, para 29)

This particular (and favourite) quotation is, in itself, one with which it is virtually impossible to disagree: who could seriously suppose that we should *not* value and make available in schools 'the best that has been known and thought' – always presuming that we could reach a well-founded agreement about what that *was*? However, Arnold's *actual* agenda in his celebrated discussion of culture is both more specific and more controversial than the popularly cited phrases 'sweetness and light' and 'the best that has been thought and said in the world' (Arnold, p. viii) might lead one to suppose. And what turns out to be especially interesting for our purposes here is the particular linkage which Arnold seeks to establish between the terms 'culture', 'reason' and 'the will of God' – and also between all these terms and national moral regeneration.

Culture and Anarchy proposes a very particular and *programmatic* definition of culture.[2] Arnold's 'culture' has work to do. The term is deployed to highlight and to combat what he regarded as the severe limitations and the disastrous consequences[3] of certain of the dominant ideas of his age: notably, self-satisfied non-conformity and free-market liberalism. In *this* respect, therefore, his idea of culture is far from being simply conservative – in either the literal or the party-political sense of that word. He calls upon his readers to embrace 'culture' as the basis from which to critically interrogate these dominant 'stock notions' of the period. This is nowhere more clearly brought out than in the way in which the famous (and usually decontextualized) quotation about the 'best that has been thought and said' continues:

> The whole scope of this essay is to recommend culture as the great help out of our present difficulties; culture being the pursuit of our total perfection by means of getting to know, on all the matters which most concern us, the best that has been thought and said in the world; *and through this knowledge, turning a stream of fresh and free thought upon our stock notions and habits, which we now follow staunchly but mechanically* ... (ibid., p. viii; my italics)

Culture and Anarchy sets out the cardinal deficiencies, as Arnold sees them, of the three great classes of mid-Victorian society, which he designates respectively as the Barbarians (the aristocracy), the Philistines (the industrial and mainly non-conformist middle class) and the Populace (the working class). He argues that the defects in the 'consciousness' of each of these social classes derived from the fact that their class-based perception of society was inevitably sectional and self-interested. In an expansionary era of change, the aristocracy, whose virtues, though real, were increasingly anachronistic, could no longer 'supply the principle of authority needful to our present wants' (ibid., p. 47). The middle class, meanwhile, were too strongly and too uncritically identified with the forces which were certainly transforming society but also disastrously undermining social cohesion: an uncritical belief in individual liberty, in free-market economic principles, and a pious non-conformity that was as blind to its own shortcomings as it was keenly aware of everyone else's. The Populace – sometimes misleadingly depicted as a 'playful giant' – constituted a threat to social order. This was partly because of the appalling squalor and poverty in which many working-class people were obliged to exist (largely as a result of the operation of laissez-faire economic policies), but it was also partly because they were being led astray by well-intentioned but deeply wrong-headed 'agitators'. The consequence of this overall situation was that social order and human well-being were threatened by the forces of *anarchy*.

Arnold's book proposed 'culture' as the most hopeful solution to these problems; it is primarily in this sense that his concept of culture may be termed programmatic:

> ... the essence of an epoch of expansion is the movement of ideas, and the one salvation of an epoch of expansion is a harmony of ideas. The very principle of authority which we are seeking as a defence against anarchy is right reason, ideas, light. (ibid., pp. 45–6)

Arnold defines culture in terms of disinterested enlightenment produced by the exercise of reason – hence his frequent recourse to the well-known terminology of 'right reason', 'sweetness and light', 'the study of perfection', etc. Moreover, he suggests that the only institution in mid-Victorian Britain which could accrue to itself the authority necessary for the effective dissemination of this enlightenment was the State[4] – with a subordinate but crucial role being reserved for education – primarily because only the State could hope to embody disinterested reason:

> but the question is, the action of the State being the action of the collective nation and the action of the collective nation carrying naturally great publicity, weight and force of example with it, whether we should not try to put into the action of the State as much as possible of right reason and our best self, which may, in this manner, come back to us with new force and authority ... (ibid., p. 84)

This, in his own day and in Britain, was controversial enough – as he recognized with his characteristic good humour.[5] But what was – and what remains – most seriously controversial in Arnold's concept of culture is the linkage with God and Christianity which is at its very heart. His consciousness of the ebbing of the 'sea of faith' expressed in what is now the most famous of his poems, 'Dover Beach', did not at all lead him, in the polemical writings of his maturity, to weaken his belief in the central importance of the Christian religion for right living and national salvation. In this respect he was very much the son of his father the reforming headmaster of Rugby School. The 'enlightenment' which was at the centre of his notion of culture was a specifically Christian (indeed Anglican) form of enlightenment; similarly the 'right reason' was a reason exercised in accordance with the core doctrines of the Established Church. Symptomatically, on no less than eight occasions in *Culture and Anarchy,* the telling conjunction 'reason and the will of God' recurs at salient points in the argument[6] – and this is sometimes further reinforced by reference to an appeal to a religious sensibility which is seen as part of the *natures* of the 'best' representatives of humanity:

> But in each class there are born a certain number of natures with a curiosity about their best self, with a bent for seeing things as they are, for disentangling themselves from the machinery, for simply concerning themselves with reason and the will of God, and doing their best to make them prevail – for the pursuit, in a word, of perfection. (ibid., p. 69)

For all his zeal, therefore, in calling upon his contemporaries to employ culture and disinterested reason to critically reconsider the 'stock' assumptions of the age, it turns out that certain of these assumptions were given a privileged status.[7] A certain sort of Christianity was the sacrosanct source from which the critique effected by 'culture' most fundamentally emanated. Far from being universalizable, therefore, Arnold's programmatic conception of culture turns out to be a prisoner of the most fundamental assumptions of that long Anglican, conservative tradition of thought which he so capably represented in his own time. In *our* own time, it is represented by less eminent but still influential figures such as the Rev. E. R. Norman, Baroness Cox, the Rev. George Austin, Dr Nicholas Tate, etc.

'The spiritual': possibilities and problems

Against this background, it is perhaps easier to see why, for such contemporary supporters of cultural restoration, there is a vitally important *symbolic* battle to be fought to preserve (or where necessary reinstate) traditional ways of designating certain categories of official educational discourse. As the

American sociologist Joseph Gusfield pointed out some years ago, the capacity to control the public *definition* of certain terms can be seen as highly significant in itself – even (or perhaps especially) in cases where social behaviour may be markedly at variance with these 'ruling' definitions (Gusfield, 1967). Gusfield himself discusses the issue of Prohibition in the USA as an example. For our purposes, a pertinent example is the question of school assemblies. As we have noted above, under the 1988 Education Reform Act there is a legal requirement for schools to hold daily acts of worship of a mainly Christian character. In many secondary schools, this requirement is in fact widely disregarded – sometimes for reasons of practical difficulty but frequently because not enough teachers in a given school are prepared to support assemblies of this kind.[8] It is significant that opponents of the House of Lords amendment which introduced the requirement – and these objectors included many Christians – argued that precisely this consequence would follow. Nevertheless, for certain kinds of traditionalists, the *symbolic* significance of such legislation – carrying the officially sanctioned message 'this is still a Christian country' – is itself of strategic importance.

'The spiritual' is a second case in point. As we have seen, specific and calculated intervention was needed to inscribe the term 'spiritual' into the 1944 Education Act – and the sponsors of this change clearly intended that the connotation of the term should be religious. Nor was the carry-over of essentially the same formulation into the 1988 Education Reform Act merely a matter of course; early drafts of the act did *not* include the preamble requiring schools to promote 'the spiritual, moral, cultural, mental and physical development of pupils' (Alves, 1991).[9] Since 1988, there have been a significant number of further official documents which have not only sought to highlight the importance of 'the spiritual' but have also persistently sought to tie together 'spiritual and moral development' in a manner calculated to suggest that the two constitute an indissolubly linked double entity – like Siamese twins (see, for example, National Curriculum Council, 1993; Ofsted, 1994). Thus, within symbolically important official statements about these areas of education, first, a religious dimension is imported into the category of 'the spiritual'; and then, secondly, it is suggested or implied that 'the spiritual' constitutes the real (even if unacknowledged) basis of the moral. In the statement by Nicholas Tate cited above, this double move is unusually transparent: 'this is one reason ... why children's spiritual development is so important, as the origin of the will to do what is right'. More commonly, the discourse of the documents is vague, platitudinous and tends to mix unjustified assertion with equivocation. It is worth noting that the 1993 NCC paper *Spiritual and Moral Development* has been trenchantly criticized on precisely these grounds – for example by David Hargreaves, who noted that 'among the platitudes is the renewed assertion of the particular importance of RE to moral development' (Hargreaves, 1994, p. 34) and by Pat White, who called the document's characterization of spiritual development 'a bizarre catch-all category', its discussion of moral development 'confused and deficient', adding that 'the document increases the confusion in the section in which it lumps spiritual and moral development together' (P. White, 1993, pp. 7–8).

It would, however, be a mistake to see this mix of assertion and ambiguity simply as evidence of an inability to think and write clearly about these important matters. There is nothing politically innocent about it. Documents from bodies like the National Curriculum Council or School Curriculum and Assessment Authority, unlike leading articles in *The Times* or the *Telegraph,* cannot quite come straight out and instruct teachers that their job is to indoctrinate children in favour of a particular sort of doctrinal Christianity or in favour of various traditionalist beliefs about matters which are in fact controversial in our society. But on the other hand, because of the political pressures operating upon them, neither can documents from these bodies easily address such issues openly and with candour – acknowledging not only the fact but also the *legitimacy* of moral debate in many of these areas. After all, for certain kinds of traditionalists within the Conservative Party and especially among some of those who seek to drive its policies ever further to the right, the whole point is that there *is* no legitimate debate! We are then, here, very much in the realm of the sayable and the unsayable. Official documents are constrained to sustain – at least to some extent – a *pretence* that within our culturally and morally pluralist society, we are all nevertheless 'really' in essential accord about the role schools should play in these areas – and that that role is essentially to instil traditional beliefs and values. In a rather similar way, during the lifetime of the most recent Conservative government in the UK, no Conservative Member of Parliament was prepared to publicly admit that he or she was irreligious – let alone that their beliefs were humanist or atheist[10] – notwithstanding the abundant evidence of how far the actual conduct of a minority of these same MPs departed from the religious and moral precepts they collectively sought to enjoin on others. All this is rather depressing – and it is far from clear how far the election in 1997 of a New Labour government, many of whose leading members conspicuously identify themselves with a form of Christian 'Socialism', may improve matters. Already, not a few observers have detected signs that this new government, with its huge parliamentary majority, may be embracing various forms of social authoritarianism – for example, in its determination to display 'zero tolerance' towards the so-called 'dependency culture', the 'excuse culture', etc. Nevertheless, the serious task of seeking to clarify the key terms and issues in current debates about the school's role in moral education must not be abandoned. Clarity in such matters is a precondition of progress, even if considerations of political expediency suggest that such progress may be difficult to achieve in 'the real world'.

The category of 'the spiritual' had additional educational legitimacy conferred upon it when, in the mid-1970s, it was included by a group of Her Majesty's Inspectors in a proposed new approach to constructing a common curriculum for secondary schools: the well-known HMI 'areas of experience'. In their document *Curriculum 11–16* (DES, 1977a), HMI listed eight such fundamental areas: the aesthetic and creative, the ethical, the linguistic, the mathematical, the physical, the scientific, the social and political, and the spiritual. This framework was very approximately evolved from Paul Hirst's well-known 'forms of knowledge' thesis (Hirst, 1974) – but it had a much less rigorous rationale, as is suggested by the fact that subsequently, technology was proposed as a ninth area, literacy was added to the linguistic, and the ethical became the moral. It is significant and symptomatic that in the *Supplement to Curriculum 11–16* (DES, 1977b), which included attempts to define each of the eight areas, HMI found it necessary when arriving at 'the spiritual' to offer not one but two definitions. The first of these was distinctly woolly: it suggested that 'the spiritual' should 'be concerned with matters at the heart and root of existence' and that it had to do with 'inner feelings and beliefs'. The second definition was clearer, associating 'the spiritual' unambiguously with experience 'derived from a sense of God or Gods', and it reinforced this unequivocally religious denotation by arguing that 'spiritual' in this sense was 'a meaningless adjective for the atheist and of dubious use to the agnostic'.

Now, a binary distinction of the sort proposed in this HMI document clearly has some utility, but, equally clearly, it considerably simplifies the range of meanings and associations which the term 'spiritual' actually carries in its full range of everyday uses. Briefly, these include:

(a) Spiritualism: the apparatus of mediums, seances, communication with the spirits of unique individuals who are believed to have 'passed over', etc.;

(b) beliefs in the existence of 'departed spirits': as in 'the communion of saints', individual saints, ancestors, etc. – often including (especially in popular religion) beliefs that communication, intercession, propitiation, etc. are possible and even necessary in respect of these beings;

(c) beliefs in intermediary spiritual beings who never lived on earth in human form: ranging from angels (currently the subject of various cults in the USA) to demons, devils, etc.;

(d) beliefs in lesser gods: household gods, tutelary deities, the lesser gods of the Hindu pantheon, etc.;

(e) theistic beliefs in a Supreme Being: Jahweh, Allah, God, to which certain predicates may be attached such as omnipotence, omniscience, love, justice; the paradoxical Christian doctrine of the Trinity is an example of how the 'purity' of even these monotheistic conceptions can become qualified as religious traditions develop and evolve;

(f) deistic beliefs in a first cause etc.;

(g) mystical experience of the kinds which Aldous Huxley sought to subsume under the title *The Perennial Philosophy* (Huxley, 1946), the heart of which seems to be a loss or merging of the independent self in 'the ground of all being';

a range of experiences which have been interpreted through a variety of metaphors and images within the different major religious traditions, with some of these interpretations making no reference to a god or gods: for example, the Zen conception of *satori;*

(h) a range of drug-induced 'mystical' experiences which are difficult and sometimes impossible to distinguish from hallucinations (see, among a vast literature, Castaneda, 1968; Huxley, 1954);

(i) profound *aesthetic* experience which is felt to reach levels of significance which are beyond the powers of propositional language to express – listening to late Beethoven string quartets, to take a hackneyed but nevertheless enduring example of works of art which seem to have been recurrently capable of evoking subjective experience of this order;

(j) the capacity of human beings – some of whom may be atheists or agnostics – for acts of outstanding courage, fortitude, goodness, etc. – as in the phrase 'triumphs of the human spirit'.

This list is obviously by no means exhaustive: it does not, for example, include magic, witchcraft beliefs (ancient and modern), or astrology and horoscopes (perhaps the most widely indulged form of popular flirtation with 'spiritual' influences in the everyday lives of a surprising number of people in Western societies – not least Nancy and Ronald Reagan, Boris Yeltsin, the late Diana, Princess of Wales, etc.).[11]

What drawing up a list of this kind *does* demonstrate, however, is the lack of utility of a single category called 'the spiritual' (or even spirituality) for helping to clarify aims and objectives in the area not only of moral education but also of religious education. It is not merely that the list brings together so many diverse and heterogeneous ideas, beliefs, practices, etc. An even more serious problem is that the meanings and propositions which lie at the core of certain religious senses of 'the spiritual' are precisely the meanings and propositions which many humanists, rationalists and secularists most decisively reject. To construct a curriculum domain, therefore, which aspires to bring them all together seems worse than misguided. Similarly, to suggest that in some global and inclusive way 'the spiritual' should permeate the teaching of art, music, literature, history, science, as well as being centrally represented by RE, seems a recipe for confusion and miscommunication. As far as achieving clarity in curriculum planning is concerned, we would, I conclude, do better to bracket off reference to the category of the spiritual as a guiding concept for moral education. Even within religious education, where the category of the spiritual in some of its senses must clearly continue to have a central place, careful distinctions and clarifications will be necessary. Here, the plural usage, spiritualities, may offer a route to exploring similarities as well as difference of meaning and significance.

It will not, of course, be easy to persuade people of this. For one thing, those groups discussed above who aim to preserve at least the *symbolic* presence of the 'religious/spiritual' within our increasingly secular institutions are likely to resist such a proposal. Others too, however, will be tempted to continue to have recourse to deliberately ill-defined and inclusive uses of the term 'spiritual' within education generally. For example, the requirement that schools must hold daily acts of worship (and for this to be a matter which Ofsted is charged to monitor) is a constraint which some senior teachers may feel can be accommodated if such assemblies are given a clearly (but loosely) 'spiritual' character – sometimes celebrating a diversity of religious ideas, festivals, etc., and at other times offering narratives of human moral or physical courage, service to one's fellow men and women, celebrations of human creativity, etc.[12] And in this context, it is noteworthy that certain secular organizations such as the British Humanist Association have gone out of their way to endorse an inclusiveness of this kind. For example, the association's pamphlet entitled *The Human Spirit* contains the following:

> Religious believers and Humanists, theists on the one hand, agnostics and atheists on the other, agree on the importance of spirituality but interpret it differently. Despite these different interpretations, however, *all can agree that the 'spiritual' dimension comes from our deepest humanity*. It finds expression in aspirations, moral sensibility, creativity, love and friendship, response to natural and human

> beauty, scientific and artistic endeavour, apprecia-
> tion and wonder at the natural world, intellectual
> achievement and physical activity, surmounting
> suffering and persecution, selfless love, the quest
> for meaning and for values by which to live. (British
> Humanist Association, 1993 quoted in J. White,
> 1996, p. 34; my italics)

In spite of the generous intent underlying such inclusive
sentiments, it is difficult not to feel uneasy. The statement
suggests too much common ground; it implies too easily that
vitally important differences can be glossed over; it sacrifices
clarity for the sake of an at least partially misplaced
togetherness. The phrase italicized above highlights the
problem: of course there is a sense in which we can agree
that 'the spiritual dimension comes from our deepest humanity'. But that merely displaces rather than resolves the
fundamental underlying *disagreements* over a range of further
questions about the *sources* of 'our deepest humanity'. Moreover, there is a sense in which it is not only the most elevated
but also the most *evil* deeds of which human beings are capable
that arise from their 'deepest humanity'. A romantic privileging
of one side of our human nature is a further danger inherent in
identifying a humanistic conception of 'the spiritual' with the
morally positive aspects of our existence. To call acts of human
barbarism 'inhuman' is certainly an understandable temptation
for certain kinds of humanistic thinking, but it is arguably
unhelpful if our aim is to think seriously about the full range of
our human potentialities. This tendency has long been
recognized as a weakness of those idealist 'philosophical
anthropologies' represented by thinkers like 'the young Marx',
in which the negative aspects of human behaviour have to be
explained away by resort to a theory that it is oppressive social
conditions which bring about a state of 'alienation' in which
human beings become estranged from their true and essential
humanity (see, for example, Ollman, 1971).

Religious education

What are the implications of this discussion for the future of
religious education in state schools? If we put aside 'the

spiritual' as an unhelpful term in trying to clarify the aims of moral education (and even, in some respects, the aims of religious education itself), what should we conclude about the future of religious education in state schools? One writer who has examined this issue is David Hargreaves in his 'Demos' booklet *The Mosaic of Learning* (Hargreaves, 1994). Apparently despairing of the inability of government agencies to rise above platitudinous assertion and their tendency to blame schools for failing to transmit clear moral and religious values, Hargreaves argues that, in view of the stubborn persistence of 'this conflation of moral and religious education' (ibid., p. 34), the time has come to acknowledge that:

> attempts to bolster RE since 1988 have failed: that morality is not as closely linked to religion, especially the Christian religion, as in the past; and that moral education will in the future need to be more closely linked to civic education if it is to provide a common core of values shared across communities in a pluralistic society.
>
> The notion of a non-denominational core RE to be offered in all schools as a buttress to moral education is becoming less and less viable and should now be abandoned. The multi-faith pick 'n mix tour of religions easily trivialises each faith's claims to truth. As an academic discipline it has little appeal to most children and comes before they are mature enough to engage in the necessary historical and philosophical analysis. (ibid., p. 34)

His proposed alternative has two main elements: that 'there should be more religious schools' and that *all* schools, whether religious or secular, should be required to provide 'a common core of civic education' including a significant element of *moral* education (ibid. pp. 34–5). Hargreaves offers several arguments in support of his proposition that we should permit, and indeed encourage, the establishment of Muslim, Hindu, Sikh, etc. state schools alongside existing Jewish schools and those of various Christian denominations. These include: first, the undeniable point that there is an element of contradiction if not hypocrisy in current policies of blocking the establishment of state Muslim schools while continuing to give public support to voluntary aided and controlled Christian schools; secondly, the equally undeniable fact that the creation of such schools would increase parental choice; and thirdly and most importantly, that 'such schools could confidently and without apology assert the fundamental link between morality and religious faith which is so prized by religious groups' (ibid., p. 35).

Secular schools would no longer teach religious education as part of a national curriculum, although secular secondary schools might offer RE to older pupils when they had developed the maturity necessary to understand 'a religious faith from the outside' (ibid., p.38). Hargreaves does stipulate that religious schools would have 'a duty to teach their students that morality without religion is an intellectually defensible and socially respectable position' (ibid., p.36). Nevertheless, the great strength he seems to see in such schools is that they would meet the deep desire of some parents to send their children to institutions whose ethos reinforced that of the home, and that in consequence of 'home and school being jointly committed to the transmission and living experience of a shared moral and religious culture', schools of this kind would play a key role in sustaining 'the very communities, including the family, on which (such) moral and religious convictions ultimately depend for their sustenance and development' (ibid., p.35). These schools would, in short, provide a sense of identity and belonging to the young of the communities concerned. Hargreaves cites and endorses here Rabbi Jonathan Sacks' distinction between two 'languages': 'the first and public language of citizenship' and 'our second languages', which Sacks characterizes as follows:

> our second languages are cultivated in the context of families and communities, our intermediaries be-tween the individual and the state. They are where we learn who we are; where we develop sentiments of belonging and obligation; where our lives acquire substantive depth. (Sacks quoted in Hargreaves, 1994, p. 37).

In this way, religious schools would also contribute to the maintenance of high standards of morality across society as a whole, both by sustaining a religiously sanctioned basis for morality among a significant proportion of the population, and by strengthening the authority of the leaders of local communities – not least their spiritual leaders.

How should we respond to this radical agenda which proposes such an interesting mix of iconoclasm in some areas and cultural preservation in others? One obvious objection, which Hargreaves himself anticipates, is that religious schools of the kind proposed would be socially divisive. Hargreaves denies this, partly on the grounds (outlined above) that religious schools would strengthen individual moral responsibility and thereby actually *increase* overall social cohesion and stability. This defence certainly has some plausibility, particularly in the context of a wider society which succeeded in promoting significant toleration of cultural and religious diversity. It is difficult, however, to balance this claim against an opposite concern: that the *superimposition* of religious, linguistic, ethnic and in some cases class differences can, in certain circumstances, be a basis for the most entrenched and intractable of social conflicts – as in the former Yugoslavia or in Northern Ireland or in Quebec, to take only three very obvious examples.[13] No one is in a position to reliably predict which of these different outcomes – greater integration or increased divisiveness – is the more likely were we to move to a national system of religious and secular schools of the kind proposed.

There are, however, other important reasons why it would be a mistake to accept Hargreaves' agenda. The most important of these has to do with the rights and interests of the children and young people who are destined to grow up in the contemporary and rapidly changing societies of late modernity. It is not legitimate, on *educational* grounds, to consign children in such societies to schools whose *raison d'être* is that they can 'confidently and without apology assert the fundamental link between morality and religious faith' – or, more accurately, between a *particular* morality and a *particular* faith. To do so would risk sacrificing the autonomy of these young people in favour of a misplaced respect for a reified and fossilized vision of the various 'communities' which make up late modern societies. Once again, we encounter here the fundamental division between, on the one hand, those who

169

wish, paternalistically, to bolster tradition and traditional authorities in the face of modernization and pluralism; and on the other hand, those who believe that there can and should be 'no turning back' in these respects. At issue in such cases are questions of representation and authority. Who now can legitimately claim to speak on behalf of these actually increasingly diversified constituencies which certain tradition-alists still like to think of as unified localized 'communities' based upon shared values and religious beliefs? It is very far from obvious that the appropriate answer is 'the accredited religious leaders' and those parents who support them. The doctrines and disciplines which some of these leaders may wish to instil may well become increasingly *un*acceptable to sections of the younger generation within such notional 'communities'. And this is not simply a question of the young being 'brainwashed' by 'Western' influences or the seductions of consumerism, etc. There are, and there will continue to be, *legitimate* divisions of thought and action – both between and within the generations in these 'communities' – over funda-mental issues such as women's rights, marrying out of a faith community, 'church' attendance, the truth claims of the faith, the claims of secular world-views, issues of personal and sexual morality, etc., etc. There is, furthermore, a clear possibility that among the parents who would most strongly wish to send their children to schools which would represent their own faith are some whose principal motivation would be precisely the desire to bring about orthodoxy and conformity in their offspring.[14] In *practice* moreover, it is very difficult to see how, once religious schooling became a sanctioned and widely institution-alized alternative, proper and effective safeguards could be instituted against narrow indoctrinatory forms of 'education', particularly within a school system which was increasingly legitimized on the grounds of enlarging consumer choice between differentiated types of schools.

Finally, what of Hargreaves' other main reservations con-cerning RE in state schools? He identifies three main problems:

(a) that parental support for RE is based on unrealizable expectations that the teaching of the subject can function as 'a kind of social antiseptic' to protect young people from moral danger;

(b) that RE as an academic discipline has little intellectual appeal to most children as well as coming too early in the process of their moral and cognitive development;

(c) that RE in state schools has, partly in response to pressures of multiculturalism, too often become 'a multi-faith pick 'n mix tour of religions' which 'easily trivialises each faith's claims to truth' (ibid., p. 34).

Let us consider each of these arguments in turn.

(a) Hargreaves is clearly right to claim that most parents express support for RE. This is clearly attested by the available survey evidence. And he is probably also correct that the main reason for such support has less to do with a belief that it is important that children should understand something about *religion* specifically, than with the understandable desire of parents that, if possible, schooling should somehow morally inoculate children so they are less likely to succumb to 'the ubiquitous dangers of drugs, sex and crime' (ibid., p. 32). Hargreaves is also correct when he argues that RE *alone* is not equipped for this kind of task and that moral education should be part of a much broader educational endeavour that includes civic education. All this, however, would come as no surprise to most teachers of RE, very few of whom have ever sought to justify their subject in these terms! If significant numbers of parents support RE for the wrong reasons, the problem which is raised is that of *re-educating the parents concerned,* not marginalizing or abolishing RE from the curriculum of the great majority of state schools.

(b) This brings us to the second contention, which is really two claims packaged into one. It may indeed well be the case that RE as a discipline has limited appeal to pupils. *Why* this is so is more debatable – but it cannot be unconnected with the low status of the subject in terms of credible educational *credentials.* We should note, however, that RE is not alone in this respect. Personal and social education, as well as citizenship education, notoriously suffer from a similar problem, such courses being perceived by many pupils as occupying valuable curriculum time which could be devoted to 'proper subjects' – i.e. subjects which lead to additional GCSE grades. The root problem here is the entrenched *instrumentalism* of many pupils and parents – an instrumentalism which is likely to be further reinforced by the growing preoccupation of the two main political parties with raising 'standards', the use of performance indicators, and the like. The strategy which Hargreaves advocates, of *replacing* RE with civic and moral education, therefore seems unlikely to overcome this problem of perceived irrelevance. *All* such subjects are likely to be seen as largely irrelevant if judged by such narrow criteria. But this is not a good *educational* reason for neglecting them.

The claim that RE is introduced too early, before most children 'are mature enough to engage in the necessary historical and philosophical analysis' (ibid., p. 34), raises rather more complex issues. Hargreaves is surely correct that there are significant difficulties in coming to understand a complex 'form of life' such as a religious faith 'from the outside' (ibid., p. 38). Nevertheless, what he seems to fail to recognize is that such problems are by no means unique to religion. For example, coming to an 'inward' understanding of the culture of, say, medieval England, or (to take a more limited example) of French Impressionist painting, also poses formidable challenges. Anything approaching a *developed* understanding and 'inward' appreciation of such matters requires extended study, exposure to a wide range of relevant experiences, grappling with conventions of representation that are initially unfamiliar, etc. None of this has stood in the way of the National Curriculum prescribing history study units (for quite young children) on aspects of medieval England, or a focus on the techniques of French Impressionism in National Curriculum art. Moreover, this has been justified in the terms of the vital educational importance of inducting children into their cultural heritage: the 'high culture' of their nation and of Western Europe. Perhaps regrettably – but also inevitably – there is a sense in which schoolchildren are *always* too immature to apprehend such matters in anything like their full complexity. (So, for that matter, are many adults!) But then, education in schools is often necessarily an exercise in legitimate simplification. How else did any of us come to understand any area of complex human activity? Once again, the conclusion has to be that Hargreaves has provided no distinctive reason why RE should be removed from the curriculum, nor a convincing account of why the subject should not be taught to younger children.

(c) This brings us to Hargreaves' final argument: his characterization (or more accurately character assassination) of contemporary RE as 'a multi-faith pick 'n mix tour of religions' which risks trivializing each separate faith's claims to truth. Once more, there is an element of validity in this criticism, at least in some instances, but not of an order that would justify the conclusion that RE should no longer be part of a common curriculum for all children. In our multi-cultural and multi-ethnic society, there are two major justifications for teaching children about religions (plural) rather than simply about Christianity. One is that a major *general* focus of liberal education should be to promote an appreciation of the nature of human understanding, and that this must include certain aspects of religious thought and experience. As Charles Bailey has put it: 'to gain some sense of man's quest for religious understanding is to gain an understanding of man's attempt to understand himself' (Bailey, 1984, p. 117). Clearly, this objective requires some attempt to develop an appreciation of certain *general* features of religious thinking and experience: for example, an exploration of the kinds of fundamental questions with which religion is concerned, the nature of the distinctive concepts that figure in religious discourse, the place of religions in human history, conflicts between theological and scientific modes of understanding, etc. This would seem to require, if not the systematic study of a number of discrete religious traditions, then at least a knowledge of examples drawn from a diversity of kinds of religion – including, perhaps, those of pre-literate societies. In a multicultural society like modern Britain, a second important justification for religious education has to do with combating ethnocentric modes of thinking and promoting a respect for the achievements of cultures outside the Western European orbit. And although it is essential here not to fall into the trap of virtually *identifying* cultural difference with religious difference (as certain well-meaning but tokenistic approaches to multicultural education in schools have certainly risked doing), it would be no less fallacious to ignore the significance of religions in the development and flowering of many non-Western cultures.

To conclude on a more consensual note. Hargreaves rightly argues that non-denominational schools (and even the formally secular schools which he advocates) would have a duty to help their students to appreciate that for many religious people, *moral* behaviour, even if it is capable of independent justification, is also likely to be regarded as religiously sanctioned and grounded (Hargreaves, 1994, p. 36). Similarly, Bailey suggests that much is to be gained by encouraging young people to understand – but to understand clearly – the nature of the connections which often exist between religion and morality:

> Both religion and morality can ... be inquired into as great human practices. Indeed, for most people without religious and/or moral considerations there would be no overriding framework of consideration from which to approach inquiries into social, political or economic matters. This is further to emphasize the point that the divisions between these practices are not logical but idiomatic, divisions of significant focus of attention.

He continues, however, with the following significant clarification:

> I do not mean to suggest by linking religion and morality together that they are *necessarily* linked. A person can clearly be moral (and immoral) in ways other than religious ways, and according to principles not dictated by religion. That they *can* be so separated, whilst for some people *not* so separated, is one of the things that pupils must come to see. A liberal education does not set out to make pupils religious, but neither does it set out to prevent them so becoming. It does and should set out to bring pupils to some understanding of religion as a great influence in historical and contemporary affairs. (Bailey, 1984, p. 123)

Conclusion

This chapter has been something of a ground-clearing exercise. First, it has sought to identify a number of obstacles to clear analyses of the real tasks which schools face in the sphere of moral and civic education – the most important of these obstacles being the persistent attempts that have been made to conflate 'the moral' with both religion and 'the spiritual'. Secondly, it has suggested that because of the diversity of overlapping and contradictory meanings which attach to it, the category of 'the spiritual' has little utility in clarifying appropriate aims and objectives for moral education, though clarification of the various meanings attaching to 'spirituality' remains a central task for religious education. Finally, it has been argued that the important task of developing better programmes of moral education and citizenship education should not be pursued at the expense of the teaching of religious education.

Notes

1. A modified version of this wording, incorporating a reference to 'a broad and balanced curriculum which promotes the spiritual, moral, *cultural*, mental and physical development of pupils', is also part of the preamble to the 1988 Act.

2. My use of the term 'programmatic' here follows that of Israel Scheffler (Scheffler, 1960). In his usage, the term 'stipulative' definition refers to a definition offered for the sake of argument and/or economy – and in order to facilitate communication or discussion. 'Programmatic' definitions, on the other hand, are those linked to some implied programme of action, and 'according to Scheffler, should be inspected not for their effects in enabling economy of utterance, nor for their relevance to prior usage, but rather for the moral and practical questions raised by the programme of action which they imply' (Lambourn, 1996, p. 155).

3. Among these disastrous consequences were the effects of 'over-population' evident especially in London. Arnold's work as one of Her Majesty's Inspectors of Schools made him directly aware of the living conditions of the children of the urban poor, and he did not hesitate to draw upon this experience:

   > I remember only the other day, a good man looking with me upon a multitude of children who were gathered before

us in one of the most miserable regions of London – children eaten up with disease, half-sized, half-fed, half-clothed, neglected by their parents, without health, without home, without hope ... (Arnold, 1869, p. 152)

4. In this respect (as well as in others which will be discussed later), Arnold is very much part of the tradition of that long line of Tory and conservative cultural analysts which can be traced back through 'men of letters' like Coleridge, Wordsworth, Southey to eighteenth-century writers like the legal theorist William Blackstone (see Mathieson and Bernbaum, 1988).

5. Arnold is acutely though cheerfully conscious that he is engaged in a battle on several fronts with a range of adversaries which included *The Times*, the *Daily News*, etc. as well as his 'liberal friends' (utilitarians and others). The following catches a characteristic tone in *Culture and Anarchy* (a text that is far from solemn): 'And here I think I see my enemies waiting for me with a hungry joy in their eyes. But I shall elude them!' (Arnold, 1869, p. 43).

6. The phrase 'reason and the will of God' occurs on the following pages of the John Murray popular edition of *Culture and Anarchy* (9th reprint, July 1961): p. 6; p. 21; p. 30; p. 49 (twice); p. 69; p. 92; p. 153.

7. The limitations, or at least highly contestable implications, of Arnold's conception of culture 'in practice', as it were, are evident in some of the conclusions to which he was led on popular issues of the day. He was, for example, a supporter of the vigorous suppression of mass popular protest, for fear that it would precipitate a descent into ungovernable anarchy. And in spite of his very marked sympathy for the plight of the urban poor and his critique of free-market liberalism as one of the causes of this situation, his 'answer' to the problem of population increase among the Populace was a strikingly Malthusian and voluntaristic suggestion that the poor should be educated to understand that no man has a moral right to produce more children than he can afford to bring up decently:

> ... to bring people into the world, when one cannot afford to keep them and to keep oneself decently and not too precariously, or to bring more of them into the world than one can afford ... is just as wrong, just as contrary to reason and the will of God, as for a man to have horses, or carriages, or pictures, when he cannot afford them, or to have more of them than he can afford. (ibid., p. 153)

8. The Annual Report of HM Chief Inspector of Schools for the school year 1994–95 acknowledged that:

> A significant number of secondary schools fail to meet the legal requirements of collective worship. Most non-compliance is *attributed* by schools to a lack of suitable accommodation. However, some schools are ingenious in overcoming such difficulties ... However, where teachers are reluctant to lead collective worship these attempts break down, even if well-prepared material is provided. (Ofsted, 1996, para. 214; my italics).

9. Admittedly, the subsequent inclusion of this part of the preamble was neither controversial nor contested, and indeed the 'spiritual' had been given additional educational legitimacy as a result of its being designated as one of the well-known HMI 'eight areas of experience' which rather briefly influenced approaches to curriculum planning in the later 1970s and early 1980s (DES, 1977a, b).

10. According to Paul Routledge, writing about UK Members of Parliament in 1996:

> There are 47 openly declared humanists ... in both houses of parliament, but not one of them is a member of the Conservative Party. A Tory MP has admitted to being gay, but none will confess to being godless ... The 26 MPs willing to advertise their irreligiousness through membership of the Parliamentary Humanist Group are all Labour, although private estimates suggest that six Liberal Democrats do not believe in God either. There are also 21 unbelieving peers, again mostly Labour ... After 33 years, the Parliamentary Humanist Group cannot call itself an All-Party Group because no Tory will join ... (Routledge, 1996, p. 6).

11. The dilemmas which this increasing diversity of 'spiritual' beliefs and practices in contemporary society poses for the 'established' religious authorities are considerable. This was very clearly illustrated by the publication in 1996 of a report commissioned by the Church of England and the Council of Churches in Britain and entitled *The Search for Faith and Witness*. According to the Religious Affairs Editor of the *Guardian*, the report warns that:

> people are increasingly turning to New Age spiritualities and superstition in an eclectic 'pick and mix' approach to religion which could lead to the collapse of our civilisation ... The Bishop of Rochester warned that the drift away from orthodox Christianity could lead to social disintegration with individuals floundering in a spiritual vacuum: 'the drifting of belief without belonging to any institution is bound to get more and more eclectic ... People's need to

believe remains strong but they're relying on all sorts of dubious things and exotic phenomena'. (Bunting, 1996, p. 9)

A core problem for the supporters of 'orthodox' belief in such a time is, of course, precisely the undermining of *tradition* as a source of authority in contemporary society. In a market place of spiritualities, an authoritative basis for identifying 'genuine' as against 'false' spirituality becomes increasingly difficult to locate – let alone enforce!

12. The government requirement that Ofsted school inspections 'must evaluate and report on the school's provision for the spiritual, moral, social and cultural development of all pupils' (Ofsted, 1995), has been the stimulus for renewed and lively public debate about the meaning of 'the spiritual'. A notable contribution is the book *Education, Spirituality and the Whole Child* (Best, 1996; a collection of papers originally delivered at a conference held at Froebel College, London, in 1994). This text reflects a wide range of views about the interpretation and utility of 'the spiritual' and spirituality in education. However, as the book's editor points out, some contributors invested the spiritual with a clearly religious connotation while others argued for more inclusive interpretations:

> The spiritual is conventionally thought of as to do with *religion*. Some contributors have approached spirituality from positions of personal faith, or from the convictions of those committed to education within church schools... Here, spiritual *leadership* is seen as crucial. Others... argue for a concept of spirituality and spiritual maturity which is universal and not premised upon theism... (ibid., p. 344)

13. Cf. Ralf Dahrendorf's well-known argument that the intensity of social conflict tends to be positively associated with the superimposition of different social bases of division between social groups (Dahrendorf, 1959).

14. There is evidence, of its nature limited, that, in some instances at least, the issue of separate religious schools may be bitterly contested *within* certain 'communities'. Discussing aspects of the education of Muslim girls in Bradford, for example, Saeeda Khanum has warned:

> ... very few have acknowledged the 'hidden agenda' behind the demands of religious fundamentalists: an attempt to stifle dissent and exert absolute control over the lives of women in the community. It is no accident, nor is it an act tinged with racism, that Muslim religious schools are referred to not as 'Islamic denominational

schools' but as 'separate' or 'segregated' by those who have a particular idea of the kind of community they want to foster – both those who want the schools and those who oppose them. (Khanum, 1995, p. 287)

References

C. Alves (1991) 'Just a matter of words? The religious education debate in the House of Lords', *British Journal of Religious Education,* 13/3.

M. Arnold (1869) *Culture and Anarchy: an Essay in Political and Social Criticism* (London: John Murray).

C. Bailey (1984) *Beyond the Present and the Particular: A Theory of Liberal Education* (London: Routledge and Kegan Paul).

R. Best (ed.) (1996) *Education, Spirituality and the Whole Child* (London: Cassell).

British Humanist Association (1993) *The Human Spirit* (London: The British Humanist Association).

M. Bunting (1996) 'Neo-paganism: a threat to society', *Guardian* (12 November), p. 6.

C. Castaneda (1968) *The Teachings of Don Juan: A Yacqui Way of Knowledge* (Berkeley: University of California Press; Penguin Books edition, 1970).

R. Dahrendorf (1959) *Class and Class Conflict in Industrial Society* (London: Routledge and Kegan Paul).

DES (Department of Education and Science) (1977a) *The Curriculum 11–16* (London: HMSO).

DES (1977b) *Supplement to The Curriculum 11–16* (London: HMSO).

P. Gilliat (1996) 'Spiritual education and public policy 1944–1994' in R. Best (ed.), *Education, Spirituality and the Whole Child* (London: Cassell).

J. R. Gusfield (1967) 'Moral passage: the symbolic process in public designations of deviance', *Social Problems,* 15/2 (Fall), pp. 174–88.

D. H. Hargreaves (1994) *The Mosaic of Learning: Schools and Teachers for the Next Century* (London: Demos).

HM Government (England and Wales) (1944) *Education Act 1944* (London: HMSO) Section 7, p. 4.

HM Government (England and Wales) (1988) *The Education Reform Act,* (London: HMSO) Sections 6, 7 and 8, pp. 4–6.

P. H. Hirst (1974) *Knowledge and the Curriculum: A Collection of Philosophical Papers* (London: Routledge and Kegan Paul).

A. Huxley (1946) *The Perennial Philosophy* (London: Chatto and Windus).

A. Huxley (1954) *The Doors of Perception* (London: Chatto and Windus).

S. Khanum (1995) 'Education and the Muslim girl' in M. Blair, J. Holland and S. Sheldon (eds), *Identity and Diversity: Gender and Experience of Education* (Clevedon: Multilingual Matters Ltd in association with the Open University).

D. Lambourn (1996) ' "Spiritual" minus "Personal-social" = ?: a critical note on an empty category' in R. Best (ed.), *Education, Spirituality and the Whole Child* (London: Cassell).

M. Mathieson and G. Bernbaum (1988) 'The British disease: a British tradition?', *British Journal of Educational Studies*, 36, pp. 126–74.

NCC (National Curriculum Council) (1993) *Spiritual and Moral Development: A Discussion Paper,* (London: National Curriculum Council).

Ofsted (Office for Standards in Education) (1994) *Spiritual, Moral, Social and Cultural Development: A Discussion Paper,* (London: Office for Standards in Education).

Ofsted (1995) *The OFSTED Handbook: Guidance on the Inspection of Secondary Schools* (London: HMSO).

B. Ollman (1971) *Alienation: Marx's Conception of Man in Capitalist Society* (Cambridge: Cambridge University Press).

P. Routledge (1996) 'God may be dead – but not if you're a Conservative MP', *Independent on Sunday* (12 April), p. 6.

I. Scheffler (1960) *The Language of Education* (Springfield, IL: Charles C. Thomas).

N. Tate (1996a) 'Education for adult life: spiritual and moral aspects of the curriculum' paper delivered to SCAA Conference on Education for Adult Life, 15 January 1996 (London: School Curriculum and Assessment Authority).

N. Tate (1996b) 'Curriculum, culture and society', paper delivered to SCAA Conference on Curriculum, Culture and Society, 7 February 1996 (London: School Curriculum and Assessment Authority).

J. White (1996) 'Education, spirituality and the whole child: a humanist perspective' in R. Best (ed.), *Education, Spirituality and the Whole Child* (London: Cassell).

P. White (1993) 'Citizenship & "spiritual & moral development" ', *Citizenship – The Journal of the Citizenship Foundation*, 15/1.

11

After Spirituality: Some Connections between Theology and Philosophy

Paul Grosch

Moral and spiritual discourses

T he title of this chapter refers, of course, to Alasdair
MacIntyre's now famous thesis concerning the collapse of
meaning in moral discourse. The central argument, part
philosophical, part historical, is presented in his 1981 book
After Virtue: A Study in Moral Theory[1] and continued in
Whose Justice? Which Rationality?[2] and *Three Rival Versions
of Moral Enquiry.* [3] The argument presented here is similar to
that offered by MacIntyre, but instead of the problems
embedded in morality, it is concerned with some of the issues
central to spirituality.

The language, meaning and tradition of spirituality has
fallen into some kind of chaos as a partial consequence of the
contemporary lack of historical understanding when it comes
to matters spiritual. My tentative and not entirely original
claim[4] is that there have been (at least) two major historical
rifts in the development of spiritual belief and practice which
have led to a distorted understanding of the nature and scope of
spirituality, so that our current discourse about it is rendered
partially meaningless and somewhat rootless. The first rift is
the almost complete colonization of spirituality by the Roman
Catholic church during the Scholastic period. Prior to this,

there existed in intellectual thought in general and in both philosophy and theology in particular the recognition that some rational progress in metaphysics, epistemology and morality could only be made if there was some version of an all-encompassing spiritual attitude towards whatever inquiry was being undertaken. This, generally took two forms: (a) a belief in the necessity of engaging in some set of individual and collective spiritual exercises which would guide both minds and bodies; and (b) a basic humility and reverence born out of reason, because reason attempts to fathom the mysterious relationship that exists between self and others, and between self and the cosmos. Such exercises and inquiries were not to be undertaken lightly, either in religious or in philosophical contexts where self-understanding and development were regarded as paramount. It was only during the Scholastic period, according to Pierre Hadot, the French philosopher and historian of antiquity, that a radical and substantive distinction between *theologia* and *philosophia* was finally drawn.[5] As a consequence the birth of modern philosophy accepted the firm distinction between theology and philosophy and assumed that spirituality, from then on, was simply a matter for the theologians and those of a particular religious persuasion, but clearly had no place in philosophy. This division, with spirituality judged neatly to be the province only of religion and theology, continued largely unquestioned until, by the middle of the twentieth century, one of the inevitable conclusions of this split had finally been reached. With the advent of Logical Positivism, only the propositions of science and logic remained as the respectable core discourse governing philosophical activity and investigation, at least within the Anglo-American analytic tradition. Spirituality was rendered as something either (a) purely mystical, about which nothing could be said,[6] or (b) only of religious significance, about which much could be said, but none of it of any philosophical significance.

The second rift is a contemporary one and is twofold in character. First, there has been a decline of interest in the kind of spirituality articulated by traditional theology. This, in turn, is partly a consequence of the growing secularization which has viewed mainstream or standard modes of religious belief and practice as irrelevant at best and a form of social control at worst.[7] Second, and clearly following on from the first, with the turning away from any serious intellectual and moral engagement with religion, there has occurred a similar turning away from any equally serious intellectual and moral engagement with spirituality.[8] What, then, has filled its place?

Two things (at least) have tended to fill the void left by a full appreciation of the rich tradition of spirituality. First is an almost semi-divine belief in the self as a purely autonomous, self-defining and self-regulating individual.[9] But this newly-created, post-Enlightenment individual needs a secular priest-hood to which it can turn in times of stress, doubt and fear. Consequently, we witness the emergence of a new post-modern priesthood of psychology and psychotherapy with its attendant initiates of counsellors, analysts and therapists with a panoply of specialist techniques for getting us to recover, reinvent and redirect our broken selves. The central point is not just that the psychologist, the psychiatrist and the therapist have now filled the secular void once occupied by the priest in the confessional, but that the 'language game' of psychology has replaced the language game of theology, with the result that what is now almost lost is the deeply spiritual and mystical nature of what it means to be a human being in a world that, logically and scientifically, need not have existed, but in fact does. And this very fact alone is an awesome thing. As Wittgenstein famously puts it: '6.44   It is not how things are in the world that is mystical, but that it exists'.[10] In a contemporary world governed by the implicit but all-pervasive ideology of the empirical sciences, with the precise recording of outward behaviours, the quantification of measurable outcomes and the closed prescription of human performance, there is little space for the critical reflection on matters mystical or the problematic expression of things spiritual. In other words, the secular, empirically-based culture of much mainstream psychology has us and the world all but sewn up.

MacIntyre argues something similar by carefully sketching out the three principal figures of the modern age: the bureaucratic manager, the aesthete and the therapist. The Enlightenment with its over-optimistic emphasis on the power of pure reason has led, in culture as well as in philosophy, to the final division between fact and value. Hence, it is now the task of politicians, economists and lawyers, as well as scientists, industrialists and technicians, to deal in the world of facts, while the world of value is relegated to the church and the occasional academic institution. In a world of fact the bureaucratic manager reigns supreme, self-confidently able to make radical and often disastrous decisions about local, national and international communities, decisions predicated on the triple mantras of effectiveness, efficiency and expertise, each of which serves to sustain power and authority.[11] I say decisions, never judgements, because judgements, in the writings of Aristotle, do not simply involve an added moral dimension, but are themselves expressions of a moral discourse which underpins all human conduct and inquiry. Instead, our contemporary bureaucratic manager sees himself (the gender ascription here is specific) as operating in a morally neutral world. The aesthete, the second of MacIntyre's characters, is a rather sad individual, the never-ending seeker for new experiences and the modern consumer of both persons and things. Finally, we are presented with the therapist, the character whose task it is to keep the 'whole sorry cultural show on the road'.[12] In essence there are three kinds of therapist. First, there is the professional therapist concerned with repairing the mental stability of individuals within a deeply divided society; second, there is the organizational therapist masking as consultant, staff development officer or company counsellor, whose job it is to steer the goals and aspirations of individuals so that they match more precisely the objectives of the corporation; and thirdly, there is the cultural therapist in the unintentional guise of the chat-show host whose task, it seems, is to massage an alienated, disfranchised and disempowered population through another week in order that they do not have to inquire too deeply or closely into the 'meaningless and superficiality of life'.[13] This contemporary cultural disaster, for MacIntyre, is the consequence of the failure of philosophy to recognize the historical error of its ways in subscribing to the Enlightenment project of sacrificing almost everything to the dictates of pure reason. Culture is now reaping the poor harvest sown by philosophy in the eighteenth century.

My contention, however, based on Hadot's reasoning, is that the mistake occurred not with the Enlightenment in the eighteenth century but with the separation of *theologia* from *philosophia* which, effectively, occurred during the late medieval period, a period dominated by the Schoolmen, when philosophy finally relinquished any authority in the realm of spiritual belief and value and became instead simply a conceptual tool for the continuation of a particular form of neutered theology, a theology which had itself separated the rich wisdom of spirituality from the cold and austere calculations of a rationalist religion.

The second thing to have filled the void is the growing interest in Eastern religions and philosophy, with an especial accent on Hinduism and Buddhism. As traditional Western religions and their weakened spiritual content have lost their appeal, people have turned to what they see as a set of deeply engaging, rewarding and liberating spiritual doctrines which appear to have no equivalent in the standard religious communities of the Christian denominations. It is interesting to note that in Eastern philosophical doctrines, the spiritual element has not been divorced from the logical or reasoned accounts of the world and a person's place within it. Within Eastern philosophy,[14] and in particular the three influential Vedanta schools of non-dualism, qualified non-dualism, and explicit pluralism, there is a clear acknowledgement that *theologia* and *philosophia* do not just sit side by side but are inextricably and fundamentally linked. Hence, there is not the same split between religion and philosophy, or theology and philosophy, in Hindu thought as there is in Western intellectual life.

Sometimes there is a syncretistic element in the development of new religious groupings, in which adherents 'go shopping', as it were, for a belief system that may include preferred modes of worship, spiritual contemplation, community ritual and highly esoteric accounts of the nature and origin of the world and its inhabitants. So, for example, in some of the more fringe or marginal expressions of the New Age movement we may find a patchwork quilt of astrology, Eastern mysticism, pseudo-scientific creation theories, and shallow or rootless metaphysical speculation about the cosmos and its meaning. All of this may then be combined with dubious forms of ritual worship and manipulative psychological practice, resulting in the exploitation of those who are most vulnerable.[15]

The argument just sketched out is similar to that used by MacIntyre in relation to moral theory and practice. As I have already suggested, MacIntyre claims that contemporary under-standings of morality are both confused and confusing as a consequence of the eighteenth-century Enlightenment project which attempted to place moral reasoning upon a purely rational and contextually unbounded footing. The failure of this project opened the door to a succession of moral theories, each of which attempted to right the rational wrongs of what went before until we finally end up with emotivism, the moral theory which evades the central issues of morality altogether by claiming that (a) an unbridgeable logical gulf separates the world of fact and the world of value; and (b) any ethical utterance or behaviour is, therefore, simply the expression of personal preference by a so-called autonomous individual. Hence, emotivism is often referred to as 'Boo–Hurrah Theory'. So, for example, if I claim that euthanasia is morally wrong, all I am doing is uttering a statement of emotional preference, irrespective of the many and varied rational arguments I may deploy in order to support my claim. The rational arguments I bring to bear on the issue simply mask the underlying emotive nature (and reasoned basis) of my preference. Ultimately, then, all responses to ethical statements are reducible to the Boo–Hurrah type. They are nothing other than individual expres-sions of approval or disapproval, given my personal and emotionally-based attitude towards whatever ethical dilemma is under question. This is the bleak social and intellectual landscape which philosophy now surveys and for which it has been partly responsible. My analysis tentatively claims a similar landscape in respect of spirituality. We now have, if you like, a generally applicable theory of spirituality which underwrites the personal preferences of the autonomous individual; preferences based on emotional responses to the range of fundamental dilemmas in human existence. It would seem then, that the traditional resources of spiritual insight and teaching to be found in both theology and philosophy are no longer at the heart of the contemporary discourse about spirituality.

However, my analysis differs from MacIntyre's in its fundamental optimism. Despite some of the intellectually conservative stances suggested so far, my claim that the two rifts just mentioned, as well as the Enlightenment project which MacIntyre blames for the collapse of moral reasoning, have been, and continue to be, healthy expressions of individual and collective scepticism towards, and creative reactions against, stifled and ossified systems of religious and philosophical thought and practice. Without these sceptical responses, radical critiques and creative reactions (some of them extreme), traditional and mainstream theology and philosophy would not, perhaps, be in a position to reconstitute themselves in a coherent, meaningful and above all, relevant, manner. By 'relevant' I mean 'capable of being seen and understood as having both an inclusive meaning and purpose for all individuals and communities'. In particular, at least one kind of feminist critique is leading us forward by (a) helping to deconstruct the past; and (b) injecting some passion and urgency into the present.[16] MacIntyre's account of morality is, to say the least, pessimistic, even claiming that the Enlightenment project should never have taken place. This is a false premise and belief. Historically it is, in any case, a piece of hopeless and reactionary speculation. So, what are some of the historical origins of spirituality within the philosophical tradition? Before any attempt to answer the question, some further description of the problems inherent in contemporary philosophy needs to be undertaken.

Spirituality, mysticism and philosophy

The professionalization of philosophy has, unfortunately, led many philosophers away from the origins of the discipline. Aristotle variously argued that philosophy emerges as a consequence of our marvelling at the vast enigma of the cosmos – a semi-mystical wonder at the beauty, magnitude and complexity of the universe and humanity's place within it. Philosophy's central task of attempting to render at least some of that size, beauty and complexity both intelligible and comprehensible is, however, not at odds with the affirmation of the explicitly spiritual proposition that not everything can be explained in a systematically coherent manner, that some elements of our understanding are, in Wittgenstein's celebrated phrase, 'mystical': '6.522 There are, indeed, things that cannot be put into words. They make themselves manifest. They are what is mystical.'[17]

However, it is well known that Wittgenstein's *Tractatus* defined the task of philosophy rather too narrowly. He claimed that all that could be said in a meaningful fashion, namely, the propositions of science and of logic, could be said clearly. Anything else, strictly speaking, could not be said at all. This, effectively, consigned to the void any metaphysical statement about theology, morality and aesthetics. In other words, God, ethics and art cannot, philosophically, be spoken about in any meaningful way. This is not to say, though, that thoughts, ideas and imperatives, as well as feelings, beliefs and values associated with them, are neither worthy nor important; it is just that they are incommunicable in a strict philosophical sense. Indeed, for Wittgenstein, they are the most important matters of human conduct and concern. They are what life is for, and once we have examined the propositions of science and logic we will be able to recognize how little we have achieved and understood. It is then possible, in Wittgenstein's famous analogy, to climb up the ladder, throw it away and be able to 'see the world aright'.[18] There is, however, the danger here of conflating the spiritual with the mystical. I suggest that they are synonymous but not identical. The self which relates to self and to others – that profound fact of one's own existence impinging upon or affecting the existence of all others, however maximally or minimally – underwrites the spiritual, that strange breath of life which unites rather than separates human lives. But more strange still is the knowledge of one's actual, albeit contingent, existence in an existing universe which allows for selves or spiritual entities to impact upon each other. That is what is mystical.

On this reading, the *Tractatus* is the key text to understanding both the importance and the collapse of spiritual insight in philosophical inquiry and practice. What the *Tractatus* does is to point to the central paradox in much modern philosophy: on the one hand, a belief in the absolute centrality of the spiritual and mystical element in human life, conduct and belief, but on the other, a subscription to the view that we must narrowly prescribe the limits of philosophical inquiry; the limits being governed by the supposedly pure facts and logical possibilities of scientific propositions wholly uncontaminated by any metaphysical speculation. In this sense, the *Tractatus* is the final logical conclusion of the enterprise begun in the late medieval period when philosophy and theology began to part company in a systematic manner.

Fortunately, Wittgenstein later acknowledged the mistake in the *Tractatus* and replaced his narrow picture theory of language with the equally famous language game analogy.[19] Although Wittgenstein denied that the language game analogy could be extrapolated into a fully-fledged theory, to all intents and purposes it is a theory of sorts. Instead of philosophy being confined to science and logic, Wittgenstein argued that there are innumerable language games, science and logic being but two. Religion and theology, morality and behaviour, art and aesthetics, are also language games, all equally valid and philosophically legitimate. Part of our purpose, as human beings equipped for dialogue, is to examine each language game in which we find ourselves, in order to clarify its rules and rituals, its grammar and meanings. When we have done this, our mistake will be seen to be to judge the values and truth claims of one language game by the rules and grammar of another. On a trivial level, therefore, we cannot judge the game of rugby by the rules of cricket, in the same way that we cannot expect to judge the status of meaning contained in a religious game by using the conventions of science. Both language games are internally rational and coherent; what is irrational and incoherent is to determine the ultimate truth-claims of one game by the conventions governing another.[20]

By carefully examining its origins as well as its new potential as a home within which all language games can be explored (though not judged), philosophy can legitimately reclaim some stake in the language of spirituality which, by both design and default, it has lost and in one sense, partly rejected. I argue not only that philosophy can do this, but that it ought to if it is to remain true to its own heritage and purpose. This, of course, is not the same as saying that all philosophy should succumb to contemporary spiritual beliefs, discourse and practice, but that philosophy should rightfully recognize that some notion of spiritual content and conduct is both historically and categorically part of the philosophical *modus operandi*.

Philosophy: a way of life?

On this note I now turn to a recent work, *Philosophy as a Way of Life*.[21] Here, Pierre Hadot discusses the original place, scope and purpose of philosophical inquiry in ancient Greece under the title 'Spiritual exercises'.[22] These spiritual exercises Hadot traces through Greco-Latin antiquity and demonstrates their similarity to the later spiritual exercises of the Christian tradition. What are these exercises? How have they been codified? And do they have any relevance today? Hadot examines them under four main headings, each of which is about the need for learning: (1) 'Learning to live'; (2) 'Learning to dialogue'; (3) 'Learning to die'; and (4) 'Learning how to read'. These four tasks of learning are considered to constitute a life-long spiritual pursuit. This pursuit is not about the short-term skill acquisition which allows one to make a conventional success of this life, a success measured in terms of product, performance and outcome; instead it is about the rich and variegated long-term cultivation of dispositions or virtues: the careful development of the *aretai*,[23] of human excellences or qualities of both mind and character. This is the kind of learning which Hadot commends, and which is central to what it means to engage in spiritual exercises in a philosophical sense, one which is closely connected to a religious conception of the spiritual life.

First, 'learning to live' involves a series of daily commitments to the improvement of the individual self specifically as a member of the philosophic community, but the commitments are by no means the exclusive preserve of those engaged in philosophical inquiry; indeed, they are open to anyone who cares to listen and observe. Two separate, but comparable, lists of daily commitments to a regime or discipline are recorded by Philo Judaeus of Alexandria (30 BCE–50 CE).[24] They map out the following:

> research *(zetesis)*, thorough investigation *(skepsis)*, reading *(anagnosis)*, listening *(akroasis)*, attention *(prosoche)*, self-mastery *(enkrateia)*, ... indifference to indifferent things, [and] reading, meditations *(meletai)*, therapies of the passions, remembrance of good things, self-mastery and the accomplishments of duties.[25]

To a greater or lesser degree, these exercises are at the heart of the four great philosophical schools of Greek and Roman antiquity: Platonism, Stoicism, Aristotelianism and Epicureanism.

Second, 'learning to dialogue' concerns the internal process of talking with oneself – a dialogue with one's soul or mind. Here, the classic figure is, of course, Socrates. It is often thought that Socrates was solely interested in the nature of dialogic communication with other people. He was clearly interested in that, as the Platonic dialogues amply demonstrate. But he was equally engaged in a life-long internal dialogue with himself. Hence, the famous philosophical method of Socratic dialogue becomes on inspection a dual method of talking with self and talking with others. Thus, the Socratic dialogue

> turns out to be a kind of communal spiritual exercise. In it the interlocutors are invited to participate in such inner spiritual exercises as examination of conscience and attention to oneself: in other words, they are urged to comply with the famous dictum, 'Know thyself'. Although it is difficult to be sure of the original meaning of this formula, this much is clear: it invites us to establish a relationship of the self to the self, which constitutes the foundation of every spiritual exercise.[26]

Third, there is the element of 'learning to die'. The actual pursuit of truth and the twinned articulation of both the pursuit and the truth itself are philosophically pregnant activities. Why should this be so? For a start, there is the notion of truth which, certainly in Platonic terms, is timeless and changeless, eternal and immutable. If the truths of justice, beauty and goodness are not bound by the temporal corruptibility of this world of appearances – or, in the contemporary language of philosophical analysis, the spatio-temporal framework of this physical world – then to glimpse these truths one would have to assume a perspective above and beyond this finite and limiting world.[27] To do this one would have to 'play dead' – to see the eternal and unchanging world of truth from a universal position, where any particular experience, particular body or particular thought is of almost no consequence. The ancient dualism of Platonism is here evident; the purpose is for us to escape the particular fancies and distractions of the body in order to see the world from another vantage point. Hadot points especially to *Phaedo*, the dialogue on the soul, as the chief source of theorizing about the importance of death:

Paul Grosch

> It is a fact, Simmias, that those who go about philosophizing correctly are in training for death, and that to them of all men death is least alarming.[28]

There are, of course, at least two significant problems with this kind of dualism. The first is an obvious one about the possible nature of the relationship between mind and body. There are a number of logical and empirical objections to the notion of dualism which, for example, even Descartes had to face.[29] The second set of problems calls into question even the way we think about the very problem of dualism itself. This set is grounded firmly in the feminist critique not only of dualism but of the ways in which we think and talk about traditional philosophical problems. In other words, the entire edifice of Western philosophical thinking, with its emphasis upon what are, essentially, masculine conceptions of reason, is justifiably called into question.[30]

Four, 'learning how to read', is crucial. Despite the range of differences between the various philosophical schools of antiquity, and the varying emphases placed upon spiritual understanding and development, all of them are committed to a detailed understanding of particular key texts, or sacred works. The point is not that such texts contain the last authoritative word on an issue; rather that they help us individually and collectively to meditate on certain 'truths' which are apprehended either immediately or after a period of contemplative reflection. These texts provide starting points, as it were, of personal journeys of intellectual and moral growth at the heart of which is a deeply spiritual acknowledgement of the limits of our own understanding.

Why should this acknowledgement be spiritual in character? The reasons are twofold: first, we recognize the limitations of our moral and intellectual development, yet occasionally we entertain a strange, almost intuitive notion that some form of unified understanding is within our grasp. Whey should this be so? Do not science, history and philosophy demonstrate that a complete account of human existence and its meaning is ever beyond us? Why then the continued search? Why the constant re-articulation of the central questions if we know, prior to the asking, that they will not and cannot be answered? This is a matter of no small spiritual significance.[31] Second, we

192

acknowledge, and sometimes experience, the deeply held mystical nature of human existence itself, apart from the enigmatic nature of our wanting to get to the root of it all. Certain mystical or spiritual experiences, ones that affect the entire 'breath' of life upon which our existence depends, can and do occur especially for those whose lives have been spent in attending to the kinds of exercises thought so necessary by the philosophical schools of antiquity and the great religious traditions. The nature and content of these mystical and spiritual experiences are varied: some are utterly ineffable or incommunicable; some are partly communicable, perhaps through analogy or poetry; and some, because of their simplicity and straightforward veracity, speak to us meaningfully almost in an instant.

The art of reading, then, is what is important, rather than mere 'barking at print' or silent acquiescence at the apparent wisdom of the written and uttered word, blind obedience to a carefully crafted doctrine, or, as in modern technocratic philosophy, uncritical acceptance of the 'wff', the well-formed formula of symbolic logic. This, perhaps, is where post-modernism can help. In privileging the reader as much as the writer or the hearer as much as the talker, we can begin to reinterpret the ancient spiritual wisdom that was once common to both philosophy and theology, but which was later colonized by theology and relinquished by philosophy. Finally, it was either abandoned or ignored by theology, or alternatively anaesthetized through theology's arrogant pursuit of a singular doctrine, or metanarrative, that served as the precise interpretation of the one indivisible truth. But what philosophy has long suspected is that truth is a much more slippery entity than one might suppose. The conflicts between coherence and correspondence theories of truth, and between redundancy, semantic and pragmatic theories, have all eventually given way to a more cautious, conditional, contextual and provisional account of truth, partly summed up in Lawrence Johnson's 'Thinking Person's Axiom One: If you think you have the answer – you are wrong'.[32] Basil Mitchell, commenting upon the analytic philosopher Peter Strawson, tells of the 'romantic' flavour of Strawson's writings, despite their commitment to analytic precision. Strawson, it is admitted, is as equally engaged in the semi-mystical quest as the rest of us. Strawson's twin notions of the 'pictures of ideal forms of life' and 'the profound truths about man and the universe'[33] lie at the heart of the key texts of culture, what Strawson himself terms the 'literature of the maxim',[34] that vast body of literary, spiritual, theological and philosophical works that exhibit the multiplicity of profound truths about the human condition and the range of meanings attached to it.

According to Hadot, what is significant here is the transformative nature of these four key areas of philosophical practice. Each is an acknowledgement of the spiritual dimension of our inconsequential physical existence. Aristotle was well aware that to lead an ethically justifiable life literally meant a lifetime's application of certain rules, habits and customs that would govern both mind and character. Ultimately, for Aristotle, the purpose was to lead a happy life according to reason, but no person could be called truly happy until the end of life had been reached. One's whole life needs to be governed by these exercises of body and spirit or character and mind. One cannot expect that the immediate apprehension of a rational moral injunction will suddenly give life a morally clear horizon. Life itself is messy, disorganized and unpredictable, full of disparate 'goings-on'.[35] The submission to these spiritual exercises, recommended in one way or another by the four principal schools of Greek philosophy mentioned above, is to engage in a 'form of life', to participate in a language game. The game is not trivial but serious, indeed it is about the very conduct and expression of life itself. The particular life led by any particular individual is indicative of, and partakes in, the universal life characterized by the catch-all conceptual phrase of 'being human'.

The medieval break

So, when did the form of life encompassing spiritual and intellectual activity become fractured? Hadot's brief answer is that the break began with the Schoolmen.

> With the advent of medieval Scholasticism ... we find a clear distinction being drawn between *theologia* and *philosophia*. Theology became conscious of its autonomy *qua* supreme science, while philosophy was emptied of its spiritual exercises

which, from now on, were relegated to Christian mysticism and ethics. Reduced to the 'handmaid of theology', philosophy's role was henceforth to furnish theology with conceptual – and hence purely theoretical – material.[36]

And contemporary philosophy, according to Hadot, with the exception, perhaps, of Nietzsche, Bergson and some of the existentialists, has continued to play this purely conceptual role. The role takes one of two forms, either as a formal systems-builder, or as a detached, second-order spectator of the systems built by others. Philosophy offers either a purely rational and normative set of complex theories or an imperious collection of meta-analyses of first-order activities. For the sake of historical simplicity we may say that in the first camp we have the great system-builders of Descartes, Spinoza, Leibniz, Kant and Hegel, with, for example, Jürgen Habermas continuing in the same broad tradition. In the second camp we have the formidable sceptics in Hume, Schulze and Clifford, with, for example, two such widely differing characters as P. H. Nowell-Smith and Richard Rorty conducting the same kind of semi-detached analysis.

How exactly did the break occur and who inaugurated it? Unfortunately, Hadot himself is not specific. He simply mentions that H. Happ argues that it was Francisco de Suárez, the sixteenth-century Spanish Scholastic philosopher, who established the first fully-fledged intellectual or conceptual 'system' which did not depend exclusively on the works of either Plato or Aristotle. This is where historical interpretation and philosophical analysis begin to cross. Judgements about what constitutes either an epistemic or a spiritual break in the intellectual tradition are notoriously difficult to make. According to John Marenbon,[37] it is possible to view the medieval period in one or more of four ways. First, one may examine the tradition as heralding the emergence of a new and specific discipline known as Christian philosophy, in which the development of Christian theology is necessarily and inextricably linked to the refinement and use of a particular philosophical method. The results, for Etienne Gilson, were that religion became much more than a social phenomenon, as it was largely for the Greeks; moreover, it became technically and intellectually monotheistic, unlike the social polytheism of Greek religious belief. Finally, the philosophical problems raised by both Plato and Aristotle, especially those connected with a First Cause and an immaterial, ideational or purely spiritual realm, were systematically investigated from a surprisingly open-minded and self-critical theological position.[38]

Second, one may see Scholasticism as the precursor to contemporary Anglo-American analytic philosophy, in which there is an overriding preoccupation with the mechanics of logic, language and the precise construction of formal arguments. This is Hadot's claim, but one which is only minimally substantiated. Third, one could, theoretically, separate the strands of theology and philosophy and examine them independently. This view, however, is predicated on the notion that there is something specifically called philosophy which is necessarily distinct from something specifically called theology, but that these had fused with each other during the post-classical period. This notion, of course, is disputed from either of the two preceding perspectives. Hence, the idea of separating the two disciplines in order to conduct an historical analysis is a mistaken one. It is not only Hadot who claims that the close interconnection between philosophy and theology was explicit in most if not all Greek intellectual thought. Gerson's comprehensive inquiry[39] into the origins of natural theology as it is found in Greek philosophical texts points to the inherent problems of trying to place philosophy on one side of the intellectual divide and theology on the other. They are not, except in the minds of a philosophical technocrat, mutually exclusive disciplines, and so the practices that inform each are not mutually exclusive either. Hence, some notion of spirituality informs philosophical inquiry in just the same way that it obviously informs theological inquiry. Fourth (and finally), there is the much less controversial approach of simply attempting to place a topic or argument in a carefully described historical context, without drawing any firm conclusions as to its nature and status in relation to either theology or philosophy. This approach need not concern us here.

Marenbon's opening two perspectives help to substantiate Hadot's claim. Philosophy became separated from theology during the Scholastic period, and spirituality was then delivered exclusively to theology, leaving philosophy somewhat, but perhaps unknowingly, bereft.

The Contemporary break

Spirituality, left within the tradition of Western theology, continued to mine a rich vein of human and transcendental experiences, as the works of Richard Rolle, Julian of Norwich and the anonymous author of the *Cloud of Unknowing* will testify. It is not too difficult to see how the traditional methods of spiritual exercises recommended by the ancient schools of philosophy – combining as they did the twin pursuits of *philosophia* (love of wisdom) and *theologia* (talk of God) – were, in almost all respects, similar to the spiritual exercises adopted by the Church. Ignatius Loyola's famous *Spiritual Exercises* emerged from a combination of the four concerns of learning described by Hadot. During his long convalescence Loyola was handed a copy of the *Life of Christ* written by Ludulph of Saxony. It was the meditative reflection on the opening section of this text that transformed Loyola's view of himself as a living entity within the cosmos. This section begins:

> Read of what has been done [in the Gospels] as though it were happening now ... Offer yourself as a present to what was said and done through our Lord Jesus Christ with the whole affective power of your mind ... Hear and see these things being narrated as though you were hearing with your own ears and seeing with your own eyes.[40]

Through learning again how to live a life, how to respond to imminent death, how to dialogue first with himself and then with others, and finally through learning how to read and comprehend, how to negotiate with a tradition that once had no deep significance for him, Loyola gradually formulated his own spiritual exercises which have, since then, had wide appeal.

But as formal religion has declined in the West and with it the widespread formal study of theology, then the tradition of spirituality has largely fallen into disuse, especially, and most worryingly within education, the very social institution which is charged with the preservation, study and rearticulation of all of the valuable conversations of the past. For example, a collection of essays entitled *Education, Spirituality and the Whole Child* [41] published in 1996 contains almost no reference to the long, rich and complex tradition of Christian spirituality. Is it because the tradition is believed to be obsolete? I do not think so. It is, perhaps, more to do with being forced to ignore the tradition through a lack of time and space within which spirituality can be studied seriously. Teachers, showered with the absurd demands from those archetypal bureaucratic managers so carefully described by MacIntyre, have no time to reflect critically on what it is they are genuinely supposed to be doing; no space to consider professionally, the underlying aims and purposes of education in its most meaningful sense. Instead, they are the victims of what Apple calls 'intensification':[42] the constant spinning from one managerial request to another, suffering from continual monitoring, accounting, testing and appraising. It is hardly surprising, therefore, that teachers, in a position where they are unable themselves to conduct the kinds of spiritual exercises talked of by Hadot, feel ill-equipped to deal seriously with the tradition of spirituality, a tradition which is crying out to be recognized, read, listened to and interpreted. Who, for example, can quote from Richard Rolle's *Fire of Love*? Who can give even an introductory interpretation of *The Cloud of Unknowing*? Who can give an account of Loyola's *Spiritual Exercises*? In a different but comparable vein, MacIntyre laments the passing of an Educated Public (EP) which can still debate the essence and function of morality.[43] We have few discourses and practices left which can assist us. May not the same be said of spirituality? Creative but often rootless, fragmented and syncretistic belief systems and practices have tended to fill the gap once occupied by a meaningful theology, a relevant religion and a liberating spirituality, but a theology, a religion and a spirituality which have allowed themselves to ossify under the backward-looking influences of patriarchy, oppression and irrelevance.

Conclusion

I said at the outset that I am not at all pessimistic, and Mary Grey's chapter lends further fuel to this optimism. In philosophy, the methodological approach favoured by Hadot, namely, historical philosophy, based on the vision of inquiry established by Hegel and Collingwood and continued by MacIntyre, can unmask the ideology of analytic philosophy which will have no truck with spirituality or a spiritual vision. It can do this by adopting some of the techniques of the postmoderns which will help us to deconstruct the past, and reinject some spiritual content into the present. In theology and philosophy the questions posed by the feminist critique of both disciplines help towards the re-establishment of a revitalized notion of spirituality which takes seriously the condition of humankind, and which recognizes the ultimate responsibility placed on each of us, as persons first, and as philosophers, theologians and educators second, to form a set of relationships based on justice, care, compassion and liberation. The Stoic response of indifference to indifferent things but an absolute concern for the welfare of others is central to a philosophical way of life. Perhaps the carefully researched and negotiated reintegration of some aspects of theology, philosophy and spirituality will transform, radically, how we rethink the place and purpose of education within a newly-emerging culture.

For MacIntyre, in *Whose Justice? Which Rationality?* (1988), the central means of how, collectively and individually, we resolve the first major philosophical question 'What is justice?', posed in Plato's *Republic,* depends on the nature of the future relationship between theology and philosophy.[44] Perhaps through a recovery and re-exploration of spirituality the link between *theologia* and *philosophia* can be forged again. If it is not, the answers to the primary question 'What is justice?' and to the supplementary question 'How is it to be secured?' may continue to be purely academic, in precisely the same way that I have presented this argument. I am not immune to the irony.

Notes and References

1. Alasdair MacIntyre, *After Virtue: a Study in Moral Theory* (London: Duckworth, 1981). The second edition (1985) contains

Paul Grosch

a further chapter summarizing objections to the thesis and offering replies to them.

2. Alasdair MacIntyre, *Whose Justice? Which Rationality?* (London: Duckworth, 1988).
3. Alasdair MacIntyre, *Three Rival Versions of Moral Enquiry* (London: Duckworth, 1990).
4. The origin of this chapter lay in a reading of Pierre Hadot, *Philosophy as a Way of Life: Spiritual Exercises from Socrates to Foucault*, ed. A. Davidson, tr. M. Chase (Oxford: Blackwell, 1995).
5. Hadot, p. 107.
6. A paraphrase of Wittgenstein's remark: '6.522   There are, indeed, things that cannot be put into words. They make themselves manifest. They are what is mystical:' Ludwig Wittgenstein *Tractatus Logico-Philosophicus,* tr. D. F. Pears and B. F. McGuiness (London: Routledge & Kegan Paul; 2nd edn, 1922), p. 151.
7. See for example A. D. Gilbert, 'Secularization and the future' in S. Gilley and W. J. Sheils (eds), *A History of Religion in Britain* (Oxford: Blackwell, 1994) pp. 503–21.
8. There are, however, some significant exceptions; see for example G. Santayana, *Winds of Doctrine and Platonism and the Spiritual Life* (Massachusetts: Peter Smith, 1971); M. McGhee (ed.), *Philosophy, Religion and the Spiritual Life* (Cambridge: Cambridge University Press, 1992); P. Sheldrake, *Spirituality and History* (London: SPCK, 1991); and for a helpful feminist deconstruction of the issue see Geraldine Finn's essay, 'The politics of spirituality: the spirituality of politics' in P. Berry and A. Wernick (eds), *Shadow of Spirit: Postmodernism and Religion* (London: Routledge, 1992), pp. 111–22. Arguably, the most important contribution is the ongoing series entitled 'World Spirituality: An Encyclopedic History of the Religious Quest' under the general editorship of E. Cousins (New York: Crossroad/London: SCM Press, paperback).
9. The notion of the supreme individual here is not necessarily (although it may be) Nietzschean in origin. Instead, it owes its debt to three sources: the Goffmanesque inhabitor of multiple social roles; the Sartrean existential self; and the libertarian political bargain-hunter. MacIntyre describes and analyses the first two in *After Virtue* (1981 edn), pp. 30–1. The third is carefully characterized by B. Jordan, *The Common Good: Citizenship, Morality and Self-Interest* (Oxford: Basil Blackwell, 1989), esp. pp. 35–6.
10. Wittgenstein, *Tractatus*, p. 149.

11. See MacIntyre, *After Virtue,* chs 6–8.
12. P. Vardy and P. Grosch, *The Puzzle of Ethics* (London: Fount, 1994), pp. 114–15.
13. Ibid., p. 145.
14. For a helpful introduction with detailed exegetical comment on some of the central texts in the major world faith and philosophical traditions see R. Solomon and K. Higgins (eds), *World Philosophy: A Text with Readings* (New York: McGraw-Hill, 1995).
15. See for example C. Raschke, 'New Age spirituality' in P. Van Hess (ed.), *Spirituality and the Secular Quest* (London: SCM Press, 1996), pp. 203–21.
16. See for example R. Ginzberg's comprehensive critique, 'Philosophy is not a luxury' in C. Card (ed.), *Feminist Ethics* (Lawrence, KS: University Press of Kansas, 1991), pp. 126–45.
17. See note 6 above.
18. Wittgenstein, *Tractatus*, p. 151.
19. See Ludwig Wittgenstein, *Philosophical Investigations,* tr., G. E. M. Anscombe (1953; 3rd edn; 2nd reprint, Oxford: Blackwell, 1992), especially sections 23–24; pp. 11–12.
20. See ibid., especially sections 81–85; pp. 38–40.
21. See note 4 above.
22. Hadot, *Philosophy*, pp. 81–125.
23. The most comprehensive account of the 'virtues' is still that given by Aristotle in the *Nicomachean Ethics*, tr. J. A. K. Thomson (rev. edn, Harmondsworth: Penguin, 1976).
24. Philo Jadaeus, *Who Is the Heir of Divine Things?* and *Allegorical Interpretations;* see Hadot, *Philosophy*, p. 111.
25. Hadot, *Philosophy*, p. 84.
26. Ibid., p. 90.
27. See Plato, *The Republic,* tr. D. Lee (2nd edn with revisions, Harmondsworth: Penguin, 1987), esp. pp. 505–525; part 7, book 6–part 7, book 7.
28. From Plato, *Phaedo*; quoted by Hadot, *Philosophy*, p. 94.
29. See R. Descartes, *Meditations on First Philosophy: With Selections from the Objections and Replies,* tr. J. Cottingham (Cambridge: Cambridge University Press, 1986).
30. See for example Genevieve Lloyd, *The Man of Reason: 'Male' and 'Female' in Western Philosophy* (New York: Methuen, 1984; 2nd amended edn, London: Routledge, 1993, repr. 1995).
31. See for example the texts mentioned in note 8 above. For an elaboration of Santayana's position see T. L. S. Sprigge, 'Spiritual life' in *Santayana: An Examination of His Philosophy* (London: Routledge & Kegan Paul, 1974), pp 209–17.

32. L. E. Johnson, *Focusing on Truth* (London: Routledge, 1992), p. 264.
33. See B. Mitchell, *Morality: Religious and Secular* (Oxford: Clarendon Press, 1980, repr. 1985), pp. 47–8.
34. P. F. Strawson, *Freedom and Resentment* (London: Methuen, 1974), cited in Mitchell, *Morality*, p. 48.
35. The phrase is taken from M. Oakeshott, 'On the theoretical understanding of human conduct' in *On Human Conduct* (Oxford: Clarendon Press, 1975), p. 2.
36. Hadot, *Philosophy*, p. 107.
37. J. Marenbon, *Later Medieval Philosophy* (London: Routledge & Kegan Paul, 1987).
38. This, Marenbon's first, is the one that is closest to Etienne Gilson's favoured approach in his celebrated *History of Christian Philosophy in the Middle Ages* (London: Sheed & Ward, 1953).
39. See L. P. Gerson, *God and Greek Philosophy: Studies in the Early History of Natural Theology* (London: Routledge, 1994).
40. Ludulph of Saxony, *Life of Christ*, cited in G. W. Hughes, *God of Surprises* (London: Darton, Longman and Todd, 1985), p. 53. This gave rise to the subsequent text by Ignatius Loyola, *Spiritual Exercises*, tr. A. Mottola, (New York: Doubleday, 1964).
41. R. Best (ed.), *Education, Spirituality and the Whole Child* (London: Cassell, 1996). The almost complete omission of the spiritual tradition is lamented by one of the contributors; see A. Rodger, 'Human spirituality: towards an educational rationale', pp. 45–63.
42. Michael Apple, *Teachers and Texts: A Political Economy of Class and Gender Relations in Education* (London: Routledge & Kegan Paul, 1986).
43. Alasdair MacIntyre, 'The idea of an educated public' in G. Haydon (ed.), *Education and Values: The Richard Peters Lectures* (Institute of Education, University of London, 1987).
44. MacIntyre, *Whose Justice?*, p. 402.

12

Awaking the Dragon – Chaplains' Perspectives on Spiritual Development

David Nixon

T he chaplain who decides to write about working in a higher education institute risks more of a swamp than a minefield. Minefields are likely to be frightening, dangerous and potentially lethal; swamps, on the other hand, suck you in, weigh you down and suffocate you. When you add 'spiritual and moral development' to higher education you seem to double the number of wet and boggy spots. The difficulties lie in three separate areas: firstly, comparison. Universities are so different from one another that legitimate comparison is difficult. Take, for example, Plymouth and Exeter Universities, both in Devon, around 50 miles apart, one with a student population of around 16,000 and one full-time chaplain (Plymouth), the other with about 8,000 students and four full-time chaplains (Exeter). Clearly chaplains will work in different ways not only depending on personal preferences and styles, but in response to the kind of institution they are working in. The second difficulty follows on: how to move beyond personal experience to say something about the topic which may have universal meaning. A third difficulty arises from the imprecision of the phrase 'spiritual and moral development'. The breadth of meaning which this phrase encompasses suggests that it is likely that with further enquiry we find that we are agreeing to mutually contradictory concepts and so a worthwhile enterprise is undermined from the outset.

To navigate on the high ground between these sloughs may not be fully possible, but to set an initial course is important. A key word here is 'development' (often ignored in the concentration on meanings of 'spiritual' or 'moral') since this implies a movement or a process to be engaged with. Its goal is uncertain but it is somewhere ahead, in the future; there is an expectation of change. This is helpful, since to write about a process gets beyond and behind the content or facts. These are the things around which the process is formed but they do not wholly contain it. Additionally, by engaging clearly with a process others may find that similar processes are at work for them while the content is quite different. This answers to some extent the objection of institutional difference. Similarly, my hope is that by telling a personal story in a process-orientated way the particular facts do not obscure what may be happening underneath. What is beneath the surface may be of interest, if only in raising further questions. At this stage it is important not to get caught in the trap of asking 'What is spiritual and moral development?' Rather I have chosen a phrase which encapsulates what I believe that we (as a group of chaplains in Exeter) are doing. The phrase forms the title of this chapter: 'awaking the dragon'.

The word 'awaking' is used because it optimistically implies that this sense is dormant or quiescent rather than simply dead. This stems from a key idea that God is at work in these places all the time, both visibly and invisibly. This may sit uncomfortably with some clergy (especially from the C of E) who think that God can only act when they invoke her! So the notion of awaking also implies a process of uncovering. It is first and foremost a process, hence the use of present participles. The process continues, the journey moves forward, but no real completion in this life is envisaged.

The 'dragon'[1] is an important symbol though an ambivalent one. On the one hand, within Christianity, the dragon has usually symbolized evil, something to control or eliminate (as in the story of St George, for example); on the other, within a wider culture including our own, the dragon speaks more positively of mysterious power and royalty. I am suggesting here that when we begin to awake or set free the powers of human spirituality, we are unleashing exciting but strong forces. We need to be mindful of the Bible's advice in John's first letter (1 John 4:1) that not every spirit comes from God. Yet without some risk we are set to remain enthralled by the predominant culture of our institutions, so that we become little more than passive receptors. The Eastern echoes of this word are deliberate as a recognition that Christianity can re-learn important lessors from Eastern faiths about stillness and detachment. Deliberate too is the echo of the heroin-user's phrase 'chasing the dragon', since our enterprise, while not illegal, may still be challenging to contemporary secularism.

Issues of identity and relevance

In an end of year report one of my colleagues likened the experience of being a chaplain to that of his recent purchase of an old Rover 2000. The charm of the car was its essential obsolescence. Was there a parallel here with chaplaincy? He wrote:

> Does our value reside only in the charm of persons who represent a set of values and beliefs that have essentially become antiquated and thus, perhaps at most, a source of curiosity and reassurance amidst an ever-evolving context? ... do we not appear as well-meaning individuals who duplicate in a more amateur fashion the services of support and encour-agement which the University already possesses? We might appear as more casual counsellors, more amiable advisors, more available academics.[2]

Our dilemma is nicely summarized as being irrelevant, either because our frame of reference (a God-orientated perspective) is shared by so few, or because we duplicate rather poorly what the university already provides professionally. My colleague sees the doctrine of the incarnation as a way through this dilemma: God sharing with us every moment of our humanity, including suffering and death, in a particular person and at a precise time, is our permission to share the lives of particular human beings around us in their myriad dimensions. If all this

205

activity is ultimately part of the gradual realization of God's Kingdom, towards which all of creation is being transformed, then our participation is not destructive of our distinctive identity. Indeed, as we participate in the lives of those we work with and they take part in ours, so we are all caught up in this movement of transformation.

> The supportive and encouraging word spoken to a student or staff member in crisis, the holding of someone's hand as they lie dying in a hospital bed, the attempt to persuade the University's policy-shapers that people are worth more than the value which the latest form of market-led assessment establishes: all of these are very human gestures but hidden within them is the stealthy approach of the kingdom.[3]

Towards a moral society

Having established in our own terms that our position is both tenable and valuable, we have to consider whether we simply allow God to direct us grace-fully to certain places and people or whether we seek them out. There are advantages and disadvantages with both approaches, but I am aware that not everybody wishes to be cared for. There is always the image used in pastoral counselling of a person whose hunted expression reflects more the pursuit of the carers than any other problem: it is so easy to intervene inappropriately.

Taking the corporate culture of the university as an example, I want to show how a group of chaplains suggested that the management process included more than economic issues. This picks up the point made in the quotation above and forms part of the concept of re-establishing a moral and spiritual sense. It also demonstrates some of the difficulties involved.

A little history to begin: April 1994 saw the arrival of a new vice-chancellor at Exeter from a senior position in the Civil Service. By October 1994 he had written an exciting discussion document entitled 'Towards a medium and longer-term strategy' which set out some of the issues facing Exeter University, including problems, and described a vision for the next five to ten years. Responses were invited. The chaplains met and formulated a reply which praised the notion of a shared vision as a community possession. However, certain deficiencies were highlighted:

> At any one time there will be those who feel that they 'cannot make the grade', who for one reason or another find themselves to be the meeting point of an intolerable array of pressures ... In particular a professional counselling service for staff is an urgent requirement ... We are concerned not just that persons should be enabled to survive the pressures they experience, but also continue to find the University a place in which, through the communal pursuit of knowledge and understanding, their labours will lead to the enhancement of their own humanity. A University should be a creative environment of fulfilment, not one destructive of human flourishing: a place of personal formation, not least for the staff as well as the students.[4]

Needless to say, while a summary of responses to the discussion document included a desire for increased attention to be given to staff welfare including a counselling service, the final published edition made no specific commitments. It did contain this paragraph:

> The University will aim progressively to enhance the working environment for its staff, particularly seeking to ensure that employment at the University is satisfying and enables personal and organisational development to take place and that the environment is safe and healthy.[5]

Somewhat less than two years later (May 1997) and following a progressive reduction in funding, Exeter University faces an uncomfortable future. A widely circulated document attempts to square the circle of reorganizing structures (a process of larger groupings of departments into Schools) at the same time as saving substantial sums of money in the academic staff budget. Cuts of 120 staff posts are envisaged, around 20 per cent, with potential replacement of 60.

The concerns of the chaplains focused on two areas: support for staff whose jobs are directly or indirectly threatened and for Heads of Departments whose role it will be to implement 'redeployment'; and secondly, an attempt to persuade senior management to invest in counselling and career services both now and in the world left after such cuts. While our approach to staff and Heads of Department has generally been welcomed, we have had only limited success with senior management. There has been some appreciation of the inequity of the first review and production of a second, gentler in tone. At least we continue a useful dialogue here and staff welfare now lies on the agenda.

A compassionate community

Hand-in-hand with this theme of a moral society runs a parallel track of compassion. Henri Nouwen reminds us that Christian compassion – the desire to share the sufferings of other human beings – is a strange quality. He contrasts this with a popular superficial understanding of compassion, the sort which is kindness to those hurt by competition, the oil which greases the cogs of the institution. He quotes the late American Senator Hubert Humphrey who picks up a long pencil with a small eraser at the end:

> 'Gentlemen, look at this pencil. Just as the eraser is only a very small part of this pencil and is used only when you make a mistake, so compassion is only called upon when things get out of hand. The main part of life is competition; only the eraser is compassion. It is sad to say, gentlemen, that in politics compassion is just part of the competition.'[6]

By contrast, radical Christian compassion derives from our view of God as one who, becoming incarnate in Jesus Christ, 'though he was divine did not cling to equality with God, but emptied himself, taking the form of a slave' (Phil 2:6–7); a God who in Jesus shares the pains of humanity in all its aspects, especially in death. The alternative, then, in a world of fragmented individuals is to create a solidarity, a community of compassion in which we all may grow. The chaplain's role is to identify and encourage such growth amongst staff, students and in himself.

For staff, the culture created by the mechanistic approaches of university management described above leads to vicious competition for scarce resources. There are victors, victims and the walking wounded. One response to this is to provide space both physically and spiritually where staff may find peace and refreshment. I have tried to create such a space in the chapel building and to encourage staff to use it for a retreat-like period in the working day. A little more formally, I convene a group which simply shares silence/meditation there once a week. Not all buildings are suitable for this but a little imagination and effort can transform unpromising beginnings – flowers, candles, arrangement of chairs, and so on. For most people the challenge is to be quiet and reflective ('centred'); once this is glimpsed, there seems afterwards a real craving for silence.

Students are usually the recipients of whatever policy decisions are made, and ostensibly the beneficiaries. In a more subtle way they assimilate an atmosphere which may or may not model good practice. It is imperative therefore that those who talk of creating a community of compassion are not made so busy by a structured timetable that they do not have opportunities for 'wasting time' with the student population. It seems obvious that, except for emergencies, any deepening insight into people's lives is developed over a period of time and after a number of encounters, many of which appear trivial. There is no substitute for spending time listening to and observing students, thereby giving them value. It also reveals the extent to which they do not share the same world-view as the majority of chaplains.

The use of e-mail may speed communication within a rapidly moving and dispersed population. Students are surprisingly willing to talk intimately via their keyboards in something which is reminiscent of the old-style confessional box.

We too may gain encouragement from the extent to which students are prepared to support those on the margins by giving cash and time. For example Exeter students have given a local AIDS charity more than £30,000 over a period of four years and helped to paint its premises. There was considerable fund-raising very recently to provide facilities for a student seriously disabled by an accident to enable him to complete his final year.

The encouragement to share the pain of others is predicated on the assumption that as chaplains we engage in our own process, which is frequently uncomfortable. This may be as a chaplains' group with or without an outside facilitator, or on our own. At the very least we are people who reflect on what we are doing and why, honestly appraising the successes and failures. Many of us wish to be people who provide a still centre in universities which appear unbalanced in human terms; to hold on to this is an achievement in itself.

Entering the sanctuary

For many chaplains leading worship, facilitating prayer groups and encouraging Christian student societies is seen as a primary task. However, there is much that militates against this: worship in a university context is seen as an increasingly alien occupation or at best another recreational activity. (If you don't join the Outdoors Society or Wine Tasting, why not try AngSoc or MethSoc instead?) There are clear questions about the validity of campus worship as opposed to joining local congregations, and a nagging suspicion that much organization is designed to justify the chaplain's existence and her sense of purpose. However unpromising, if we are going to 'awake the dragon' in this basic area of faith, we have to engage with it.

Again, a profound understanding of our context is an essential starting point for any decisions made in this area. When we discover we are working in a culture of competition, our worship may begin as an encouragement to share gifts and resources; when most of the week lays emphasis on what is divisive and fragmentary, a moment of prayer is about creating a gentle and tender human community, which looks beyond to the Divine. When worship at first sight seems alien in the context of late-twentieth-century institutions, with a sense of history both secular and sacred, it is soon the institutions and their own systems which reveal how alienating they are to human development. Worship then develops out of the pastoral context in which it is rooted:

> There is a desire within people, however inarticulate,
> to make sense of human experience. Liturgy, by

providing a structure of meaning, helps us to respond to that desire. It also creates a safe environment to push our questions hard and face perplexity. People come to church to be with God and to hide from God, to scream at God and to embrace God, to be with others and to be with themselves, to prepare for death and birth, marriage and divorce. Worship at its best is a place where people confront the depth of their own need in the presence of God.[7]

If we are serious about our worship, a radical review of our buildings may be needed. If we have chapels at our disposal, are they really necessary? If they are, how can they be adapted so that they give the same kind of message that we give verbally, or at least do not contradict it? A chaplaincy which says that it welcomes students but whose place of worship is cold and untidy is not using its resources effectively. If we are sharing space with others (which may be an appropriate mode of community), then how is it best prepared for worshipping God in an exciting way? There may be a need in our local university community for space to rehearse and practise music or drama, to house a playgroup, to provide refreshment and so on. It is possible for a chapel to reflect a multiplicity of community needs and for all to live in harmony.[8]

At Exeter, one of our most significant developments has been to meet weekly as an ecumenical group for worship at the Catholic Chaplaincy. The group includes Methodists, Baptists, Catholics, Anglicans, a United Reformed Church minister, a Quaker and a representative of independent churches in the city. We offer something integral to our own tradition in which we participate at the level which conscience or discipline allows. This is followed by coffee and informal business (and gossip). The different styles of worship have involved unfamiliarity and some pain at our broken communion, but beyond this there is a common sense of purpose in our relationship with the rest of the university. We are enabled to minister better our of this small worshipping community than from our more isolated denominational positions. Additionally, this group has provided a degree of support to its members and recalled the full-time chaplains to links with the wider church via those who work as city ministers as well. At present we have little or no contact with other faith groups. This is regrettable, but is largely for geographical reasons.

Prayer and worship is again an area in which the chaplain himself engages publicly and privately with the process he is encouraging in others. How this happens is partly dependent on personal history and preferences. I cherish the notion of inner space and like the way that George Maloney links this to the environment we inhabit. Perhaps this concern with 'green issues' is another point of entry between the Church's tradition and the student population.

> Man [sic] was to be healthy and full of life by breathing in the living power of God. But man polluted his interior environment. What we see around us as the pollution of the air, the streams, rivers, lakes and oceans, our woods and forest and countryside, and in the jungles of our cities, is but an *icon,* a dramatic image, externalized, of what man is doing within himself in the unlimited expanses of his 'inner space'.[9]

Blocking the Spirit

If our intention is to 'awake the dragon' of spiritual and moral development, many factors conspire to inject regular doses of anaesthetic. We too as workers in this field may unwittingly contribute to this process. The chief conspirator is the debate between types of language and the worlds they derive from.[10] While our natural home lies with the spiritual world (as opposed to the mechanical one) we do better to act as reconcilers than risk being accused of fundamentalism on the other side. There is also the danger that our energies are caught up in this debate to the detriment of our actual engagement in the development process. It is frankly disheartening to witness in many official university documents the extent to which human beings are no more than economic factors. To use the words of Robert Pirsig, it is like facing an impregnable wall where no contrary argument is heard; for shorthand he calls this a 'cultural immune system'.[11] On the other hand, this highlights the role of those who live with the language of the heart but also understand the language and world of current management.

An example from another discipline may persuade us that others are in harmony with this position. Oliver Sacks, in his moving account of patients suffering the after-effects of encephalitis, underlines the need of the medical profession to see beyond the diseased body to the diseased person. He describes a whole-person approach in almost mystical terms:

> all of us have a basic intuitive feeling that once we were whole and well; at ease, at home, at peace in the world; totally united with the grounds of our being; and then we lost this primal happy, innocent state and fell into our present sickness and suffering. We had something of infinite beauty and precious-ness – and we lost it; we spend our lives searching for what we have lost; and one day perhaps we will suddenly find it. And this will be the miracle, the millennium ... This sense of what is lost, and what must be found, is essentially a metaphysical one. If we arrest the patient in his metaphysical search, and ask him *what it is* that he wishes or seeks, he will not give us a tabulated list of items, but will say, simply, *My happiness, My lost health, My former condition, A sense of reality, Feeling fully alive* etc. He does not long for this or that; he longs for a *general* change in the complexion of things, for everything to be *all right* once again, unblemished, the way it was.[12]

Perhaps as chaplains we cannot hope to make everything all right once again, to return people to how things were; but we do offer the promise of reconciliation, the possibility of living in and with the new world, and deriving sustenance from it.

I have hinted throughout that we contribute to blocking the Spirit ourselves if we are less than fully committed to being part of the process. This includes being able to stand back from our involvement and reflect upon it; to consider the effect of our work and prayers on us personally and in terms of our faith. Equally, if we do not raise our eyes from immediate concerns and 'being busy' our vision will be dimmed.

David Nixon

Conclusions – process and paradigm

In this discussion of spiritual and moral development within higher education I have used the shorthand description 'awaking the dragon' to capture what I believe to be some of the processes involved. Among these I have singled out for further comment the way in which we seek to be both faithful to our tradition and relevant to the institution in which we work. The attempt to persuade the whole university that human values are as important as economic ones and that compassion is not an optional extra are developments from this first premise. Lest anybody imagine that God has been side-tracked here, worship is seen as an indelible part of this pastoral process, which may also include the re-ordering of our buildings. All these elements are like signposts on a path on which staff, students and chaplain are engaged together, sharing each other's joys and sorrows. Lastly, I have looked briefly at what slows down the process and deflects us from 'awaking the dragon', including our own responsibilities for this as chaplains.

I should like to finish by offering a further question which is one posed to universities and the churches alike, which derives from an appreciation of both. For Exeter (as for other traditional universities) the root problem lies in concepts of self-perception. Since the rapid expansion of student numbers in the 1980s and 1990s, the percentage of the standard age cohort has increased vastly (from around 7 per cent to over 30 per cent) and a higher number of mature students have entered; yet the kind of education offered is essentially the same. For the churches declining numbers and ever-ageing congregations have reduced their influence locally and nationally, and sometimes threatened their viability, yet so much remains sacrosanct. So the question to both institutions about self-identity is this: without losing the heart of what it is to be a university or a church, how can we set up new models or paradigms which are sustainable economically yet will also nourish us spiritually and morally for the next and subsequent generations? And a second part: Thomas Merton talks about the fruit of education as providing ways or paths which lead to the igniting of a spark which is 'a self beyond all ego, a being beyond the created realm'.[13] Is there something in the processes described in this article that the universities can offer to the churches, which may act as a spark to ignite the imagination and the soul?

Notes

1. For a fuller discussion of this, see B. Rowland, *Animals with Human Faces* (London: Allen and Unwin, 1974), pp. 66–70.
2. J. T. Law, 'Chaplains' Report to the Joint Trustees' (University of Exeter, June 1996), p. 1.
3. Ibid., p. 3.
4. J. T. Law and other chaplains, 'Towards a medium and longer term strategy – Chaplains' Group response' (University of Exeter, December 1994).
5. G. Holland, *Into the Twenty-First Century* (University of Exeter, June 1995), para. 7.5.
6. H. Nouwen, D. McNeill and D. Morrison, *Compassion* (London: Darton, Longman and Todd, 1982), p. 6.
7. R. Green, *Only Connect* (London: Darton, Longman and Todd, 1987), p. 13.
8. For an excellent discussion of re-ordering churches and resurrecting liturgies, see R. Giles, *Re-pitching the Tent* (Norwich: Canterbury Press, 1996).
9. Quoted in N. Roth, *Organic Prayer* (Boston: Cowley Publications, 1993), p. 4.
10. Discussed in Chapter 5 above, pp. 79–89.
11. R. M. Pirsig, *Lila, an Enquiry into Morals* (London: Black Swan, 1992), p. 66.
12. O. Sacks, *Awakenings* (London: Picador, 1991), p. 29.
13. Quoted in K. Deignan, 'Learning to ignite', *The Way Supplement*, 84 (Autumn 1995), p. 100.

Bread Not Stones – Nurturing Spirituality

Catherine Bowness and Marian Carter

C lues to the nurturing of spirituality, in both schools and institutions of higher education, need to be imaginative whilst critically reflecting government education working papers and discussion documents. The focus of this chapter is practical. The aim is to show where and how spirituality may be emphasized or explored and how official guidelines may either help or hinder the teacher or lecturer.

Background to the debate

The word 'spiritual' is present in British educational legislation.[1] The creation of a new inspection model necessitated advice on criteria for the inspection of spirituality. The document *The Framework for the Inspection of Schools*[2] attempted to define and give criteria for assessing the spiritual development of children. Legislation recognized spirituality as underpinning the whole curriculum and ethos of the school: spirituality was not limited to religious education. It defined spirituality as 'something fundamental in the human condition which is not necessarily experienced through the physical sense and or expressed through every day language. It has to do with relationships with other people and, for believers, with God.'[3] Spirituality is acknowledged as fundamental to being human; it is always relational, since humans are social beings. For some pupils personhood and relationships receive their meaning within God. The latter understanding will be a driving force in a Church school or college.

Spirituality has a long Christian tradition: see, for example, the poet Wordsworth:

> But trailing clouds of glory do we come
> From God, who is our home:
> Heaven lies about us in our infancy![4]

The theologian Kenneth Leech writes 'I believe that we can speak of spirituality as a necessary bedrock of the foundation of our lives, provided that we understand that we are speaking of the foundation and not of a compartment. ... to speak of spirituality in this sense is to speak of the whole life of the human person and human community in their relationship with the divine'.[5] Leech is deeply rooted in the political and social expression of spirituality.

Government reports display a fascinating attempt to grapple with meanings of 'spiritual': for example, 'Spiritual development relates to that aspect of inner life through which pupils acquire insights into their personal existence which are of enduring worth. It is characterised by reflection, the attribution of meaning to experience, valuing a non-material dimension to life and intimations of an enduring reality.' The evaluation criteria were to be 'a system of personal beliefs, which may include religious beliefs; an ability to communicate beliefs in discussion and behaviour; willingness to reflect on experience and search for meaning in that experience; a sense of awe and wonder as they become more conscious of deeper meanings in features of the natural world or their experience'.[6] Later a caveat was added reflecting the importance of spirituality, yet implicitly recognizing the demise of much institutional religion. 'Spiritual is not synonymous with religious, all areas of the curriculum may contribute to pupils' spiritual development.' Subsequently the criteria were amended to 'Spiritual development is to be judged by how well the school promotes opportunities for pupils to reflect on aspects of their lives and the human condition through, for example, literature, music, art, science, religious education and collective worship and how well the pupils respond'.[7] The latest guidance criteria ask

Does the school provide its pupils with knowledge and insight into values and religious beliefs and enable them to reflect on their experiences in a way which develops their self-knowledge and spiritual awareness? Effective provision for spiritual development ... depends on a curriculum and approaches to teaching which embody clear values and enable pupils to gain understanding through reflection on their own and other people's lives and beliefs, and their environment. It relies on teachers receiving and valuing pupils' ideas across the whole curriculum, for example, in stories, in pupils' writing, art, music, history and in religious education.[8]

Spirituality becomes a concern of the whole educational establishment.

Church involvement in discussion of spirituality was expressed through a variety of documents which welcomed the priority given to spirituality but indicated a distinctive Christian emphasis. The Catholic Education Service indicated a common starting point:

It is true. 'Spiritual' means 'of the spirit'. We are, therefore, talking about the development of the essence of a unique individual. 'Gaudium et Spes' (para. 15) refers to our ability to 'surpass the material universe', to 'share in the light of the divine mind'. The continuing search for 'more penetrating truths', 'the quest and love of what is true and good' are what spiritual development is all about ... In the Catholic tradition, spiritual development is inseparable from growth in faith, from life in 'the spirit of truth' (John 15.26), as we each help to bring creation to perfection and find our own true and lasting fulfilment.[9]

The Anglican tradition within education, whilst it shares much with the Roman Catholic tradition, has a different focus. Seminal to a Church school or college is the foundation document or Trust deed which roots the institution in the Christian tradition. The educational institution is not being true to itself if it does not reflect this history. Central to Christian belief are the Great Commandments 'You shall love the Lord your God with all your heart, and with all your soul, and with all your strength, and with all your mind; and your neighbour as yourself' (Luke 10:27 RSV). There is a holism about this understanding. Thus the definition of spirituality within educational establishments which have a religious foundation will have a focus which understands the transcendent as divine, though individual members of staff and pupils may not necessarily share a Christian stance – sensitivity is therefore important. The definition of spirituality in state schools may have a different emphasis but it should nevertheless enable pupils to recognize the place of spirituality in the understanding of their own humanity, and in relationships with others and the created world. Perhaps the depth of engagement with spirituality may be expressed as a continuum.[10] The following example is based on a sense of awe arising from the natural world: spirituality may range from

> unreflected acceptance of spirituality: 'Wow! It's snowing';
> reflection: 'All snowflakes are different, isn't that amazing?';
> reflection and recognition which has an effect on living: 'Snowing, that's wonderful but the birds will need feeding in the bitter weather';
> 'seeing' the experience in the context of God: 'What a wonderful world that there is so much difference in snowflakes, and God created it all'.

The sociologist Peter Berger[11] wrote about 'signals of transcendence' which are given in and through normal human experience. People can be spiritual without being religious, yet the 'signals',[12] reflected upon, may lead to an awareness of religion. Adrian Thatcher writes of spirituality as an 'achievement-word' implying some progress has been made in our response to our selves, neighbour and God, whether through supernatural grace, human effort or both.[13]

Spirituality is a challenge to the materialism, rationalism, secularism and individualism of much of our society. It is counter-cultural in that spirituality is characterized by relationality (therefore love, truth, justice, concern for the forgotten and marginalized), the intuitive, creative (non-rational), the transcendent, God. Love of neighbour, that is in biblical terms 'the stranger at the gate' (Deuteronomy 10:18–19), is not rational: it is about self-forgetful love. Is education's use of the term spiritual as a 'secular' or 'humanist' concept, borrowed from religion, adopting religious concepts without the religion, in contrast to a spirituality rooted in a historical Christian tradition?[14]

Recognizing spirituality in education

We will look at the implications of spirituality within three areas of the educational scene: the environment of education; the process and methods of education; the content of education.

The environment of education

In recent years education has been driven by the entrepreneurial spirit of the market place. There has been a competitive emphasis between schools and within schools. In higher education the judging of academic research has been seen as devaluing personal research interests in order to create an 'Ivy League' of top research institutions, leaving the skills of teaching students to a lower order. Education has been politically driven and prescriptive rather than a desire for the realization of the pupil's full potential. For example, schools have been mindful of league tables and parental choice. Academically successful schools have attracted parent choice. Funding based on numbers of pupils has tempted governors to refuse entry to those children who might not make the academic grade. Government statements have spoken about zero tolerance of failure and refer to the need to educate people to take their place in the workforce. Recently a Muslim leader was asked for his observations on government funding for Muslim schools. He replied that if the strings attached to finance included using the British National Curriculum, then he was worried. 'Education is not about preparing for the workplace. It is about life, learning of the Creator and of humanity's place in creation.'

The ethos of the school or college, central to the fostering of spirituality, is evident in the mission statements of institutions. The diocese of Bath and Wells advises its church-nominated inspectors that school ethos 'is about the way we do things here and why we do these things. It affects the quality of relationships, pupils' aspirations and the way the school is perceived by the wider community. The school's ethos will be derived from its core values and beliefs about its purpose and the aims of education.'[15] In a Church school or college one would expect the ethos to be demonstrably based on shared Christian beliefs, values and concepts, the love of God and the love of neighbour. The glossy school prospectus should contain more than recent school positions in the government league tables. It needs to be rooted in spiritual values, reflected in the school ethos, celebrated in collective worship, underlying the admissions policy, the content of the curriculum and the discipline policy of all members of the community. The mission statement is actualized in the environment of the school or college: each dimension, the psychological, social and physical, is undergirded by the spiritual.

The psychological environment of education

Spirituality is evident when each individual is valued and accorded worth. Press reports indicate a reluctance of some schools to take children with special educational needs; an emphasis on academic success and league tables may prompt schools to refuse them admission. The recognition that each child and adult is of worth, has gifts to offer but also needs to be met, is an obvious demonstration of practical spirituality.

Young children quickly imitate the models of adult behaviour around them. Children learn to show respect as they themselves are respected. They learn through watching the respect and courtesy shown by adults to one another, for example, the relationships between academic and ancillary staff or a member of staff's relationships with both a gifted and a struggling[16] child. An example from a playgroup illustrates the point. Marie was in a corner alone. The teacher said 'She's there because she's no good, she pulls other children's hair'. Marie was 4: at that tender age she had been excluded from the community. On another occasion, a visitor to a students' classroom asked which table was for the 'thick ones'. Such labels do not provide models of respect.

Some pupils enter education psychologically damaged, perhaps the result of a broken home, or a 'reconstituted' home where they may believe that they are not wanted by the step-parent or are considered an intrusion, and a reminder of a past relationship. They may be marked by distrust, hatred of themselves and others, cynically hiding their vulnerability and sensitivity, often by loud and bullying behaviour. The spiritual need of these children is for an affirmation of worth. They need school to be a safe place, where they are accepted and where they can learn that they are of worth and can trust themselves. Other pupils need to be shown how to welcome, accept and help those who enter school with difficulties, whilst those with problems need to be shown that they are accepted and need not stand alone. This is a long, hard task. The film *Kes* and more recently *Free Willy* are good illustrations of the power of transforming relationships.

School needs to be a safe psychological environment where children can 'play out' and express strong emotions or incidents which may be frightening to them. The 'home corner' is just such a safe place. In one school the home area had been turned into a 'hospital' where there were uniforms for 'doctors' and 'nurses' and 'stethoscopes' and 'medicines' to dispense. One 4-year-old was alone on a line of chairs, sitting very still. When asked by the teacher what he was doing he looked up in great surprise, saying 'I'm dead, of course'. The teacher immediately moved him into another task, missing an ideal opportunity to help the child to reflect on his feelings and explore his experience which for him identified 'hospital' and 'death'. On another occasion, the teacher was told that Peter, a Caribbean child, had a new baby in the family. When the teacher asked him what the baby was, the sharp reply was 'Black, of course'. The anger of the child suggested that already there was a distrust bred of societal, racial discrimination. Valuing reflects the biblical insight 'we love because he first loved us' (1 John 4:19 RSV), paralleling the psychological insight that humans need love and affirmation to grow into personhood.

Older pupils and students may experience levels of oppression and exploitation. To create a positive psychological environment to enable learning, teachers must express a solidarity with the sufferers, for example listening to the silenced voices of women, who are sometimes abused by peer group male students and members of staff. Evidence of spirituality is witnessed in acts that challenge a system which allows and perpetuates the diminishing of people through, for example, the abuse of power. We must work for human flourishing, not exploitation and the treating of people as things.

When a person is regarded as a spiritual being, he or she is valued, has dignity and worth, lives in integrity and is a moral agent with responsibility for and accountability to the neighbour, whoever that is. Respect for the dignity and worth of the other, since neighbour-love is communal, recognizes our human inability to live up to the ideal of love even in the face of the suffering of others. Forgiveness and reconciliation are needed, together with a vision of life as it could be and the faith that transformation is possible.

The social environment of education

An educational environment informed by spirituality will take community seriously. It will promote learning together as a shared experience. It will affirm the individual, recognizing that as a person is loved so s/he is released to love and value others. The psychologist Michael Rutter reminds us: 'all of us live in a social environment in which our interaction and relationships with others are of vital importance to us. The essence of humanity lies in communication with other people and in common with other social animals, development of personal ties and group relationships is fundamental.'[17] Our inner self or spirit grows and is fostered in relationships, between-ness. Relationships are guided by moral values. For the Christian community these are embraced in the Great Commandments. Jesus did not prescribe values but gave a set of principles for living which need to be worked out in experience. His parables dealt with ordinary people doing ordinary things and often ended with the question 'What do you think?' It may be argued, therefore, that lists of rules and values to be transmitted in a new section of the curriculum might not be so helpful as a chance to discuss decision-making in pupils' own lives and the life of the community in which they live. For example, values are reflected in how deficiencies and handicap, talent and success, are accredited without belittling those who have not succeeded. Here too the new focus on league tables is unhelpful. A child having difficulty with reading is given extra reading lessons so that she will catch up and 'pass' the standard assessment tests. She has to miss art sessions to fit in the extra reading. She hates doing this, as the extra lessons mark her out as different from fellow pupils. She also knows that she is good at art-based activities but is missing the chance to show her peers what she can do.

Another example is the exercising of discipline in a school: is it constructive? How is the offender treated? Does discipline recognize the failures of each of us, the possibility of reconciliation, recompense, forgiveness and the desire to begin again? A National Society report suggests 'A school discipline policy should always be designed to provide a basis of self discipline. If it becomes too dependent on the staff enforcing the acceptable standards then it does not carry the seeds of further growth to maturity ... It is only be being trusted that we learn to be trusted. Within a school where every human being is accorded that respect shown to unique human beings loved by God, this should come naturally, and where there are failures, as there will be, these can be dealt with, not as disasters, but as experiences from which learning can grow.'[18]

The physical environment of education

Modern Western society is dominated by a rampant materialism. A quick fix, 'throw away' society has developed, which is frequently careless of the long-term physical environment. Thus the importance of the physical world is diminished. Is this indicative that the physical doesn't matter? Is there a dualism? Incarnation is a central affirmation of the physical body. Beauty of shape and colour in buildings can be powerful, speaking of thought, care, awareness of people's needs; it 'raises the spirit'. On the other hand, educational buildings in disrepair, or those where the needs of people have not been a priority, can lead to despair.

Education establishments decorated with displays, posters, models, exhibits can stimulate and provoke questions, raise awareness, deepen understanding. We have known schools where pictures have been borrowed from a local art gallery: children looked and were challenged to ask why the artist painted particular scenes, what was s/he trying to say about being human and living in the world? Questions of meaning and worth are thus raised.

Schools where pupils' work is handled with care and displayed tastefully speak implicitly to children of their worth and value.

Some educational establishments use their grounds for educational purposes. A primary school created a garden with a pond for fish and amphibians, nesting places for birds and habitats for butterflies. The choice of plants and stones and the position and layout of each was carefully thought out for the sake of the well-being of the wild creatures the pupils hoped to attract. The project led to the formation of a junior branch of the Royal Society for the Protection of Birds. Children spent time simply watching the birds, classifying, noticing differences and exploring the reasons why, talking about migration, wondering about flight, safety and the return journey. They imagined what it would be like to be a migrating bird. This led to a concern for the welfare of the natural world and the recognition of responsibility – awe, wonder, mystery were grounded in reality. The grounds also created a place of quiet for silent reflection.[19] Children realized their responsibility for the natural world, and the interrelationship of the web of creation. Humans are not the centre of the world. There developed a sense of humility in the face of the majesty of creation. Creating a garden raised issues of speciesism, of working for a sustainable and just life-style for all creatures, since humans live in a symbiotic relationship with nature. It led to wondering about origins and creation: to the exploring or creation spirituality and to the expression of feelings and experience in many different media, for example this poem called 'Autumn thoughts':

> As the grass turns gold the birds leave my heart
> the hedgehog scuttles as night falls
> leaves fall down in colours
> squirrels hurry around the forest floor
> the country turns to fire as celebrations come.[20]

Here the child has transcended her humanity and identified with the migrating birds. A group of children watched spellbound as a chrysalis split open and a bedraggled butterfly emerged, pushed out and shook its wings. One child said 'It's resurrected'. These are profound spiritual experiences.

225

Process/methods of education

Much classroom learning is driven by ends. It is prescriptive, rational and utilitarian, leaving little room for spirituality. The process of learning guided by spirituality will stress that 'the mind is not a vessel to be filled but a fire to be kindled' (Plutarch). The process of learning which reflects spirituality will be characterized by emphasis on intuition, experience, imagination, silence in the face of mystery, wondering, open exploration, being as well as doing, reflecting, giving 'space for the spirit', holism and making connections. For example, the Nuffield science project (launched as far back as 1968) opened with the statement 'Let us remember to dream and then we will discover the truth'.[21]

Robert Waddington recognizes that education 'ordering the process whereby children can increase in understanding and develop particular competences can signal man's essentially contingent place in the universe which circumscribes boundaries to his knowledge and experience yet allows new discoveries. This contingency is an aspect of man's finitude and sensing it is the first step on the road to humility before God.'[22] The process of education will lead us to mystery in the face of situations where there is no answer. Derek Webster locates spirituality in that divine mystery who is at the heart of human existence. Awareness of this mystery is simultaneously an awareness of God. 'Unless young people are helped not only to question, but to question the questioning: not only to intellectualize but to ponder the intellectualizing; not only to learn but to move to what lies both within and behind the learning; then they lose one of the most significant parts of education.'[23]

The Church school or college must be a place of challenge. The method of Jesus the teacher is a good one. 'Our Lord challenged his opponents – he coerced none, he invited them to seek, listen, think and perhaps most of all, to trust.'[24] The process of education in a Church foundation may be a counter-culture. 'The Christian teacher, however, will reflect upon and test the success of the teaching situation not only with educational criteria ... but ... the model of Christ as teacher – the one who enables disclosures. Christ's reference to the hidden process of growth of seeds hidden in dark, deep moist soil, might lead to reflections on education's obsession with measurement, management by achievable objectives, its pre-occupation with certified academic success.'[25]

The process of education informed by spirituality will be an 'opening of windows', not a premature forcing. It will give time and silence through encouraging reflection to struggle with the mysteries of life, discovering that a number of answers may be appropriate or silence in the face of mystery.

The process will make links across disciplines. The expressive arts and technology were successfully linked with religious education in a middle school when 11-year-old pupils used computer technology to design a quilt based on the story of the life of the Buddha. They then constructed the quilt by hand, working together as a team with classroom assistants. The finished product was a resource for a storytelling session with 5–7-year-old children at the next-door first school. The quilt now hangs in the school entrance hall as a symbol of achievement and team spirit. This illustrates a further characteristic of process for, in the spiritual dimension, both teacher and learner are on a joint venture where even the teacher is allowed to say 'I do not know the answer to that question. What do you think?'

The process of learning begins with the experience of the pupil, whatever that is. A child may be fearful of his/her own feelings of anger or jealousy. The recognition of the reality of evil within us and without is central; as Shakespeare wrote, 'this thing of darkness, I acknowledge mine'.[26] A teacher working with children at a Church of England first school (5–7-year-olds) delved into the book of Psalms to encourage her pupils to think about their own spiritual experiences. Working from the Good News Bible, her class explored creation, the wonder of an annual harvest, death, fear, joy, sadness, finding somewhere special, and the power of being still and quiet. Pupils first read or listened to a variety of Psalms being spoken or sung, and discussed their meanings for the original writer and for people throughout the ages, including our own time. They then painted pictures, wrote music, told stories, danced, made bread, planted seeds and composed their own psalms. This would appear to contradict the commonly held view that the use of biblical material in schools appears outdated and would therefore be unpopular with pupils. Biblical work, when set in the context of pupils' own lives, can encourage them to explore their own feelings about their place in the world and may offer them inspiration for their own creativity. The teacher said 'Throughout their work pupils amazed me by giving glimpses of their true selves. Most expected, but nevertheless moving, was work on Psalm 8, for example, "My favourite bit of God's creation is my Mum and Dad".' Evidence of a recent showing of *Free Willy* on television shone through in another response, a poster of a bright blue sea with a rainbow sky, and the caption "Dear God let all the whales be free".' Most telling were the results of creative writing based on Psalm 23 relating to overcoming fear. One child wrote 'I am scared of spiders and snakes and sometimes my sister, also when I get lost in a big shop without my Mum but mostly I get scared when I hear about horrible diseases and see people smoking, when I am on my bike and there is a lorry behind me it is scary. I was scared when there was a bomb in Bournemouth.' The teacher worked with her pupils, helping them to express their fears and talking about how they could be overcome. The fact that she was able to do this at all depended on the trust that the school had built between teacher and student. Finally, work on Psalm 150 expressed the joy of being alive and culminated in the sharing of things which make people happy – family, friends, pets, being in Class Five – in whole-school collective worship. During all the activities pupils were encouraged not only to speak and share their own thoughts but also to listen to the hopes and fears of others. Pupils should obviously be made aware that, for religious believers, the Bible is a sacred text, but by also treating it as a collection of thoughts about the human condition, stimulus for exploring a variety of human emotions and responses to the wider world is given. While non-religious texts may be used to encourage sensitive thinking, it could be argued that the Bible adds another dimension, often missing in discussions: the possibility of human relationships with a creator.

The process of education means taking the pupils' experience seriously as a starting point for growth and maturation. It is expressed in the following story: 'The disciple said to the Master, "Teach me wisdom and learning". Said the Master, "These are two different things. You will get learning by listening to people and reading books, by then talking and thinking about them." "And wisdom?" asked the disciple. The reply was, "You get wisdom by listening to your own story. You are a book which you have to read and study. This is very difficult and never ends. Each day there is a new page. Each moment brings a new thought, each person a new plot in the book that is you." '[27] Parker J. Palmer in his book *To Know As We Are Known: A Spirituality of Education* criticizes an education which is predominantly the transmitting of information.[28] He explores the ancient wisdom reflected in the Desert Fathers and Spiritual Guides of prayer. In essence the author uses the monastic tradition of the three disciplines: the study of sacred texts, the practice of prayer and contemplation, and the gathered life of the community. He parallels this with secular schools (study of texts, reflection on experience, and the ethos of the school) so that schools and education are inevitably and necessarily involved in spiritual formation, the attainment of self-knowledge, shared wisdom, and profound understanding of the human heart and the nature of the world.

The content of education

There is a common misconception that spirituality belongs to the religious education, religious studies or theology department or is the responsibility of the primary RE co-ordinator. Certainly the British Education Reform Act of 1988 identified two components of the curriculum i.e. religious education (including collective worship) and a National Curriculum, but spirituality was not confined to the former.

All the subjects of the curriculum are vehicles for spirituality; however, RE and collective worship are obvious carriers. The aims of religious education are to enhance pupils' spiritual, moral, cultural and social development by:

> developing awareness of the fundamental questions of life raised by human experiences, and of how religious teachings can relate to them

> responding to such questions with reference to the teachings and practices of religions, and to their own understanding and experience

reflecting on their own beliefs, values and experiences in the light of their study.[29]

The guidance of government inspectors gave clues to approaches to spirituality in Religious Education: Although religious education and spiritual development are not synonymous, religious education can make a significant contribution to spiritual development. Inspectors might consider, for example, whether religious education encourages pupils to consider life's fundamental questions and how religious teaching can relate to them; respond to such questions with reference to the teaching practices of religion as well as from their own experience and viewpoint; and reflect on their own beliefs or values in the light of what they are studying in RE.'[30] When a British government working party produced model syllabuses for religious education[31] the suggested attainment targets were 'learning about religion' and 'learning from religion'. Critics of the approach suggested that there should be another dimension: the need also to 'engage with religions', i.e. to discuss and challenge religious teaching in the light of pupils' own experiences.[32] Where a syllabus specifically mentions a study of biblical passages a focus on the frailty of humanity could encourage young people to think about their own identity within a community or to discuss major issues within society. The Jewish story of the child Moses, abandoned to his fate in the rushes, could lead to a focus on helplessness, i.e., the helplessness of a baby or of people trapped in slavery. The story of Moses leaving Egypt after committing murder can lead to a discussion of uncontrolled anger and fear. Questions of authority are raised in the story of his return to Egypt, whilst ingratitude, a common human failing, is found after the crossing of the Red Sea. Young people could be encouraged to think about the things from which they would wish to escape, how they act themselves when under pressure and whether society is fair to all its members. This could develop into a theme of what it means to be a human being in an unfair world. This should not be taken to imply that aspects of Jewish faith and the meaning of Passover should be removed from the Moses story. We are simply suggesting adding another dimension to the traditional story in addition to the religious background. Thus passages from the scriptures of the major religions may be seen to speak not only to religious people but also to humanity as a whole. Care of course needs to be taken to ensure that in discussions about human nature the religious meanings behind stories from scripture or religious rites of passage are not omitted.

Four students, all RE specialists, were recently invited to a school to teach rites of passage. They took with them their own knowledge, experience and skills, Having viewed *Eggshells and Thunderbolts*,[33] they liked the idea of taking promises as a central theme for a study of marriage. They researched the promises made in Christian, Sikh and Hindu weddings and aimed to ask pupils to think about what promises they would ask a bride and groom to make, the most important part of these weddings in all cases being the promises made before God. The teacher was frightened by this idea. 'We cannot focus on promises made at weddings because most of these children have parents who are divorced. Let's just talk about what people wear at weddings instead.' The teacher seemed frightened of the 'spiritual dimension', the most important area of the topic. Interestingly, the children wanted to talk about promises, and after the students' supervisor had talked to the teacher, the students were able to explore promises made in marriage with the children. The lesson ranged from looking at the frailty of being human, of broken promises as a reality, vision and hopes of what might be.

Identity – *what does it mean to be human?*

'Spiritual' means 'of the spirit'. Here we are talking about the growth of the essence of a unique individual. Every young person, from beginning at school through formal education and beyond, has the right to be regarded as a special individual, living a meaningful and valued life. Modern living is full of rapid change and pressures and each stage of life brings challenges to identify. At 5 years (in Britain) the child enters school, bearing the socializing patterns from the home. Immediately s/he is faced with a bewildering amount of change. Having been a member of a small family unit, the pupil becomes an individual within a large group many of whom are strangers. The school will welcome new pupils, placing them into a new class unit. However, the child will soon have to learn that, whilst they are an important member of the reception group, other class members may have needs greater than their own. At this stage RE programmes of study on 'Myself' will help move the child from an egocentric phase by helping to build relationships with others, encouraging the valuing of self and recognizing difference. Psalms of praise are of particular help here (Psalms 4:7; 40:5; 106; 150). Young children make spiritual sense of life: one very aware 3-year-old said 'Grown-ups have the babies, that's us. We grow up. Adults die. We have the babies. The babies grow up. We die and so it goes on.' Another asked her parents 'What did you do before I was born? Didn't you miss me?' Here is the beginning of a sense of belonging.

At 8–11 years, pupils have developed relationships with others and are beginning not only to notice their own feelings and responses to events and people around them but also to understand why society as a whole values and upholds certain attitudes and believes that others are wrong and should not be accepted by the community. Themes here are related to friendship, loyalty, belonging and justice.

The move to secondary school (at 11 in Britain) is frequently dramatic. The sheer size of the school itself is daunting. New subject specialisms have to be developed and a large number of teachers encountered, each with different teaching styles and expectations. Friends may change, journeys to school lengthen. Puberty is beginning, with hormonal changes which may be accompanied by massive mood swings. As independence continues and identity forms, authority is questioned. The needs of the adolescent are for adult models, i.e. those who will listen to the young person, encourage questioning, and not often be shocked. Themes at 11–14 years would include: What it means to be human: the responses of science and religion; What cost friendship?; The influence of peer group pressures; Family and what it means to belong.

From the age of 14 is a period of even more pressure, from the peer group to conform to fashionable activities and dress, from teachers to do well in examinations, perhaps even from parents to fulfil their hopes. It is also a period when pupils recognize acutely the hurt and evil in the world and a lack of justice. In the mid-teenage mind concepts of suffering, famine, wars and ecology abound. An idealism that can change the world alternates with a suicidal despair at the hopelessness of the world created by adults. This can be a stage of isolationism for pupils. Themes in the classroom need to be honest, open and encourage vision.

Pupils aged 16–18 years are making decisions about the future: Who are my real friends? What am I going to do with my life? Students become adults at 18, yet many 18-year-olds in fact have less responsibility than their earlier counterparts who waited until they were 21 to come of age. The 18-year-old adult may still live in the parental home, yet is not in most cases eligible for any adult welfare benefit until the age of 25. These adults, who are not thought of by society as adults, need time to think and prepare themselves for the world of work and leisure. Those who reach higher education have further pressures of identity raised by the sudden release for many from the restraints of home. Loneliness can be an issue. Questions of uncertainty abound: Am I up to this? Can I make it? Increasing financial pressures, new challenges of a drinking and drug culture, the awareness of sexual availability, make the first undergraduate year a time for serious thinking and adjustment.

Underlying each stage, therefore, are pertinent questions of identity. Who am I? Does life have a meaning? Why do people suffer? What is right? The educational process is a long one: indeed the current British government is now promoting a new culture of 'life-long learning'.[34] With this in mind, a spiritual education should provide a healthy environment for individual growth and place emphasis on the value of each person as they grow into maturity. For the Christian, maturity is about wholeness and salvation. Rowan Williams expresses it: 'Spirituality becomes far more than a science of interpretation of exceptional private experiences; it must now touch every area of human experience, the public and the social, the painful, negative, even pathological byways of the mind, the moral and relational world. And the goal of a Christian life becomes not enlightenment but wholeness – an acceptance of this complicated and muddled bundle of experiences as a possible theatre for God's creative work.'[35]

Death – finality or frontier?

A topic on death raises spiritual questions. Young children are fascinated by death, though they realize neither its finality nor their own mortality. At 5–7 years children may experience the death of a pet, maybe a favourite grandparent or on occasions a classmate. Opportunities can be made to engage in rituals – e.g. the burial of a pet – encouraging respect in death and special times of remembering. Story can be used, the opportunity given to express feelings in paint, music or dance; seeds found and planted can give ways into conversations about endings and beginnings. *Eggshells and Thunderbolts*,[36] at 8–11 years, illustrates some powerful work linked with memorials and remembering favourite people who have died, resulting in a natural introduction to the remembering of Jesus and the Last Supper. Pupils of 11–14 can spend time looking at different losses: hair, milk teeth, friends on moving school, loss in the natural world, the processes of growth, maturity and death. Loss is natural. How do we use it and grow through it?

Pupils over 14 years may be able to reflect more deeply on experience. Issues of personal uniqueness, interrelationships and interdependence together with a growing need for a new independence during the middle teens become more significant. The issue of death in the wider context of its link with humanity's perpetration of evil, through war and violence or within racism, becomes a topic for exploration. Teenagers often raise questions about the meaning and purpose of life. Who are we? What happens when we die? Why do we have to do this? We didn't ask to be born! Bob Geldof called his autobiography *Is That It?* This was clearly an odd title but it deliberately implied a question often on the lips of human beings – 'surely there is more to life than this, isn't there?' A teacher, who had once been a member of a silent monastic order, used to ask his pupils to debate whether death should be seen as a door or a wall.

Spirituality in the curriculum

What of other subjects on the curriculum? Language teaching which is caring, positive and affirms the individual can be a vehicle for spirituality. Storytelling is often a safe way to explore deeper questions with children. The characters in the story may not be real but the situations in which they are found might help pupils look further into difficult situations without the danger of being judged themselves. Stories from traditional children's classics may be read and discussed to good effect. Oscar Wilde's *The Happy Prince* or *The Selfish Giant* may highlight attitudes towards others, e.g., coldness, kindness, generosity, selflessness, by allowing pupils to focus on the actions and feelings of the major characters, e.g., the swallow who was prepared to die for his love of the Prince, the town officials who wanted to tidy up the community statue but had forgotten what the Prince had done for the people. The pupils could discuss what they would think or do if they were in the fictional character's shoes.

Kenneth Grahame's *The Wind in the Willows* could be used to consider an individual's perception of events and actions: did Toad steal a motor car, as claimed by the judge, or did he simply borrow it? More modern tales on thinking of others include Shirley Hughes's *Dogger,* concerning property, a favourite toy, and thinking of the pain of others; Raymond Briggs' *The Snowman,* which could be used for a focus on making and losing friends and/or death, sorrow and remembering; Roberto Innocenti's *Rose Blanche,* the stupidity of grown-ups at war through the eyes of a small German child; and for older pupils Ann Holm's *I Am David,* a boy's search for his own identity, God and his mother as he escapes from a concentration camp and makes a long journey across Europe; and Ted Hughes's *The Iron Man* with its links with ecology, creation and care of the planet. Good teachers have already spotted the richness of literature and encourage their pupils to use story as a basis for group discussion or creative writing and role play on spiritual issues. At college level Shakespeare is constantly challenging spiritual issues of the human condition, as is the work of many contemporary writers – the poetry of Sylvia Plath and the novels of Alice Walker such as *The Color Purple* are immediate examples.

Poetry, read, or written by children, can introduce spiritual moments. Whether the stimulus be a book of nursery rhymes or a Shakespearean sonnet, we encourage teachers to be brave in their interpretation of the literacy hour in primary school and English literature periods at secondary level and to make more room, even within traditional whole-class teaching, for spirituality. The beauty of good language within poetry, symbol, story and myth gives exposure to the rich resources of stories that excite and depict virtues and build character, such as the use of biographies of those who have struggled to overcome handicap and disadvantage. Queen Elizabeth II in a Christmas broadcast said of Nelson Mandela 'that most gracious of men has shown us all how to accept the facts of the past without bitterness: how to see new opportunities as more important than old disputes and how to look forward with courage and optimism. His example is a continuing inspiration.' Such stories act for pupils as exemplars of the spiritual life. Literature is an opportunity to recognize, reflect on, and be moved by the existence and experience of others.

The visual arts have a history of pointing to the transcendent. Sister Wendy Beckett wrote 'One of the mistakes we make is to think that God only comes to us through religion. Wherever there is beauty, and truth, there is God; not under his rightful name but anonymously. It doesn't work with bad art. Bad art only occupies the mind. The depths are left unchallenged. Good art puts us in touch with the transcendent.'[37] Through symbol, line and colour, pupils encounter and are able to express spirituality in profound ways. At a recent course for head-teachers of Church schools, the group was provided with creative materials – wire, clay, tissue paper, material, card, ribbon, lace, plant pots, garden canes. They were asked to work individually or in pairs. The process involved looking at the materials, feeling them, and letting them 'speak' of the transcendent. The results surprised everyone. One teacher had begun with a clear idea of what she wanted to do, imposing her 'will' on the materials, but it didn't work. She had to look and feel the clay that she had chosen as a medium. The resulting form was of something beautiful and enriching.

Music offers much to spiritual education. Pupils of all ages can be encouraged to develop the skill of listening, perhaps finding empathy with the composer or the players in the orchestra or group. They may be encouraged to think about what emotions the music evokes for either the composer or the listener. They may wish to compose their own music.

With their emphasis on examinations, literacy and numerical skills and the need to prepare pupils for employment, is there a danger of all creativity being squeezed out of educational establishments? Being creative for its own sake, rather than for certification, may be one area where spirituality comes into its own. Perhaps we need to encourage educational institutions to give some time for dreaming, no matter how much pressure there is to move up the league tables. The joys of the arts, music, dance, drama, painting and creativity for its own sake are vital for a full and rich human experience. The technological age is here to stay, but it should assist human development, not stifle it.

Mathematics is not simply instrumental but also about discovering awe and wonder which underlie order and pattern, discovering beauty in mathematical formulae and recognizing the insights given to maths, for example, through the Hindu and Muslim cultures of Indian and Arab scholars.

Science education may be able to create an alternative concept to a science which frequently has been dominated by power and profit, exploiting animals and polluting the physical world. An education which depends on intuition and inspiration will challenge dualism and see the inter-relatedness in the natural world. Value and respect for the physical world may engender feelings of awe and wonder in the face of the rich diversity and interdependence of the natural world, the mystery of life, humanity's role as stewards of creation. Pupils can be encouraged to show respect in observing plants without picking specimens, gathering only live species or insects that can be returned to their natural habitat, observing creatures in their natural habitat and context if possible rather than in the classroom. Within sex education, pupils can be encouraged to recognize themselves as created, sexual beings, marvel at difference and delight in complementarity. A spirituality of sexuality may be expressed in life-giving ways, in giving and receiving of love, care, respect and wanting the best for the other as against the misuse of bodies to exploit others.

Collective worship remains a controversial issue. Within Christianity believers celebrate their shared humanity in the context of their Christian faith. In an educational community, even one with a religious foundation, it cannot be assumed that all who gather together for worship are practising members of a faith community who would be familiar with ritual or liturgy. In an educational context, collective worship cannot mirror adult forms of worship. The ages, aptitudes and interests of the participants must be considered. A 14-year-old pupil from a multi-faith school explained 'Worship to us should not be old-fashioned, or only about sick or dead people'. Similarly, a pupil at a Roman Catholic high school said 'Worship could be entertaining. Religion does not have to be boring.' Perhaps in spiritual terms more focus needs to be put on the word 'collective', then worship could become the heart of the life of a community which comes together to share and to celebrate what the institution values or to mark special occasions. It is from this togetherness that spirituality grows. Sometimes collective worship offers comfort in grief, for example, reactions to the shooting of the young children at Dunblane or the death of a member of the community. It can become a communal celebration of achievement in overcoming difficulties, or a successful sponsored walk.

Although worship implies a relationship with God, members of the community who do not confess a religious faith also deserve time for reflection and celebration. They too can touch the spiritual. The use of music (popular or classical), dance and poetry are invitations to encounter mystery. Successful worship often involves a sharing of the participants' own creative response to the world around them. Removed from the constraints of the traditional 'hymn–prayer sandwich', creative collective worship can offer the spiritual dimension to all participants.

As we approach a new millennium, it is a good time to reflect about individuals and the future. Is the latter to be one of hope or danger? Are there real fears? Our vision is a future not driven simply by industry and the computer but one that can add to the technological age the space to breathe, grow and dream, to give 'space for the spirit'. Spirituality is at the heart of the life of the Church school or college which is richly enabled to witness to one who said 'I came that they might have life, and have it abundantly' (John 10:10 RSV).

Notes

1. The Education Act of 1944 lay dormant. However, it was reiterated in the 1988 Education Reform Act which was set within a broad context, that of promoting 'the spiritual, moral, cultural, mental and physical development of pupils and of society'.
2. Ofsted, 'The framework for the inspection of schools', Part 2 of the *Handbook for the Inspection of Schools* (London: DfEE, August 1993), p. 21.

3. National Curriculum Council, *Spiritual and Moral Development* (London: NCC, April 1993).
4. William Wordsworth, Ode 'Intimations of Immortality' (1807), stanza 4.
5. Kenneth Leech, *The Eye of the Storm* (London: Darton, Longman and Todd, 1992), p. 16.
6. NCC, *Spiritual and Moral Development*, p. 21.
7. Ofsted, *Framework for the Inspection of Schools* (London: HMSO, 1995), p. 19, section 5.3.
8. Ofsted, *Guidance on the Inspection of Nursery and Primary Schools* (London: HMSO, October 1995), pp 83–4. To the extent that spiritual insights imply an awareness of how pupils relate to others, there is a strong link to both moral and social development.
9. Catholic Education Service, *Spiritual and Moral Development Across the Curriculum: A Discussion Paper for the Professional Development of Teachers in Catholic Schools* (London: Catholic Education Service, 1995), pp. 11–12.
10. There is a parallel here with collective worship, which covers a range of participants, staff and pupils, from those who have no formal religious beliefs to those who are committed to a living faith. The importance of celebrating shared values and acknowledging shared failure is communal, helping non-believers to the 'threshold' of worship as traditionally understood.
11. Peter Berger, *A Rumour of Angels: Modern Society and the Discovery of the Supernatural* (Harmondsworth: Pelican, 1969), pp. 70–96.
12. Berger noted five signals: the sense of order; the phenomenon of play; the experience of hope; the concept of damnation – a sense of cosmic injustice to be put right; the fact of humour.
13. Adrian Thatcher, ' "Policing the Sublime": A wholly (holy?) ironic approach to the spiritual development of children', in Jeff Astley and Leslie J. Francis (eds), *Christian Theology and Religious Education* (London: SPCK, 1996), p. 120.
14. The Christian mystics St Teresa of Avila and St John of the Cross, for example, could not speak of 'spiritual' without reference to the love of God and the love of neighbour.
15. Diocese of Bath and Wells, *Framework for Inspection* (1996), p. 2.
16. In Britain the word 'statemented' is used to refer to a range of the child's special needs.
17. Michael Rutter, *Maternal Deprivation Reassessed* (2nd edn; London: Penguin, 1981).
18. D.W. Lankshear, *A Shared Vision: Education in Church Schools* (London: National Society, 1992), p. 64.

19. The creation and setting 'apart' of a quiet place or area in an educational establishment is central for the fostering of spirituality, not to indulge a private, individual narcissism, but, in the words of the mystic Thomas Merton, 'I meditate not to escape the world but to listen more intently to its voices'. Similarly, the encouragement of silence and meditation allows 'space for the spirit'.

20. Amy Illingworth, aged 7.

21. Nuffield Foundation, *Nuffield Foundation Science Teaching Project* (London: Nuffield Foundation, 1968).

22. Robert M. Waddington, 'No apology for theology' in L. J. Francis and D. W. Lankshear (eds), *Christian Perspectives on Church Schools,* (Leominster: Gracewing/Fowler Wright, 1993), pp. 43–4.

23. Derek Webster, 'A spiritual dimension for education?' in Leslie Francis and Adrian Thatcher (eds), *Christian Perspectives for Education* (Leominster: Gracewing/Fowler Wright, 1990), p. 362.

24. Alan Brown, *The Multi-Faith Church School* (London: National Society, 1992), p. 9.

25. Waddington, 'No apology for theology', p. 45.

26. Shakespeare, *The Tempest,* Act 4.

27. Derek Webster, *Collective Worship in Schools* (Cleethorpes: Kenelm Press, 1995), pp. 123–4.

28. See Parker J. Palmer, *To Know As We are Known: A Spirituality of Education* (San Francisco: Harper and Row, 1983).

29. *Model Syllabuses for Religious Education,* Model 1: 'Living Faiths Today' (London: SCAA, 1994), p. 4.

30. Ofsted, *Guidance on the Inspection of Nursery and Primary Schools,* pp. 83–4.

31. *Model Syllabuses.*

32. V. Baumfield, C. Bowness, D. Cush and J. Miller, *A Third Perspective* (Exeter, 1995).

33. *Eggshells and Thunderbolts: RE and Christianity in the Primary Classroom* (CD ROM and video pack; BBC and Culham Institute, 1993).

34. See *The Learning Age: A Renaissance for a New Britain* (London: HMSO, 1998).

35. Rowan Williams, *The Wound of Knowledge* (London: Darton, Longman and Todd, 1990) p. 2.

36. See note 33 above.

37. Sister Wendy Beckett, *The Times* (16 February 1994).

Name Index

Apple, Michael 198
Aquinas, Thomas 63
Aristotle 93, 184, 187, 194, 195, 196
Arnold, Matthew 9, 155, 156, 158, 159
Ashenbrenner, George 84
Austen, Jane 156
Austin, George 159

Bach, J. S. 156
Bailey, Charles 173, 174
von Balthasar 66
Bauman, Zygmunt 38, 39
Beck, John 9, 10
Beckett, Wendy 236
Bellah, Robert 18, 87
Benedict, St 15
Benjamin, Walter 19, 124
Berger, Peter 219
Bergson, Henri 195
Berry, Thomas 23
Blatch, Baroness 95
Bledisloe, Viscount 155
Bolton, Andrew 7
Bonhoeffer, D. 50
Bowness, Cathy 11
Briggs, Raymond 235
Buber, Martin 93, 104
Bulger, James 90

Cantwell Smith, Wilfred 131, 132
Carey, George 90, 92, 153
Carey, William 97
Carr, David 112, 114, 119
Carter, Marian 11
de Certeau, Michel 63, 69
Clifford 195
Collingwood, R. G. 199
Compson, Jane 149
Constantine 93, 94, 95, 100, 101
Cousins, Ewert 112
Cox, Baroness 95, 154, 159
Cranmer, Thomas 7, 100
Cromwell, Oliver 96

Dalai Lama 134
Davie, Grace 143
Descartes, René 192, 195
Dickens, Charles 38
Diana, Princess of Wales 143, 164

Elizabeth II 238

Endean, Philip 86
Erricker, Clive and Jane 7, 8, 9, 142, 143, 144, 145, 147
Erricker, Jane 116

Fiorenza, Elisabeth Schüssler 19, 25, 120
Ford, David 16
Freire, Paulo 136

Gadamer, Hans-Georg 18
Gardner, Howard 136
Geldof, Bob 234
Gerson, L. P. 196
Ghazali 145
Gilliat, Peter 155
Gilligan, Carol 21
Gilson, Etienne 195
Ginott, Haim 121
Grahame, Kenneth 235
Green, Arthur 147
Gregory of Nyssa 64
Grey, Mary 4, 5, 6, 7, 8, 9, 10, 33, 37, 49, 50, 84, 91, 103, 104
Grosch, Paul 10
Gusfield, Joseph 160

Habermas, Jürgen 195
Hadot, Pierre 182, 184, 189, 190, 191, 194, 195, 196, 197,198
Hanson, Bradley 66
Happ, H. 195
Hargreaves, David 161, 167, 168, 169, 170, 171, 172, 173, 174
Hay, David 125, 126
Heelas, Paul 114
Hegel, G. W. F. 195, 199
Helwys, Thomas 96
Henry VIII 100
Hick, Edward 98
Hillesum, Etty 20
Hillman, James 20
Hirst, Paul 162
Hughes, Shirley 235
Hughes, Ted 235
Hull, John 104, 115, 117, 120, 122
Hume, David 195
Humphrey, Hubert 208
Huxley, Aldous 163

Ignatius, St 81, 82, 84
Innocenti, Roberto 235

241

Name Index

Subject Index

Subject Index

religious studies 8
religious teaching 230
religious tensions 13
remembering 20, 33, 34
Reorganized Church of Jesus Christ of
  Latter Day Saints 92
ritual 55

sacrament 22
Scholastic period 181, 182, 196
Scholastic theology 10
Scholasticism 196
school as church 7, 100
School Curriculum and Assessment
  Authority 5, 35, 41, 45, 49, 52, 90,
  129, 154, 156, 161
science 232
science and religion 55
secular humanism 1, 40
secular schools 168
secularism 16
secularization 1, 2, 8, 16, 91, 125, 142,
  143, 151, 182
sectarianism 62
self 21, 42, 46, 47, 145, 183, 188
self-identity 111
self-realization 111
self-transformation 127
self-understanding 126
Sermon on the Mount 101
signals of transcendence 219
Sikhism 107
Sikhs 98
social development 36, 91
social gospellers 97
social justice 2
social principle 93
society 43, 93
Society for the Study of Christian
  Spirituality 57
sociology 69, 87
soul language 20
special educational needs 221
specialization, academic 68
spirit 96, 213
spiritual autobiography 20
spiritual development 2, 8, 9, 35, 36, 91,
  102, 108, 124, 125, 128, 155, 160, 161,
  203
spiritual education 112, 132, 134, 135,
  136, 137, 139
spiritual exercises 190, 197
Spiritual and Moral Development (NCC
  Paper) 161
spiritual theology 66
spirituality 1, 3, 4, 6, 7, 9, 10, 51, 55, 57,
  58, 65, 67, 68, 70, 86, 104, 111, 112,

115, 116, 121, 125, 126, 143, 147, 151,
  175, 181, 182, 183, 216, 217, 218, 221,
  222, 229, 230, 233, 238
spirituality, models of 114
spirituality, relation to theology 59, 66,
  71, 86
spirituality and ethics 69
spirituality and psychology 70
state 93
Stoicism 190
Sufism 55, 145, 146
'survival after extinction' doctrine 146
systematic theology 60, 64, 73

Theologia 61
theologies of creation 21, 22
theologies of liberation 16, 19
theology 6, 23
theology, absence in shaping RE
  practice 2f.
theology of education 3
theology of human person 68
theology as prayer 63
theology of transformation 7
theoria 61
Third World 104
Toronto Blessing, The 13
tradition 25
traditional theology 86
traditionalist position 154
traditionless model 144
trainee teachers 107
Transcendent, the 38, 125, 143
transformation 6, 16, 34, 50, 83
transformation of power structures
  128
transformation theologies 4, 5, 10, 16,
  17, 91
transformative philosophy 10
transforming relationships 222
trilemma 14–17
Trinity, the 67, 72, 146
truth 14, 34, 48, 56, 62, 127
typology 94

universalism of love 39

values 37, 38, 39, 40, 41, 42, 45, 46, 47
visual arts 236

Westminster College 103
whole child 90
world faiths 52
'World Spirituality' series 112
worldlessness 149
worship 35, 90, 113, 155, 160, 210, 211,
  237, 238

yoga 80